Foreigners,
Aliens,
Citizens

First published by Birch Leaf Books, 2020

British Library Cataloguing in Publication Data

A CIP catalogue record for this book is available
from the British Library.

ISBN 9780956467799 (print)

Printed by Parkers Design and Print, Ramsgate,
Kent CT12 5GD

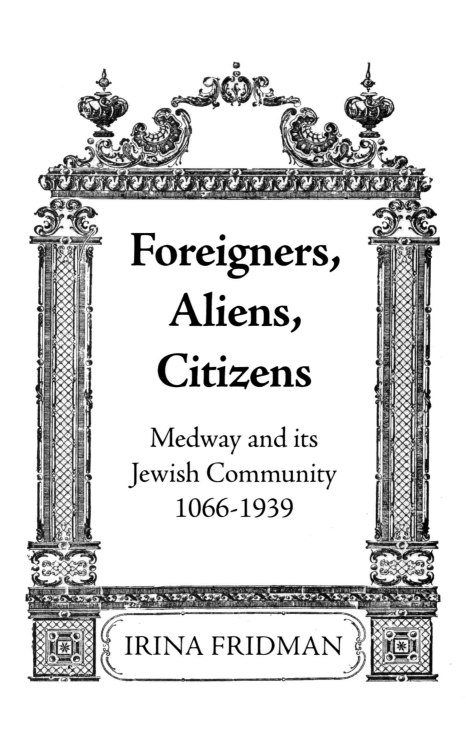

Foreigners, Aliens, Citizens

Medway and its Jewish Community 1066-1939

IRINA FRIDMAN

Contents

Foreword

Like many people who have lived or worked in the Medway Towns, I have often walked past the Chatham Memorial Synagogue in the High Street that runs between Chatham and Rochester. This stretch of the High Street is much quieter in the 21st century than it would have been when this iteration of the synagogue was built in 1869. It is possible to grab a couple of moments to read the foundation stone, and reflect on the history of the community for whom this was and remains an important part of their lives.

Buildings are an important way in which we can engage with the past, as we can look upon them, walk into and through them, and start to imagine how previous generations might have felt or what they might have done in that exact spot. Other buildings dominate the history of the Medway Towns: Rochester's castle and cathedral grab the attention of anyone coming over the bridge between Rochester and Strood, itself an important piece of infrastructure with an ancient history. Chatham Historic Dockyard, Upnor Castle and the various Napoleonic forts around the towns remind us of the area's strategic military and naval importance over the centuries. With such imposing structures dominating the skyline, it is perhaps easy to forget that there are other stories and other ways of understanding the development of the Medway Towns and its people. The history of the Jewish community in the towns is a story that richly deserves telling because of what it can add to our understanding of both local and national histories, and Irina Fridman is supremely well-placed to do this.

I met Irina when I brought my social history students to the Medway Archives to introduce them to sources that they could use for their projects on the history of the Medway Towns. With her professional background in local studies librarianship, Irina has an exceptional understanding of where to find this history in the archives and how to bring it alive. Irina draws upon archival sources now in the Medway Archives, and has also painstakingly tracked down papers in collections at the Jewish Museum, the British Library, and the Victoria and Albert Museum, for example. The result is a book that takes the reader on a journey through the history of the Jewish community in the Medway area from the 12th century to the 1930s. On the way, we learn not only about the everyday lives of individuals in the towns, but also the impact of national and international developments on the community. In doing so, we also gain fresh perspectives on the development of the towns, with a different way of seeing how those landmark buildings, bridges and fortifications and the social, economic, cultural and military changes they brought with them were experienced over time.

Foreigners, Aliens, Citizens: Medway and its Jewish Community, 1066-1939 is a very important addition to the history of the Jewish community in the United Kingdom, providing rich and fresh insight that will appeal to a wide variety of readers.

Dr Kate Bradley
Reader in Social History and Social Policy
School of Social Policy, Sociology and Social Research
University of Kent, May 2020

Irina Fridman

A word from former president of Chatham Historical Society

I became convinced some time ago that a definitive history of the Jewish presence in the Medway Towns needed to be written. After all, at a thousand years old, the community was one of the earliest in the country, and yet there has been little of note written about it. This has constituted a significant gap in both the historiography of British Jewry and the history of the Medway Towns.

My conviction was reinforced after I read Irina's two booklets on the subject, the most recent of which was a celebration of the Chatham Synagogue entitled *A Fitting Memorial*. Modest though these booklets were, Irina had demonstrated that a wealth of hitherto untapped sources was awaiting detailed scrutiny. Using them would require commitment and time though, because not only were they extensive but they were also scattered among various public repositories and private collections.

There was a lot of work to be done, and I was so glad when Irina told me she had decided to take on this task, because I can think of nobody who is more qualified or equipped to do the subject justice.

After several years' hard work and dedication, Irina has finished this undertaking, and it does not disappoint. On reading it, I was struck by Irina's mastery of the sheer amount of material at her disposal. A lesser researcher could have been overwhelmed by not only the quantity, but also the diversity of the sources, from medieval pipe rolls to 20th-century newspapers. Irina, however, was equal to this task and used the material to produce this authoritative work.

I also appreciated the way in which the author weaves the development of Medway's own Jewish community into the story of the national experience. She never loses sight of this, thereby preventing her book from falling into the

11

parochial trap common to so many works of local history.

The extensive footnotes and appendices provided by Irina bear witness to the scope of her research and commitment to this project.

After reading this book, I was left with two overriding impressions of Medway's Jewry after their return in the 18th century. The first was their determination to establish a community and the tenacious way they set about it. The second was the speed in which this was achieved and the way in which the leaders of the established non-Jewish community accepted the Jews' presence and honoured individuals. Irina's accounts of the Levy and Barnard families bear witness to this.

The subject was fortunate in getting the author it deserved. Irina Fridman has produced a much-needed book that will surely remain definitive for the foreseeable future.

Brian Joyce
President of Chatham Historical Society (2008-17)

Introduction

The Jewish presence in Rochester, Chatham and their environs goes back to the 1100s. After the readmission in the 17th century, the members of Jewish community, one of the oldest in the country, played a prominent role on the national scale, with some achieving international acclaim.

I was given various snippets of information about the community when, in the early days of my work at the Medway Archives and Local Studies Centre, I was preparing an introductory exhibition about Jewish life in the Medway Towns. Directories listed a substantial number of Jewish businesses and there was a collection of Jewish records in the archive. However, my search for a comprehensive study revealed only two publications by Michael Jolles that he produced between 1998 and 2000 — his transcription of *The Chatham Hebrew Society Synagogue Ledger, 1836-65*, and a book, *Samuel Isaac, Saul Isaacs and Nathaniel Isaacs*. Additional references to the community discovered in Geoffrey Green's *The Royal Navy and Anglo-Jewry, 1740-1820* (1989), and Cecil Roth's *The Rise of Provincial Jewry* (1950) gave a tantalisingly brief description of Chatham Jewry, which posed more questions than it provided answers. Time was pressing and, using whatever material was at hand, I produced a small booklet accompanying the exhibition. Later, intrigued by the absence of information about the medieval period, despite the commonly used image from the 13th-century *Textus Roffensis*, I discovered references to Jews associated with Rochester in Joseph Jacob's *The Jews in Angevin England* (1893).

Over the years, having received numerous requests from descendants to find records relating to their Jewish ancestors from Chatham and Rochester, and discovering more and more information about community members and the role they played within the area and beyond, it became apparent that an in-depth study was required to fill in the gap in both local and Jewish historiography.

So, this book is about the relationship between the Jewish community, the first non-Christian community in the area, and the Gentile community of the Medway Towns. It is about the way the nature of this relationship was influenced by factors such as legislation and military campaigns. It also touches upon the position of the Medway Jewry within the context of Anglo-Jewish history as a whole. And it is also about people who shaped this area, their families and their experiences. Additional information, which was not imperative to the story, but might be of great interest to the readers, is in the notes to each chapter.

While I was writing the book, the country was undergoing several changes, some of which echoed the events from previous centuries. The referendum in 2016 — the so-called Brexit vote, the result of which had been influenced by a whipped-up nationalistic agenda and anti-immigration feeling — paralleled the agendas and events from earlier centuries with similar rhetoric. The perceived fear of 'a stranger' has been exploited to impose restrictions for settling in the country with 'skills' being a substitute for 'religion'.

At the same time, in November 2019 the Church of England's Faith and Order Commission published a document entitled *God's Unfailing World* encouraging Christians to rediscover the relationship of 'unique significance' between two faiths, worshipping one God, with scriptures shared in common. It acknowledges that over the centuries the attitudes towards Judaism were providing a 'fertile seed-bed for murderous antisemitism'. The church urges Christians not only to repent the 'sins of the past' towards their Jewish neighbours but also to be alert to and actively challenge such attitudes or stereotypes.

The narrative of this study pauses just before the Second World War. The devastation of European Jewry during the war is known, but as the witnesses are dying, the terrifying memories of the events in the mid-20th century are fading and transform themselves into a blurry image, the testimonies and records become just a recounting of events from long ago — too remote to affect personally, creating a potential danger of repeating the same horror. Until we start educating ourselves to understand the past and learn our lessons from it, we are bound to fall prey to demagogues and descend into the same devastating narratives again.

This book is intended as a starting point. More research needs to be undertaken to understand the Jewish history of Rochester in the 12th and 13th centuries. Stories about local Jewish women are yet to be explored — in the masculine world of the Medway Towns dominated by soldiers and sailors, their lives often remain hidden.

I would like to thank the Jewish Historical Society of England and Kent Archaeological Society for their grants, which made research and publication of this book possible. I would also like to thank the descendants of the Barnard, Halpern, Hyman, Levy, Lyons, Magnus, Pyke, Salomons and all other families for sharing with me their family stories. My heartfelt gratitude to all those people, whose overwhelming generosity, advice, and encouragement helped me along the way. To Kate Bradley, Ruth Brown, Catharina Clement, Chris de Coulon Berthoud, Maria Diemling, Dean Irwin, Michael Jolles, Anthony Joseph, Brian Joyce, Simon Mills, Nathan Nicholls, Steve Nye, Ari Phillips, Stephen Rayner, Richard Reader, Jonathan Romain, Alison Thomas, Pauline Weeds — my special thank you. Your contributions allowed me to complete this project and make it as good as it can be — all the mistakes are entirely mine.

Irina Fridman
Chatham, September 2020

Foreigners, Aliens, Citizens

Chapter 1

The First Community:
From William the Conqueror to Edward I, 1066-1290

The earliest arrival of Jews to England is steeped in mystery. Historians agree that before the Norman Conquest Britain was known to Jews: a few might have been part of the Roman army or visited the country as single traders or travellers.[1] Small-value coins, which could be easily carried in pockets and originating from the Jewish homeland, were found in Bingley Moor in Yorkshire, dating back to 41-43 CE — reign of Herod Agrippa; at a Roman fort at Melandra, Derbyshire, dating from the First Bar Kokhba Revolt in 66-72 CE; and in London from the time of the Second Bar Kokhba Revolt in 132-135 CE.[2] The researcher Shimon Appelbaum also mentions a silver ingot found at Richborough, Kent, in 1915 with a stamp dating from the late fourth century, which gives a link in the evidence of the Jewish participation in the production and trading of silver between France (Gaul) and Britain at the time. The proximity of England to the Continent meant that some continental Jews probably visited England before the 11th century, and an occasional family might have even resided here. However, the general consensus among historians is that it is still impossible to ascertain the existence of a settled Jewish community in the British Isles.

It was the conquest of the isles in 1066 that prompted Jews to put down roots in England. Historians disagree on the precise reasons for settlement. Some suggested a bribe made by William the Conqueror to the Rouen Jewish community; others mentioned some Jewish financial backing for William's invasion fleet. Some historians even claimed that William's mother was Jewish, pointing to a common Jewish name of the time, Dieulecresse and its variants, which is in essence the Conqueror's battle cry 'Dex aiae' or 'God aid me', and the name Manser, which derives from the Hebrew 'mamzer', *ie* 'bastard', as William was also known.

If there is no solid basis to the above 'conspiracy theory' to convince the majority of historians, there is no doubt among researchers regarding William's connection with the Jewish community. To operate successfully in the new country, it was useful for William to have French-speakers, who were also loyal to him.[3] In addition, Jewish commercial skills, expertise and personal capital would make the newly conquered country more prosperous. Jews were known for their strong reputation as dealers in plate, coin, luxury goods and money-lending.[4] As they resided mainly in urban areas, and were not tied to the land or farms, Jews were more mobile than most.[5]

From the royal perspective, money-lending was the main and the most useful function of the Jews. It had little to do with the perceived Jewish aptitude for dealing with finance, but with differences in biblical interpretation in the Talmudic and Canon Laws. Money lending is permitted as such, but Exodus 22:24, Leviticus 25:35, and especially Deuteronomy 23:20, stipulate that 'thou shalt not lend upon interest to thy brother'.[6] Talmudic interpretations argue about the term 'brother' to include Jews and non-Jews alike, though some settle on a narrow interpretation of the term as referring to a Jew. As an act of kindness and goodwill you are not to charge him interest, which you can do to the strangers, *ie* not belonging to the same faith. Canon Law, however, at least in theory, adopted a wider interpretation of 'brother', applying it to everyone. Generous and inclusive as it may seem in principle, in reality there was hardly anyone who was prepared to make a loan without charging interest, to make a profit, or at least compensate for defaulters. And so, to minimise Christian dealings with money and interest, or to appear to do so, it became convenient to have non-Christian Jews as the principal money-lenders.

In 1070 William addressed the status of the Jews and gave them the utmost protection: 'the King would treat both their persons and property as his own'[7]. However, within the next 200 years this promise proved a double-edged sword.

At first, Jews settled in the 'seat of the royal power' — London. For the

English population, resentful of any foreign influence, they were a double-minority — foreigners and non-Christian, and as such an easy target. Jews remained in London until 1135,[8] after which they formed communities across the country. The Jewries tended to be established in county towns — permanent places of the sheriff, the king's official.[9] Until now, the consensus among historians had been that every community settled in the close proximity to the castle, where Jewish lives were governed by a royal constable, who could also ensure their safety.[10] However, latest research reveals that the protection of the Jews, apart from in London, was largely delegated to the local civic authorities.

Research into the existence of the medieval Jewish community in Rochester presents more questions than answers and resembles a puzzle with most pieces missing. No historian has ever written on the subject. However, there is no doubt that Jews resided in Rochester and its vicinity in the 12th and 13th centuries: the place possessed all the attributes for their settlement there. Rochester was on the main road to the Continent, at a convenient distance from London, and at the major crossing of the River Medway. Rochester also had its own castle from about 1127 and a religious house, the Cathedral Priory of St Andrew, established in 604.

However, there is a total absence of any surviving physical sign in Rochester relating to the Jews. If Canterbury, which had its community by 1187, still has its Jews Lane, and the site of the former synagogue is known, Rochester offers no hints to the existence of the community during the 12th and 13th centuries. Of course, for Jews to practise their religion there was never a compulsory requirement to have a synagogue — a small community could have practised in someone's house. Was the community ever big enough to require a purpose-built synagogue, especially as this was not an easy matter in the 13th century?

In 1222 the Council of the Archdiocese of Canterbury sought to prohibit the construction of new Jewish places of worship. Later in 1253, it would be decreed that there should be no synagogues apart from the places where they existed during King John's reign.[11]

The paucity of surviving records scattered in various rolls and transaction deeds do not represent a true picture of the community that resided here. What factors influenced the survival, or more precisely lack of, records relating to the Jewish community in Rochester? Was it anything to do with events throughout the 13th century, such as the Rochester Castle sieges? Was it because Rochester was on the main thoroughfare for crusaders travelling to Dover and the host to the Knights Templar? Or was it something else entirely? What was the relationship between the Jews and the citizens of Rochester?

Rochester, a city established by Romans, is described in the *Domesday Book* (1086) as a place enclosed by the walls of 23.5 acres[12], and containing 16 households (Canterbury contained 262). In comparison with other places it paid very little tax, £20[13] with only three households deemed wealthy enough to do so. There were 18 villagers, six smallholders and eight slaves in addition to the monks of the priory.[14]

The dominating establishment of the area was St Andrew Priory, originally founded in 604 and re-established after the conquest by Lafranc, Archbishop of Canterbury, in 1083 during his visit to Rochester. The priory comprised 22 Benedictine monks, the same order as St Augustine Priory in Canterbury. Among them they elected a prior and bishop. However, from 1124, the bishop became appointed by the king. In addition to his appointment by Henry I, he was also an outsider and not a monk. From that moment, the bishop's duty changed, and he became more of an occasional visitor hardly known to his monks than part of the priory 'family'. He had his own household, separate from the monks of the priory and his own, much lower, revenues.[15]

The 12th-century records mention two fires, which had major consequences for the priory. The first fire occurred on 3 June 1137 when 'the Church of St Andrew, Rochester, was burnt, and the whole city, together with the offices of the bishop and monks.' The second fire was on 11 April 1179. According to the contemporary chronicler Gervase of Canterbury, the church 'was reduced to a cinder … All the offices and the whole of the city within and without the walls were also burnt'[16]. On both occasions to rebuild the city and the priory with its offices required money, and most certainly it required more than the income would allow. Loans would have been obtained.

Despite a common perception that only Jews were able to provide a loan, there were several ways to obtain one: from the local civic community, from the tolls, from Christian merchants or indeed from Christian financiers: William Cade was a well-known 12th-century name. Unfortunately, no records survive, and we can only speculate. Coincidentally, the first reference to Jews connected

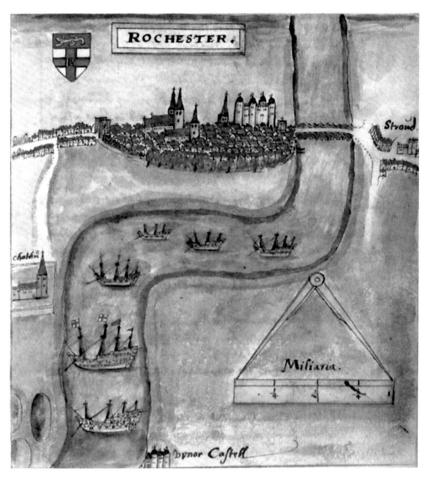

This very early map of Rochester and surrounding area comes
from William Smith's *The Particular Description of England, with the
Portraitures of Certaine of the Chiefest Citties and Townes* c.1590. The
city, established by the Romans, would look the same for many centuries

to Rochester appears in the Pipe Rolls of 1180-82, straight after the second fire, when Ysaac of Tchernigov, Russia, possibly the first Russian to set foot on English soil, and Ysaac of Beverly 'render count of 10 marks to be quit of a charge that they said to 'have exchanged' or 'minted' (cambivisse)'[17].

In 1186-87 records we find another name, Benedict of Rochester, who appears in the records twice: the first time in regards to his financial dispute with Radulfum (Ralph) of Rochester and the second time when he 'renders count of one mark of gold for having his deeds which the sheriff holds'.[18]

We need to bear in mind that Rochester as a surname only means an association with the place either through birth, residence or business connections[19], but does not prove that a person either was born or resided there permanently. However, it does indicate that Benedict of Rochester was connected to the city.

Throughout the 12th century, the Jewish population in the country increased, having been encouraged to settle in England by the kings, and bolstered by the expulsion of the Jews from the Ile de France in 1182. Could it be that Rochester became home to more than three Jews?

In 1185 Baldwin, Archbishop of Canterbury, gave this see to his own clerk — Gilbert of Glanville, a native of Northumberland, and at the time Archdeacon of Lisieux in Normandy. On his appointment Glanville 'found the bishopric very ill furnished, with mean and destroyed buildings; he shewed the solicitude of a Martha, and in the first place erected the cathedral buildings which had perished in the fire' …[20]

The appointment of Glanville, an outsider and a secular bishop, served a twofold purpose for both, Henry II and the archbishop: to curb the monks' independence and establish a strong barrier against the encroachment of Rome. Understandably, in their turn, the monks viewed Glanville with great suspicion. In addition, the revenues of the priory were much larger than that of the bishopric. Tension started bubbling under the surface.

At the time, the Jews of England were given the privilege to be tried in courts in most cases in accordance with Talmudic Law (homicide, arson and rape excepted) — protection granted by Henry I, and confirmed and extended by

Rochester Castle, its cathedral and the early bridge over the Medway

Henry II. They were allowed to hold property as tenants-in-chief to the Crown. Despite the prohibition, abbeys and minsters borrowed money from the Jews on the security of items of divine worship, and even relics of the saints, as was the case of Bishop Nigel of Ely, who pledged relics with the Jews of Cambridge. The business deeds were kept in the cathedral treasuries, commonly used for protection of the valuables in emergency. Jewish women and children found shelter in monasteries at times of unrest. Jews even took part in monastic politics as they did in Canterbury, when in 1187 Jews sided with the townsfolk and smuggled food and drink to the monks of Christ Church Priory during their 18 months' siege by Archbishop Baldwin. They even prayed for the monks 'in their synagogues', according to Gervase of Canterbury.[21] At the same time, however, hatred of Jews was increasing, and by 1189 it was running high. The Jews had already experienced accusations of ritual murder and violence against them in Norwich in 1144, Gloucester in 1168, Bury St Edmunds in 1183, and Bristol in 1183. In addition, in 1179 the Third Council of Lateran under the Pope Alexander III urged Christians to minimise their contact with Jews.

On 3 September 1189 a Jewish delegation tried to present an address to Richard I during his coronation in Westminster but were refused. Some of them were swept up by the gathered crowd and pushed inside. One Christian, having spotted Jewish delegates, remembered the king's order against them and started beating one of them. The result: a full-scale attack and massacres that raged all over the country during the following months. As Jews were under the direct protection of the king, the attacks were 'an assault on his dignity and power as well as the purse'.[22]

Richard was eager to start his crusade, and so the royal orders were dispatched ordering sheriffs across the country to ensure that the Jews were left in peace. No other action was taken. By December 1189 the situation calmed down only to flare up again once Richard left the kingdom. In February 1190, riots against Jews took place across the country. They culminated in York on 16 March 1190, where the entire Jewish population of the town, estimated at 150, who took shelter in the royal castle, were massacred by a local mob.

Kent witnessed no riots or massacres. The only record of that time relating to a possible attack on Jews referred to a fine of 10 marks imposed on Ospringe, a village on the route between Rochester and Canterbury, for failing to take appropriate action when 'one of the king's Jews [was] discovered dead'. The entry was as a result of non-payment.[23] So, most probably there was no attack, and the death was unrelated to the bloody events across country. Canterbury's Jewish population escaped unscathed, perhaps indicating an unusually peaceful relationship with the local population.[24] There are no surviving records relating to Jews in Rochester, if there were any, but given the above examples, we can probably assume that Jews in Kent generally felt much safer than Jews in other counties.

There was no immediate reaction from the king in relation to the massacres of his subjects. Only on 22 March 1190 Richard confirmed that 'all the customs and liberties which King Henry, our father, had granted and by his charter confirmed to the Jews of England and Normandy, to reside on our [lands] freely and honourably ...'[25] Crucially, this charter was granted only to certain Jews of London: Isaac, son of Rabbi Josce, and his sons and their men; it was only in 1201 that King John's charter was extended to include others.

Richard departed from England on crusade in the summer of 1190. It lasted until October 1192. On his way back from the Holy Land the king was captured and imprisoned in Dürnstein Castle, Austria. A ransom of 100,000 marks (about £66,000) was required and was duly provided. Overall, to finance the crusade and contribute to the ransom, Jews paid eight per cent, though they were only 0.25 per cent of the total population. They paid the tallage — an

The tomb of Bishop of Rochester Gilbert de Glanville (*d.*1214) in Rochester Cathedral. An anonymous chronicler, in recording his death, gleefully adds 'that he was buried like Jews and heretics'

arbitrary tax levied by the king, of £1,333 at the start of Richard's campaign, followed by £3,333 in addition to £2,000 contribution to the ransom.[26] The list containing 271 Jewish names, who were able to contribute, included some Kentish names — Jacob from Canterbury who contributed £115[27]; Benedict of Rochester, who contributed £3 6s 8d and Simon of Malling, who paid £1 3s 4d.[28]

Based on the contribution towards Richard's relief from the captivity, we may assume that the Jewish community of Rochester, if indeed there was one, was not as numerous or as wealthy as the Canterbury Jewry, which ranked third with £235 19s 4d after London and Lincoln. There is only one identifiable name, that of Benedict of Rochester, contributing towards the release of Richard I, whereas Canterbury's list contained 20 residents. Also, Benedict's name appears on the Canterbury list, raising a question of whether he was actually living in Rochester.

Meanwhile, the tension between the monks and Bishop Glanville erupted into full-blown confrontation. And that confrontation included Jews. In 1193, eager to teach the monks a lesson by showing them he was in charge, and at the same time wishing to consolidate his standing with his superiors by contributing towards the king's release, and probably to increase his slender income, Glanville appropriated two churches from the monks — Aylesford and St Margaret's in Rochester. He also convinced the prior, Ralph de Ross, to surrender some meadows along the road to Frindsbury to establish Newark Hospital and home for St Augustine monks: '... Bishop Gilbert's gift in free alms of all that part of a meadow near Strood belonging to the priory as enclosed by a certain ditch, and all the land the priory holds lying between the hospital building and the Augustinian house near the main road leading to Frindsbury, and extending from the wall of the Augustinian house as far as the meadow ditch on the north.'

The prior stated that in exchange for assenting to this gift, the bishop had given him 'thirty pounds to rescue the priory from the hands of the Jews, had finished the cloister in stone and had had an organ made for it.'[29]

No record of the original loan between the Benedictine monks and the Jews survived and we do not know what the loan was advanced for. According to the author of 1772 publication *The History and Antiquities of Rochester and its Environs* the monks probably borrowed the money in supporting their unjustifiable contest with Glanville. The author, firmly siding with the bishop continues: 'The monks were under the greater obligation to their bishop, because the interest due upon it [the debt of £30] was enormous. Glanville likewise gave them sundry utensils and ornaments, which are enumerated, in the Registrum, and the following books, viz *Bartholomaeus Adversus Judeos*, and the *Pentateuch*, in two volumes.'[30]

Whether the money was borrowed to fund the feud between the monks and Glanville, or whether it was the loan to restore the establishment after the fire of 1179, we will probably never find out. What is clear though, that the Rochester monks turned to Jews for a loan. Furthermore, the loan was advanced by several Jewish 'financiers' indicating that to provide the sum required they needed to form some sort of an alliance. We do not know how many of them formed this alliance, but we can infer that none of them was wealthy enough to advance the whole sum or could solely bear the risk of providing it. There is no indication as to whether those were Canterbury Jews or even Jews from London. However, bearing in mind the discrepancy of wealth between the Jews from Canterbury and Rochester in the sums advanced towards the release of Richard I, it is plausible that the Jews who advanced £30 to the monks were either local or connected to Rochester.[31] The conflict between the monks of Rochester and Strood lasted for over the century, long after Glanville's death in 1214.[32] The Rochester priory monks gave up on the struggle only during the reign of Edward I, after they were ambushed and beaten up by the monks at Strood, when under the pretext of inclement weather, they tried to pass in procession through the hospital grounds.[33]

The general impression is that all medieval Jews were moneylenders and of the same class. However, even our simple examples above dispel this impression. The historian Vivian Lipman suggests that medieval Anglo-Jewry was divided into three classes. The first and the smallest one was wealthy Jews, a class normally associated with an official position within the community. Then came the class in the middle, and then 'the poor', which was probably true for those residing in small towns or in villages or rural areas. Both Lipman and another historian, I. Epstein, mention other occupations apart from moneylending or taxpaying — peddlers, clerks or agents of the richer Jews, doctors, teachers, cheese and fishmongers, tailors and pawnbrokers. In regard to the latter, pawnbroking was not registered in the way the moneylending was.[34] Taking into account the size of Rochester, its low tax, the only name with a relatively small contribution towards Richard's release from captivity and several moneylenders in relation to the establishment of the hospital, suggests that the possible community consisted of several 'middle-class' families, and quite possibly of several poor ones, who do not appear in any records.

On his return from the crusade in 1194, Richard established a system of *archae* — chests, containing business transactions and guarded by four chirographers (clerks), two Jews and two Gentiles.[35] By 1194 five or six *archae* were already established, one of them in Canterbury.[36] During the 13th century, at its peak, 26 *archae* were mentioned; by 1290 only 17 remained.

As we can see from above, to provide a loan, to create a transaction, to ask for protection, the local Jews would have to be in contact with the monks and the officials. On a day-to-day basis, the contact was probably even greater than we imagine. Monks and the officials would be using Latin and Norman French. Jews, especially those from the wealthier classes, were probably trilingual. Apart from Hebrew, which clearly set them apart from Gentiles, for contracts and legal language they would use Latin. A large number of records regarding Jews were written in Latin, suggesting that those who were involved in moneylending transactions were fluent in it. They also spoke and wrote in French, and probably used it as an everyday language. They even preferred to use French names for their daughters. It is also reasonable to suppose that as time progressed, they acquired sufficient knowledge of English to communicate with locals.

The diet of English Jews complied with *kashrut* (Jewish dietary laws) and would probably differ in some ways from the diet of their neighbours. It might have been better even for poor Jews, who would regularly have fish, such as tuna, carp, herring and salmon, meat in the form of pies and bread and wine — the last two were the most important for *kiddush*, or benediction.[37] However, in comparison with their continental co-religionists, English Jews were somewhat lax regarding their dietary laws, and English rabbis seemed to be comfortable with this laxity. Jews had no scruples in eating non-Jewish bread. Indeed, Rabbi Isaac ben Peretz of Northampton even declared that fresh non-Jewish bread was preferable to stale Jewish bread. There was some import of wine, but there were Jewish vintners in Oxford, and Isaac of Colchester even had his own vineyard. It was known for the Jews to drink with Christians.[38]

St Andrew's Priory in Rochester had its own brewhouse, bakery and a vineyard and there is a great possibility that Jews would buy their food and drink there. Furthermore, Rochester wine was mentioned in one of later Jewish publications; the Vines, a park in the centre of Rochester is an echo of those times. We will never know with absolute certainty, but the idea in itself seems plausible enough.

Jews had already experienced accusations of ritual murder and violence against them in Norwich in 1144, Gloucester in 1168, at Bury St Edmunds in

1183 and at Bristol in 1183. It is interesting, then, to recall a murder relating to Rochester, which occurred in 1201. William, a native of Perth, who was passing through Rochester when on pilgrimage, was 'martyred outside the city of Rochester and … buried in the cathedral church of Rochester with glistening of miracles.'[39] The subsequent shrine of a saint[40] attracted many pilgrims, worship and donations, which increased the priory's income and its status. The fascinating part in this story is that Rochester monks did not jump to conclusion regarding the murderer by pointing an accusing finger at the Jews, despite precedents in other parts of the country. A blame-the-Jews accusation was almost ideal and could have been used against their presence and their perceived privileged position in the country. If there were Jews in Rochester at the time, the absence of murder accusations provides us with more proof of unusually peaceful relationship between Jews and people of Rochester.

A similar 'protection' of Jews happened in Canterbury, during the massacres elsewhere in 1189-90 when no Jew in Canterbury suffered harm. A couple of years earlier, during the conflict between the monks of Christ Church Priory and the archbishop, the Jews sided with the monks. Both religious houses, Christ Church and St Andrew, belonged to the Benedictine Order. Could it be that the Benedictine Order was more tolerant and friendly towards Jews?

In 1210 while in Bristol, King John demanded from his Jews a tallage, or tax, of 66,000 marks (£44,000). That was in addition to the tallage of 1207 when he demanded £2,666 13s 4d as well as a levy of one-tenth of the value of their bonds. To make them pay, the entire Jewish population was imprisoned, and some tortured. For example, Abraham of Bristol, who was taxed £10,000, had his teeth extracted one by one until his resistance broke down. Even the poorest had to contribute or leave the country.[41] It is probable that many preferred the latter option. In 1213, further inquiry was made into their property and the next year Jews were made to pay again. The impecunious were imprisoned at the opposite end of the country. Many Jewish houses were confiscated and given to royal favourites. In 1215 John ordered that those who left the country due to their inability to pay were not permitted to return until they paid their debt and submitted £2 to the Treasury.[42] It is known that by 1206 Canterbury Jewry numbered about 100 souls, but there is no record relating to Rochester around that time. We know, however, that Rochester Jews were not as wealthy as the Jews of Canterbury. Were they the ones who were unable to pay and hence left the country?

On death of King John in 1216, he was succeeded by his son, Henry III, then a nine-year-old. His regent, Hubert de Burgh, Sheriff of Kent and Surrey and later Earl of Kent and a governor of Rochester Castle, was determined to restore stability and order. Jews were encouraged to return to the country, and the wardens of Cinque Ports were instructed to let them pass freely. The Jewish population in England started increasing again, and in 1219 we find the last reference to Benedict of Rochester. This time he acts as an agent for Josce Presbyter, Arch-Presbyter of Jews, the chief official for the Jews in England. The matter relates to a financial dispute regarding the arrears of mortgage.[43]

Throughout the 1220s Rochester's defences were strengthened, and in 1230 Rochester paid tallage of 15 marks (about £10), though it was still a very low tax in comparison with Canterbury, which paid 100 marks (about £67).[44] However, despite such a big discrepancy in tax paid by the cities, which reflected in the size of each place, on 28 March 1231 Henry III ordered the Sheriff of Kent to send to Westminster six of the richest Jews from Canterbury, and as many from Rochester, with arrears of tallages.[45] This is the only record explicitly stating not only the existence of the Rochester Jewish community but also the number of Jewish families wealthy enough to pay tax. The equal number of richest Jews from Rochester and Canterbury implies that at that time Rochester Jewry was on a par with Canterbury. Does that mean that the Rochester community was of the same size: about 100 souls?

The church's hostile position towards Jews increased in the 13th century. It also reinforced Henry III's attitude towards his Jewish subjects. In 1215 the Fourth Lateral Council with Archbishop of Canterbury Stephen Langton in attendance, attempted to compel Jews to pay church tithes, and for the first time, fearing romantic encounters and sexual intercourse between Jews and Gentiles, proclaimed an obligation for the Jews to wear a tabula, a distinctive badge, to identify them. In addition to the visual distinction between Jews and Gentiles, the Jews were also verbally condemned as 'perfidious'. They were commonly referred as 'Devil's disciples', sorcerers (possibly because of their better hygiene, and as a result lower mortality rate, especially in childbirth), murderers, necromancers, poisoners, cannibals, and international conspirators among other similar descriptions. The main goals were either to destroy them, or better still, bring them into the fold, convert them, thus claiming the victory of the righteous religion, Christianity.

In 1232, Henry III established a house for converted Jews in London — Domus Conversorum. The Jews willing to convert would stay in the house, forfeiting their property to the Crown. Instead, they would receive a weekly stipend — 10d for men and 8½d for women. After an appropriate time spent there, they would be sent to various religious houses across the country to adjust to their lives as Christians. Rochester had its own share of converts. The Fine Rolls for 1254 and 1255 record three male converts, all of whom bore the name of John in the memory of Henry's father.[46] The Domus would stay open till the beginning of the 17th century.

Meanwhile, the number of religious houses, entrepreneurs and households dealing with Jewish financiers and profiting from those dealings increased. One of the examples connected to Rochester is the manor of Great Delce, which was in the possession of Andrew Bukarel, Mayor of London, who lost it to the king in 1239 for his debts to Elias L'Eveske of London. The royal family usually took its share from the profits of Jewish lending, but also used their position for their own profit. They provided patronage and protection for several individual Jews who probably had a very direct relationship with the royal family and their officials. Edward I's uncle, Richard of Cornwall, used Jewish financiers and often seemed to have intervened on their behalf.

Richard's sister-in-law, Eleanor of Provence, wife of Henry III, was hostile towards Jews and benefited from the finance they provided by receiving payments from their profits. Her income came from her lands, received as a dowry. It was boosted by 10 per cent on any voluntary fines over £6 13s 4d that were made to the Crown — part that was known as Queen's Gold. While Eleanor was young, Henry III ensured that he collected and allocated money to her. In 1237 those sums were used to buy jewels, to enhance her chamber at Westminster, and to help build a church for the Dominicans at Canterbury. By 1254 the queen controlled her financial matters herself and was appointing her own officials, who handled the day-to-day running of her affairs. From time to time the queen accepted Jewish bonds taken directly from the *archae*; sometimes she insisted on cash only. She had a growing portfolio of Jewish debts and favoured certain Jews. Her attitude, however, changed suddenly in 1275 when she sought permission from Edward I to enter the convent and demanded the removal of all Jews from her dower towns.[47]

By the mid-13th century, the role played earlier by monasteries in buying up debt-encumbered lands was open to many others. In the 1240s, Walter de Merton, a Chancery clerk and later on the Bishop of Rochester (1274-27 October 1277), a future founder of Merton College, Oxford, and a future chancellor to Edward I, acted as a commissioner with the task to examine the state of the royal lands in Kent, Essex and Hertfordshire. He purchased the manors of Malden, Chessington and Farley that were encumbered by Jewish debts. When the possibility of a cheap purchase presented itself, he would increase his portfolio, which by the 1270s comprised land in and around Oxford and Cambridge, lands at Barkby and Grantchester Mill, and property, houses and manors in Oxford, London, Cambridge, St Aldgate, Ibstone in Oxfordshire, Cheddington in Buckinghamshire and manor of Kibworth Harcourt in Leicestershire. The lands and manors were bought by clearing debts and paying them to the Jews.

Walter de Merton was also 'spin-doctoring' and forming government policy on the state of the lending market in addition to boosting his own status and increasing his personal financial wealth. The historian Robin Mundill suggests that in 1269 he may even have advised Henry III and Lord Edward, the future King Edward I, in preparing new legislation in response to baronial complaints. Concerned that too many annuities — investments entitling the investor to a number of annual sums, similar to today's credit arrangements — had been placed in circulation, that year the Crown banned Jews from taking out new fee debts and limited the way in which Christians could sell these on. In 1271, a further piece of legislation prohibited Jews from holding a freehold in manors, lands, tenements, fees or tenures of any kind. This effectively left Jews legally able to deal only in cash and commodities and quite possibly resulted in higher interest rates on loans. The mandate also stipulated that all fee debts, lands and tenures that the Jews had made or negotiated before 1271 were to be discharged as quickly as possible, and that the Christians involved were to pay off the principal only. Not only did de Merton exploit Jewish lending but he also showed other Crown servants how they could use shrewdness and inside information of royal business affairs to become both wealthy and influential.[48]

In 1241, a mere 10 years after six rich Jews from Rochester were sent to Westminster, the so-called 'Jewish Parliament' was held to apportion among themselves a tallage of 20,000 marks demanded by Henry III. One hundred and nine representatives from 21 Jewries assembled. However, only one name relating to Rochester is recorded — De is Ruff (Rochester), who also appears in the London list as De Isac' Ruffo, who paid 32 shillings tax.[49] Does that imply that the community was transitory? Did the relationship between the population and Jews became so sour that the Jewry did not survive? Were the bishops of Rochester hostile to the extent that Jews felt compelled to leave? Did the city have enough prosperous clients to deal with? Or was the competition too fierce, as the neighbouring Strood was the base of the Knights Templar?

Temple Manor in Strood, founded in 1160, was given to the Knights Templar by King John and confirmed in the 11th year of King Henry III (1226-27),[50] probably for financial services that Templars provided to the Crown. There is a mystery surrounding the importance of the manor: hardly any documents regarding it exist. So far, the consensus has been that the manor was not a preceptory — the estate supporting the living-in community, subordinate to the order — though its complex of buildings followed the preceptory model. They included a hall, a buttery, a kitchen and a chapel. If Strood manor was not a preceptory, it meant that there were no residents, who were knights, sergeants, chaplains and free servants, each dining at their own table and wearing different livery.[51] However, records from the 1220s show the opposite was true. The records show three disputes between the Templars and the bishop and the monks of Rochester. The first financial dispute, initiated by Benedict, Bishop of Rochester, was in regard to the arrears of the 20 shillings rent of the mill and 4s 3d in rent for Cokelestan (Cuxton), for which the knights paid five marks.[52] The second one, of 1222, was concerning the lands of Shamel [Hundred]; Frindsbury, Denton [near Gravesend]; Strood, Dartford and Rochester and a 'certain arm of the sea (fleta) in Strode'. The dispute was resolved when William, Prior of Rochester, warranted to the Templars the above land and the Templars warranted to the prior 'salt rent' and 4s 6d rent.[53] The third dispute between Knights Templars and Benedict, Bishop of Rochester, requested him to follow the Archbishop of Canterbury with regard to the Hundred of Shemel by the bishop's men of Halling and Cokelestan [Cuxton]. The Templars would relinquish their right to five shillings in yearly rent from the bishop's men for the arrears. However, the bishop was to pay five shillings in yearly rent to the Templars and '12d yearly which Templars used to pay to Bishop for a certain meadow in Strod [Strood] called the meadow of Stephen Aurifaber and 4s a year received from the mill which Symon de Belesse held in Cuxton in fee of the Bishop at a rent of 8s which Bishop used to receive from the said mill'.[54]

In all three disputes the Templars were represented by Alan Martell, Master of the Knights Templar in England, which implies that Martell stayed in the manor on those occasions. To provide hospitality to the most senior knight, the manor would have had to have sufficient number of sergeants, chaplains and servants. That elevates the status and importance of Strood manor as a Templars' place of residence. It was also the most valuable property of the Templars in Kent, with its rental value of £11 18s. The importance of the manor is also supported by the 19th-century local historian Henry Smetham who, quoting William A. Scott-Robertson, mentions: 'The manor was one of importance. The Hundred Roll of 1274 mentions 32 of its principal tenants of men of Strode, who were withdrawn by the Templars from doing suit and service in the Hundred Court of the City of Rochester.'[55]

The Knights Templars were among the wealthiest and the most powerful of the Christian military orders.[56] As crusaders, they were particularly hostile to Jews. To quote Thomas F. Tout: 'This hatred was based not only upon the attitude of the unbeliever natural to an order of crusading knights but also the commercial hostility of a society of bankers interested in cosmopolitan finance to a rival commercial community whose command over capital and international relations made them the chief competitors of the Templars in this sphere.'[57] As rival creditors to the Crown and the Church (it is known that bishops of Rochester held their accounts in the New Temple in London), they were hostile to Jews. So, what was the position of Rochester Jews, who lived with this neighbour? Or perhaps the community existed, but comprised exclusively non-prosperous Jews, who never appeared in any records? No documents have emerged to provide any clues.

The baronial uprising of 1258-66 saw Rochester and its vicinity caught in the midst of the conflict. As troops led by Simon de Montfort and Gilbert de Clare were approaching the city in 1264, Jews, fearing the worst, were trying to save themselves and some of their assets. Aaron of Sittingbourne left his two bags, containing two fine linen mantels and cloaks and four silver buckles, with some other valuables with his neighbours, Alan and Dionisia, who in their turn locked the bags in a chest in the church, presuming it would be safe. Aaron took away the key. Upon arrival, the troops demanded from the citizens of Sittingbourne to surrender Aaron on the threat of burning the city down. Facing the town's destruction, Alan confessed that the Jew had left, but his possessions were in the church.[58]

The account of Matthew of Westminster in Frederick Smith's book on Rochester describes the defence of the castle and the city by Roger de Leyburne and the horrors inflicted on the city and its residents by Simon de Montfort:

'Entering … the whole City, and whatever was in it, became … the prey of the spoilers. Moreover, unsheathing their swords, the diabolical partisans entered the church of the Blessed Andrew, and crucified its sons, and all who were found therein through fear or for worship, with the Lord who suffers for his elect; violently carrying off gold and silver and other precious things thereof. Many valuable things also, among others the royal charters and other muniments of the Church of Rochester in the prior's chapel were destroyed and torn to pieces. Certain Monks also of the same church were that night imprisoned and guarded. Armed Horse-men, too, on horses riding round the altars, with wicked hands dragged out all who fled to them … The Sacred places, as the oratories, cloisters, chapter, infirmary, and all the divine oracles, were converted into stables for horses, and were everywhere filled with the uncleannesses of animals and the filthiness of corpses. On Saturday that is the eve of Easter Day, the barons took the outer bailey of the Castle, and the Earl of Warren with his men retired into the tower. The besieged then stoutly defended themselves for seven days, and many both within and without were wounded and slain. But on the seventh day, that is, the Saturday following, the Earl took to flight with the army; Simon hearing that the King was coming to the succour of the besieged.'[59]

Rochester was recorded as a place of Jewish settlement in 1262.[60] After reading the above account one wonders whether any Jews of Rochester survived this violence. Simon de Montfort, known for his strong anti-Jewish sentiments, would have not hesitated to massacre the Jews and destroy any records. The records between 1253 and 1266 of the Plea Rolls of the Exchequer of the Jews are lost, probably destroyed by his order.[61]

In 1272 Henry III imposed another tallage on Jews, which resulted in £71 paid by four Jews of Canterbury with no contribution from Rochester, showing a significant financial hardship borne by the communities. By that time Jews were already barred from many occupations and they were not allowed to own land outside towns, nor permitted to farm. After 1271 Jews were allowed to own only their own residence or let it to other Jews.[62] Nor were the Jews permitted to be employed in any capacity by Christian households.[63]

Edward I succeeded to the throne in 1272. His policy towards his Jewish subjects crystallised three years later, on 25 April 1275, and was summed up by a Rochester chronicler: 'And it was particularly forbidden for the Jews to practise unrestrained usury. And so that the King was able to keep them apart from Christians he ordered that they should wear the tablets of the Law in length and width as a sign on the outside of their outer garments.'[64]

Later that year proved that the king embarked on what has become known as 'Edwardian experiment'. In his *Statutum de Judaismo* in 1275 he decreed that every Jew, male or female, above the age of 12 were to pay chevage (poll tax) of 3d. To balance out the restrictions and the chevage, Jews were allowed to trade in wool and grain and agriculture. They were to make to landowners advances of money, without interest, to be repaid, and in the case of Kent, in corn.[65] Trading and agriculture required a capital, already lacking because of the extortionate sums of numerous tallages, and a fundamental reorientation, which would take at least one generation to take effect. Jews were given a mere 15 years to do so.[66]

To help his reform Edward issued royal licences for Jews to trade in several towns, including Rochester. Contemporary Jews realised the intention of changing them from moneylenders into merchants and bring them into line with the accepted Christian business practices. They complained. The Jews petitioned the king, pointing out that they would not be able to compete with

Christian merchants, as they had to buy at dearer prices and could not to sell dearer. They also claimed that despite continued royal protection, the Jews were unable to take their goods out of *archa* towns for the fear of being robbed, whereas Christian merchants could do so freely.[67]

To help his reform, Edward issued royal licences for Jews to trade in several towns, including Rochester. Rochester possessed a royal licence, allowing Jews to trade, which implies that there were Jews who lived in Rochester at the time. This in its turn means that Rochester Jewry must have recovered from the horrors inflicted on the city by Simon de Montfort in the 1260s.

However, another record suggests otherwise. By royal decrees of 1245 and 1253 Jews were not permitted to live in any city that did not possess a royal *archa*, and as evidence suggests Rochester did not have one. A royal order of 8 December 1276 permitted 'Salle de Roucestria and Hake Poleyn, Jews, to dwell in the city of Rochester in the houses wherein they previously dwelt until the King shall otherwise ordain'.[68] The inference is that both Salle and Hake had been living in Rochester for some time, and to do so required the king's permission. Indeed, we find an earlier record, 13 November 1273, mentioning Hake, where he is referred to as Hak of London. However, the king's writ is addressed to John de Cobham, then Sheriff of Kent. The fact that the writ was addressed to the official in Kent means that Hake had been already living in Rochester in 1273.[69] Indeed, in 1275 Hake paid four shillings for a writ of residence in Rochester.[70] The payment and that he had to obtain the royal permission implies that the city did not have a Jewry.

On 18 June 1290 the sheriffs were issued instructions to seal the *archae* in the whole country by 28 June. A month later, 18 July, the official Edict of Expulsion informed the sheriffs of the counties and the Constable of the Tower in London that all Jews had been ordered to leave England by 1 November 1290. The sheriffs, bailiffs, barons and sailors of the Cinque Ports were also to ensure that the Jews with their wives, children and goods (the ones that were not forfeited to the Crown) suffered no injury or harassment during their departure.[71] Cecil Roth referrs to this date, 18 July 1290, which coincided with the fast of ninth of Av (Tisha B'Av), as an 'anniversary of manifold disasters for the Jewish people'.[72]

By that time, it is estimated that only about 2,000 Jews remained in England (at its peak the overall community had about 5,000). Most possessions were left behind, and several disturbances were recorded. At Queenborough, Henry Adrian, the captain of one of the ships decided to administer 'justice' himself. Having pretended that the ship had foundered on a sandbank, he asked the Jews to disembark while refloating. When they did so, he jumped back on board, shouted at them to call on Moses to help them and took off with whatever meagre Jewish possessions he had on board. The Jews drowned when the tide came in. Adrian was eventually captured and spent two years in Sandwich jail.[73] It is not clear what happened to the Jewish possessions.

Another act of violence, this time probably taking part in Rochester itself, was portrayed in the early 14th-century *Rochester Chronicle*, written by one of St Andrew Priory monks — three Jews, wearing their tabula — badges, depicting tablets with 10 commandments, which Jews had to wear to be distinguished from the Christians,[74] are being threatened by a Christian swinging a club at them. One Jew has raised his arm to protect himself as the others seem to try to negotiate with the attacker. Although the chronicle was written much later and may contain some artistic licence, there is no doubt that it depicts a hostile scene.[75] If one is to assume that Salle de Roucestria and Hake Poleyn stayed in Rochester until 1290, could two of the three Jews be them? Probably not, and judging by that last record of 1276, there was hardly a Jewish community in Rochester at the time. Those could have been Jews just passing through on their way out of the country. Whoever those individuals were, the presence of Jews in Rochester, the significance of Jewish connection to the city over two centuries was such that it was deemed necessary to immortalise them and their expulsion in the chronicle.

After the expulsion, only Jews who converted remained; perhaps some stayed illegally. Records neither show a significant increase in baptisms, nor reveal anything about those who decided to stay on illegally.[76] The expulsion of Jews from the country marked the end of the first Jewish community in Rochester.

Chapter 2

Out/with the Jews
1290-1656

Having expelled its Jews in 1290, England thus asserted the superiority of its Christian faith. Jews who preferred to convert in exchange for permission to stay entered Domus Conversorum, established by Henry III in 1232. Out of a list of inmates between 1280 and 1308, which contained 80 residents in the year of expulsion, only five or six names were connected to Kent, at Gillingham and Canterbury:

❖ Christina de Gellingham (though she might have been from Gellingham in Dorset)
❖ Robertus de Cant' [Canterbury]
❖ Gregorius de Cant'
❖ Matill' de Cant'
❖ Ermedruta de Cant'
❖ Elena de Cant'[1]

However, a complete list of residents from 1330 gives us a large number of Jewish names from Brussels, Spain, France and Acre (in today's northern Israel), with a small sprinkling of names associated with English towns of Leicester, Dartmouth, Exeter and Kingston. No names appear in connection with Rochester, confirming that no Jews from the city remained in the country after 1290. The number of residents steadily declined and seven years later, by the end of 1337, there were only 13 residents — two men and 11 women.[2]

The city of Rochester celebrated the supremacy of Christianity and expulsion of its Jews 52 years later, when in 1342, Bishop Hamo of Hythe commissioned a new decorative door to the cathedral's Chapter Room, which can still be seen today. Two female sculptures, eclipsing the doorframe represent the Church and the Synagogue. The figure of the Church carries a pennant and a staff in one hand and a model of the church in the other; the other, a beautiful blind-folded woman wearing a mantle, is the Synagogue. She is poised and pathetic, holding her broken staff and the Tables of the Law with their rounded tops reversed.[3]

There are also four figures above the Church and the Synagogue, two on each side. It seems there is no consensus as to who these figures represent. Some suggest that the four figures are four Evangelists, or the Doctors of the Church: St Augustine, Gregory, Gerome and Ambrose.[4] However, according to the historian W.H. St John Hope, two lower heads, which are veiled, are Jewish doctors, and two upper ones, with bare heads are Christian — their upper position once again asserts the supremacy of papal power.[5]

Having rid itself of the Jews, the Crown and the priory turned to strengthening their position in the city, most notably during the middle and the latter part of the 14th century. Temple Manor, such a significant player the previous century, became the property of the king once the Knights Templars were

Facing page: the chapter door of Rochester Cathedral with the figures, representing the Church and the Synagogue, before the 1890s. The figure of the Church was 'restored' by the architect Lewis Nockalls Cottingham, who carried out the cathedral restoration in 1825-30. Either deliberately ignoring the iconographical significance of the figure, or being ignorant of its importance, he decorated it with the mitred bearded bishop's head. The mistake was corrected only in the 1890s by the efforts of Miss Louisa Twining, writer on ecclesiastical iconography and a major social reformer.

disbanded in 1312. The manor lost its function and became a farm.

In 1344, during the reign of Edward III the new city wall, though built entirely upon the property of the monks, once more extended the boundaries of the city towards the south. In 1368 extensive and expensive (£1,200) repairs were carried out in the castle supervised by John the Prior.[6] The bastion was added to the northeast angle of the city-wall, and a new stone bridge over the Medway at Rochester was finished in 1391, paid by Sir John de Cobham and Sir Robert Knolles.

The monks, having secured the king's grace by supporting his efforts in strengthening the city's defences, were also active on their own account. They built a new wall along the north side of the priory, where their property adjoined High Street, and in other directions they completely isolated themselves from the rest of the city. No doubt the tensions between the resident monks and the Rochester citizens, notable in the previous centuries, were still bubbling underneath the surface, which resulted in establishment of St Nicholas Church next door to the cathedral for the benefit of ordinary folk.[7]

Despite having rid itself of the Jews, the country's fear of them persisted. The Jew became a bogeyman to be feared and hated in equal measure. This attitude pervaded the literary works of the period, the most famous, *The Prioress's Tale*, being written between 1387 and 1400 by the prominent literary name associated with Kent: Geoffrey Chaucer.

The tale is told by the Prioress during the pilgrimage to the shrine of St Thomas Becket at Canterbury Cathedral. According to the experiment conducted in 2012, when a group of enthusiasts re-enacted the same pilgrimage, the story is narrated in Cobham Woods near Rochester.[8] We can only speculate of the significance of that, if it is true. However, it is interesting to note that the shrine of St William of Perth in Rochester Cathedral never acquired such prominence as Becket's.

Chaucer's story tells the audience about a Christian boy who, when walking through the Jewish ghetto on his way to and from school, offended Jews by singing praise to Virgin Mary. Infuriated by his piety, Jews kidnap and kill the boy; but despite his throat being slit, the child still sings and his song leads his mother to the place, where his body has been thrown. The Jews, Satan's agents in the world, are tortured and executed, while the boy is given a digni-

Temple Manor, Strood: the most valuable property of the Knights Templars in Kent. It became the property of the king once the knights were disbanded in 1312, and turned into a farm

fied burial and declared a martyr. The story echoes the familiar narrative of accusations against Jews in ritual murder in the 12th and 13th centuries, legal proceedings following the events, reports of the proceedings and songs and sermons 'inspired' by them. The Prioress's tale about the death of a pious child, though a fiction, provides the listeners with the impression of truthfulness. It reminds the audience of what their own children once risked and affirms the Jews' hatred against Christians. The message is clear: as long as Jews live among us there always will be child murders. England is very fortunate to be clear of them.[9] Were citizens of Rochester familiar with the story? If they were, their reaction to it would probably be as intended — fear and hatred.

However, no expulsion applied to any group of people, no matter how strictly enforced, can ever be absolute. Also, as time passed, memories of the persecution became distant and dim, and after the Jews' expulsion from Spain in 1492, England seemed an attractive option for some exiles. A small number of them resided in London until the negotiations of a marriage between Arthur, Prince of Wales, and Catherine of Aragon, daughter of Isabella of Castille and Ferdinand of Aragon. However, during the negotiations, King Ferdinand formally protested against the presence of Jews in England: after all, he was the initiator of the Spanish Inquisition. King Henry VII solemnly reassured the Spanish sovereign that any Jewish fugitive from the inquisition, discovered in England, would be mercilessly prosecuted. However, no records indicate that the promise was ever enforced.[10] Furthermore, after the expulsion from Portugal in 1496, some of the Portuguese Conversos reached England and settled in London as well.[11] It is considered that there were about 37 householders of crypto-Jewish community from Spain and Portugal, who settled in England.[12] But the main change regarding Judaism, if not Jews themselves, occurred during the Reformation triggered by Henry VIII's desire to extricate himself from Rome and assert his own supremacy.

It all started with the king's matrimonial problems. The biblical authority for his desire to annul his long-standing marriage to Catherine of Aragon, who became Henry's wife after the death of Arthur, was in Leviticus 18:16, which stated that the marriage between a man and his brother's wife was categorically forbidden. However, Deuteronomy 25:5 expressly prescribed such an alliance, if the brother had died childless, for his name to continue. The problem of interpretation was highly complicated and the importance of Hebrew tradition for the correct understanding of the holy text suddenly dawned on both sides of the dispute. However, there were no Jews in England or in Spain to ask for advice, and both sides had to seek guidance in the Jewish quarters of Venice.[13]

In January 1534, parliament passed legislation against the exercising of papal power in England. The act also included the transfer of the religious houses from the Pope to the king.[14] Bishop John Fisher of Rochester refused to acknowledge the king's supremacy in ecclesiastical affairs, just as earlier he had refused to sign in favour of Henry's marriage to Anne Boleyn.[15]

Within the next five years the parliament passed another two pieces of legislation relating to monasteries. The first declared the suppression of the monasteries with an annual income of less than £200, and their possession granted to the Crown. The second act established the Court of Augmentations of the Revenues of the King's Crown to manage the acquired properties. The subsequent Act for the Suppression of Religious Houses in 1539 announced the end of all their establishments in England.[16]

At the time there were 36 religious houses in Kent, including St Andrew's Priory in Rochester.[17] In 1540 the monks lost their possession of the cathedral, which they had enjoyed for more than 450 years. The animosity between the monks and the bishops started with Bishop Glanville in the 12th century, and seems to have continued with his successors. In the 15th century, William Wells, who became the Bishop of Rochester in 1437, conducted an inquiry into the monks' behaviour and deviation from the St Benedict's rules, one of which prescribed silence to be kept at most times and in most quarters of the priory. As an anonymous author writes in his publication of 1772: 'The monks not only exercised the faculty of speech (the singular prerogative of a man) at times and in places when and where he [the bishop] judged they ought not; but had made a practice of abusing it by licentious and idle talk, and by keen invectives against each other.'[18]

The numbers of the monks also dwindled over the years. At the time of its establishment by Lafranc in 1083, the priory comprised 22 monks of Benedictine Order, the same order as St Augustine's Priory in Canterbury; by 1540 there were only six residents.[19] There were also offences regarding their knowledge and manner in educating the young. According to the above-mentioned publication of 1772, the rudiments of grammar were taught only occasionally.

However, the gravest concerns were related to their ecclesiastical knowledge. The monks were so ill-qualified that, already in the early 14th century, Bishop Hamo of Hythe was mortified by their ignorance in the doctrines and duties of the Holy Scriptures. His concern was such that he presented them with a set of books, which the monks and the neighbouring clergy could consult, in hope that they would be able to 'perform the proper office of their profession.'[20] There is no record to find out whether the monks' ecclesiastical knowledge improved by 1540. If it did, it was undoubtedly too late. On 20 June 1542 'the dean and chapter of the cathedral church of Christ and blessed Virgin Mary of Rochester' created a new establishment comprising a dean, and six canons or prebendaries, with other ministers necessary for the appropriateadministration for divine service. Newark Hospital in Frindsbury, near Strood, founded by Bishop Glanville in 1193, also came into the king's possession.[21]

The European Renaissance interest in antiquity, humanism, Judaism and Hebrew studies manifested itself in England in establishment of chairs of Hebrew in Oxford and Cambridge in the 1540s.[22] Paul Fagius, a notable German theologian and humanist, was appointed to the chair of Hebrew at Cambridge in 1549.[23] A year earlier, Richard Bruerne was appointed regius professor of Hebrew at the University of Oxford. It is interesting to note that Bruerne's interest in Hebrew and Judaism, though natural for a scholar of his calibre, landed him into much trouble throughout his life.[24]

Despite the prohibition of Jews from setting foot in England, the Crown always referred to Jews or turned a blind eye to their presence, when it was suitable to do so. Already in 1309 Magister Elias — from his title, a physician or rabbi — was given a safe conduct by Edward II to come to England to treat 'certain matters relating to Us'.[25]

Henry VIII had strong commercial relations with the Mendez Trust in Antwerp established before 1525. The connection was so important that when Diogo Mendez was arrested in 1532 for Judaism, *ie* for following Jewish customs and practices, Henry VIII intervened for his protection.[26] English ports were also used as a safe stop-over for Spanish exiles on route to Netherlands after 1536 when King Charles V allowed New Christians to settle in the country. Many refugees never proceeded to Antwerp, but settled in England, thus expanding the crypto-Jewish community.[27]

In addition, London was also a host to a small community of Italian musicians and their families, such as the Bassanos, Kellims and Lupos, who came at the invitation of the Crown.[28]

However, with the accession in 1553 of Queen Mary and reinstatement of Catholicism, England became at least as dangerous as Spain for those communities. The crypto-Jewish settlement dispersed but already by the close of the reign of her predecessor, Edward VI, there were tiny communities of Conversos in London and in Bristol.[29]

During the reign of Elizabeth I (1558-1603), the 'secret' settlement of Jews in the country continued, encouraged by the possibility of tolerance free of Roman Catholicism. During the war with Spain they were used by London merchants for trade with the Peninsula[30] and as Elizabeth's secret agents, working for Walsingham and Cecil. The dangers their work presented were not only from the outside, but from within the country. This could easily result in a death sentence, as in the case of Dr Roderigo Lopez, the personal physician to the queen and a secret agent for Cecil. At the instigation of King of Spain, Lopez was accused of plotting to poison Elizabeth. He was arrested in October 1593 and executed at Tyburn on 7 June 1594. He was undoubtedly innocent of that particular charge, though his methods and aims might be found dubious for people far removed from the intricacies of cloak-and-dagger organisations.[31]

The most prominent feature though in Lopez's trial and execution was his origin. And the propaganda machine, reiterating the messages of Jew-hatred and influencing public opinion, worked well. The most popular play on the London stage at the time, *The Jew of Malta*, was written by the Canterbury playwright Christopher Marlowe. The Jew of Malta, whose name, Barabas, was in itself an affront — the original Barabbas was a prisoner released by Pontius Pilate in preference to Jesus, with approval of the Jews (see Matthew 27:16-26).[32] Marlowe's Barabas seemed to anticipate the character and the fate of Lopez.

Just a few years later a revenge comedy by Shakespeare, *The Merchant of Venice*, transformed the Jew into an object of ridicule, sarcasm, and revenge. Shylock, the play's representative Jew, in his naïvety, believes that by strict adherence to the rules, both Jewish and Venetian, one can discharge his duties to friends and strangers. But his fidelity to the rule of law is criminalised by the play. Shylock is a bad Jew, representative of all Jews, who therefore are bad, and as a result, their loyalty to Judaism is bad. In comparison, Antonio, a respected and prosperous merchant, defaulter on his loan, is portrayed as a victim, who nevertheless is prepared to change his view of Shylock and act with true Christian charity — offer him 'an olive branch of conversion'.[33] As the writer Anthony Julius points out, Shylock is an English Jew — wicked, malignant, despised, but conquerable and tolerated due to his usefulness as a financier.[34] It is worth speculating whether Shakespeare visited Domus Conversorum when gathering information about Jewish dress, manners and religious customs. He was also probably familiar with the publications in English containing the conversion speech by Nathaniel Menda, a Hebraist and biblical scholar, probably from Morocco, and a powerful sermon by the Puritan preacher John Foxe, the author of *Foxe's Book of Martyrs*. Both published in 1578 and sold widely.[35]

There is no proof that Rochester residents were acquainted with *The Merchant of Venice*, though it is of course, possible that some saw the play in London, or that it was performed in Rochester, though no record survives. There is, however, a much greater probability that Rochester citizens saw *The Jew of Malta*. Between 1592, the first recorded performance, and 1597 the play was staged by various troupes including Queen Elizabeth's Men (or Her Majesty's Players) and Admiral's Men, who performed it more than a dozen times between May 1594 and June 1596.[36] Queen Elizabeth's Men and Lord Admiral's Men performed in the city every year between 1591 and 1597 (with the gap year in 1593), as indicated by the mayor's accounts. For example, during the trial of Dr Lopez, the accounts for 1594-95 show that Her Majesty's Players received a payment of 20 shillings for their performance on 22 February; Lord Admiral's Men performed in the city on 11 March, for which they were paid 10 shillings.[37] There is no mention of the title of the play on either occasion, but it is highly probable that at least one of the performances was *The Jew of Malta*, considering the popularity of the play that year. It is not hard to imagine the audience's response to it.

So, officially without Jews, but in reality with them, Rochester arrived in the 17th century — an era of tumultuous change.

Chapter 3

The Return
17th century

The interest in Judaism and Hebrew studies continued in the 17th century. So did their suppression. In the second decade, John Traske, a Church of England clergyman published a number of works that deviated from mainstream Christian teachings. More significantly, he also adopted a great number of Jewish ceremonies, including the adherence to *kashrut* (Jewish dietary laws) and the strict observance of the Jewish Sabbath on Saturdays. A charismatic preacher, very soon he acquired many followers. The danger to the establishment was obvious, and on 19 June 1618 Traske was sentenced for 'detraction and scandal on the King's most excellent Majesty', and for 'a seditious practice and purpose to divert his Majesty's subjects from their obedience' after he wrote to James I trying to convert him to his cause. Star Chamber sentenced him to be degraded, fined, whipped, pilloried, branded, to have his ears nailed to the pillory, and to be imprisoned at the king's pleasure. 'Having endured state torture and facing a lifetime in prison, Traske opted to reassess his theological position.'[1]

Despite the short lifespan of this Judaising sect, Traske's influence and his teachings spread and reverberated long after his trial, reaching up to the House of Commons. The measures to counter Traske's influence ranged from the expulsion of Thomas Shepherd, MP for Shaftesbury in Dorset, from parliament for his sympathy for Traske's teachings in 1621, to a bill regulating the observance of the Sabbath. In relation to the bill, the Archbishop of

Canterbury was arguing in favour of excluding the word 'Sabbath' from the vocabulary altogether because of 'the aptness of divers to enclyne to Judaisme as the newe sect of the Thraskites.'[2]

However, the mood of toleration among some sections of English society seemed to be catching. In 1648, Edward Nicholas published *The Apology for the Noble Nation of the Jews and All the Sons of Israel*, calling for the extension of goodwill towards the Jews for their past sufferings in England. This was one of the typical publications of that time.[3] Then in December 1648, during the trial of Charles I, the Council of Mechanics passed a resolution extending tolerance to all religions 'not excepting Turkes nor Papists nor Jewes'. The Council of War endorsed this 'universal toleration. However, opposition was strong, and in *The Agreement of the People*, the manifesto proposing constitutional changes to the state, the toleration was limited to Christians only.[4]

Rochester, though traditionally royalist, was, however, governed by supporters of Oliver Cromwell during the Civil War. We do not know whether they were supporters of the universal toleration that would have included Jews. The only local reference relating to Jews we find is in a sermon of John Warner, Bishop of Rochester, published anonymously in London during 1648 after the execution of Charles I. Invoking a familiar 'blame-the-Jew' technique, it was entitled *The Devilish Conspiracy, Hellish Treason, Heathenish Condemnation, and Damnable Murder, Committed and Executed by the Jewes, Against the Anointed of the Lord, Christ their King.*[5]

In January 1649 the Council of Officers considered a petition from two Baptists from Amsterdam, Joanna and Ebenezer Cartwright, who motivated by the notions of Christian charity and brotherly love, were requesting the readmission of Jews to England and permission for them to trade. The council decided to investigate the matter at a future date.

The next attempt to allow Jews to settle in England was considered by the Council of State barely over two-and-half years later, on 10 October 1651. This time it was submitted by Menasseh ben Israel, a rabbi from Amsterdam. In December 1652 the council sent Menasseh an invitation to visit England, with a pledge of safe conduct. However, the outbreak of the First Dutch War prevented his visit.

The war aimed to establish control of the seas around England, protecting

English trade from foreigners and compelling the Dutch to acknowledge the English monopoly of trade with its colonies. In truth, the English were copying Dutch trading techniques, and permitting Spanish and Portuguese Jewish merchants to settle in England fitted very well into this policy. During debates on the subject, Martin Noell, a brother-in-law to the Secretary of State John Thurloe, who was a partner in East-India ventures, a merchant to the Baltic and the Caribbean and a major tax-farmer, said in a speech in parliament: 'The only reason that the Jews of Venice had to wear red hats was that they had no State which could protect them.'[6] As a result, once the war was over, Cromwell was swayed to look into the readmission of Jews. Menasseh ben Israel was advised to visit England and to submit his petition on behalf of the Jewish nation to the Lord Protector.

What attracted Menasseh ben Israel specifically to England? For once, it is known that he was profoundly influenced by the prophecy: 'When he shall have accomplished to scatter the power of the holy people, all these things shall be finished,'[7] meaning that only when the dispersal was complete and the Deuteronomic prophecy was fulfilled, could redemption begin. To resettle Jews in England was to hasten the process. In addition, England presented a very specific interest and importance, because throughout medieval Jewish literature 'Angleterre' was literally translated into Hebrew as 'katzeh haaretz' — the angle, the limit, the end of the world — the notion that was reflected in the verse of Deuteronomy: 'And the Lord shall scatter thee among all peoples, from the one end of the earth even unto the other end of the earth.'[8] For Menasseh, the resettlement of Jews in England became the matter of international importance. He also thought this idea would appeal to Christians, such as Henry Jessey, the rabbinical scholar and founder of the Puritan sect the Jacobites, who shared his interpretation of the prophecy. So, in 1655 during his visit to England, Menasseh submitted his petition 'on behalf of the Jewish nation', *The Humble Addresses, to the Lord Protector,* asking permission to settle in England and practise religion publicly, freely and without fear of persecution. However, the request and the ideas expressed in the petition annoyed some parliamentarians, and great agitation ensued. Rumours about the dangers of readmitting Jews widely circulated in London and, no doubt, in the provinces. One fanciful accusation stated that Jews were buying St Paul's Cathedral to convert it into a synagogue. They had already made an offer of £500,000, and the only obstacle to the sale was that parliament insisted on £800,000.[9]

One of the most virulent opponents to the readmission was William Prynne, a prominent politician and the Keeper of the Records in the Tower of London. He revived the familiar blood accusation, but when that failed, argued that as Jews were 'banished out in 1290 ... never to return,'[10] it would be unlawful to allow Jews to live in the country. The same year he published *Short Demurrer to the Jewes Long Discontinued Barred Remitter into England.* He asserted he had consulted the original records.

On Tuesday, 4 December 1655, in the Council Chamber of Whitehall, a conference of representatives of political, theological, legal and business walks of life gathered to decide:

i) Was it lawful to admit Jews to England?
ii) If yes, would the country admit them?
iii) If it is decided that they are to be admitted, then on what terms and conditions?

Very quickly it became apparent that there was no legal prohibition preventing Jews from settling in England. But did the English want Jews to settle here? A small number of religious leaders were in favour, but the majority were against. They argued that Jewish customs and 'their worship or religion is not only evil in itself, but likewise very scandalous to other Christian churches.'[11] Merchants vigorously insisted that allowing Jews in would only enrich foreigners and would cause the decline of English trade. Even those who were in favour, wanted to impose stringent conditions which included:

i) That they may not be admitted to have any publicke Judicatoryes, whether civill or ecclesiasticall, which were to grant them terms beyond the conditions of strangers.
ii) That they be not admitted eyther to speake or doe anything to the defamation or dishonour of the name of our Lord Jesus Christ or of the Christian religion.
iii) That they be not permitted to doe any worke or anything to the

prophanation of the Lord's Day or Christian Sabbath.

iv) That they be not admitted to have Christians dwell with them as their servants.

v) That they bear no publicke office or trust in this commonwealth.

vi) That they be not allowed to print anything which in the least opposeth the Christian religion in our language.

vii) That, so farre as may be, not suffered to discourage any of their owne from usinge or applying themselves to any which may tend to convince them of their error and turn them to Christianity. And that some severe penalty be imposed upon them who shall apostatize from Christianity to Judaisme.[12]

The conference produced no result and the petition reverted to the special committee of the council for its consideration, though everyone knew that Cromwell would have the final word on the matter. Meanwhile, Jews were quietly meeting for prayers in the privacy of their homes. By the end of February, it was clear that the Lord Protector would not provide a direct answer. Having realised that the question of their formal readmission was closed, on 24 March 1656 the Jews submitted another petition, this time simply asking for permission to 'meete at owr said private devotions in owr Particular houses without feere of Molestation' and establish a cemetery 'in such place out of the cittye as wee shall thincke convenient'.[13]

Meanwhile, another war broke out, this time between England and Spain. Robles, a merchant residing in London, was denounced to the authorities as a Spaniard, resulting in all his goods being seized. Robles submitted a request for the restitution of his property, stating that he was not a Spaniard, but a Portuguese 'of the Hebrew nation'. In May 1656 Robles was reinstated in possession of his property. If he were a Spanish Roman Catholic, his position at the time of war would have been precarious, but as a refugee Jew, he was safe. The case in its essence thus established the legality and legitimacy of the residence of Jews in England. Cromwell, a cunning politician, was unwilling to directly confront the anti-Jewish mood in the country; on the other hand, he did not wish to be deprived of the advantages that the resettlement would bring. Consequently, he pursued an oblique policy of endorsing Jewish resettlement without formal authorisation.[14]

Following Cromwell's implicit permission to settle, a first private synagogue was established in December 1656. It was based on the first floor of a house on Creechurch Lane in the City of London. The small community comprised about 27 males, Spanish and Portuguese Jews, mostly the heads of families.[15] They were merchants, jewellers, brokers, or wholesaler's agents and a handful of domestic servants.

Immigrants were mainly recorded as lodgers. As foreigners, or 'merchant strangers', they could not own land. At the same time, they were unable to trade if they did not have a dwelling. As a result, immigrants took tenancy for years of a dwelling house as incidental to their trade. People were anxious about letting to aliens, partially because if the foreigner gave up his tenancy the remainder of the term would become forfeited to the Crown instead of reverting to the landlord.[16]

By 1690 another synagogue appeared in London, at Duke's Place, this time for the Ashkenazi Jews, and the overall community grew to 35 families. In comparison with Sephardi Jews, these immigrants were very poor. They had fled from persecutions in countries such as Poland and Bohemia, where they had lived in densely populated settlements. They looked different, they wore peculiar dress and their names were constructed in a different manner. They had always lived openly as Jews in their tight-knit communities, preserving their identities as Jews. They had not intermarried with Christians or assimilated; their religious knowledge and practices were much more intense; and their Hebrew pronunciation was different. Between themselves they spoke Yiddish, a language unintelligible to the Sephardim. Many were destitute. In their countries of origin their interactions with people outside their immediate communities were minimal, and as a result, their secular knowledge was limited. They were usually small artisans, builders, repairers, painters, handymen, porters or dealers in second-hand goods. They survived by whatever means and often did not prosper. The Christians regarded them with great suspicion and disgust, and it would be the image of an Ashkenazi Jew they would have in mind when accusing Jews of crime later on.[17]

With the restoration of the monarchy from 1660, anti-Jewish agitation was revived. The death of Oliver Cromwell in 1658 had already unleashed a campaign against the Jewish presence in England with some clerics, MPs and their constituents praying for the banishment of the Jews and confiscation of their property. In December 1659, Thomas Violet brought a case against Jews to court. Basing his statements on Prynne's *Demurrer* he argued that settlement was illegal, and that the law should be upheld by banishing the intruders. Not being satisfied by the judicial opinion that there was no illegality in admitting Jews to England and by Mr Justice Tyril's refusal to take action, he published a tract, asserting that the existence of Jews and their worship in the City of London was 'the great dishonour of Christianity and public scandal of the true Protestant religion.'[18] Following the judge's advice, Violet also applied to the Privy Council, personally marching to the Whitehall and delivering his application to the Lords.

Violet's campaign received great support from the City of London Corporation, which feared competition from the Jews, whom Cromwell had granted the right to trade with native merchants on an equal footing. The City was also eager to preserve traditional methods of trading, no matter how outdated they were. The lord mayor and aldermen joined Violet in his campaign, saying that Jews were a swarm of locusts, that they corrupted religion, that they presented a threat to English women, that they endangered public security, and that they ruined trade. They beseeched Charles II to advise parliament to expel 'all professed Jews out of Your Majesty's dominions, and to bar the door after them with such provisions and penalties as in Your Majesty's wisdom shall be found most agreeable to the safety of religion, the honour of Your Majesty, and the good and welfare of your subjects.'

The anxiety among Jews about the uncertainty of their state in England was high, and they appealed to the king asking for his protection. On 7 December 1660, the House of Commons received a note from the king 'desiring their advice thereon'. This action was soon known to the public, which prompted Violet to publish another venomous pamphlet attacking the Jews. Ten days after the council's meeting, the privy counsellor Denzil Holles presented a royal message to the Commons, but different from the earlier one adopted by the Privy Council. It asked advice not on whether Jews should be banished or not, but desired the question of 'protection of the Jewes' to be considered.[19] The Commons concluded that 'there was no law which forbade the Jews' return into England', and Cromwell in guaranteeing the Jews certain privileges had really not granted them any new ones, but had simply pledged himself to prevent parliament from restricting the logical consequences of their fundamental legal right of settlement.[20] The expulsion of Jews in 1290 related only to Jews residing in England at the time, and because it was only an order, it did not have the permanency of the law. Subsequently, it meant that, from the legal perspective, Jews were free to settle in England.[21] Once it was concluded that the edict of 1290 was not valid any more, Charles was happy to follow Cromwell's decision.

In general, the legal position of the Jews in this country had been established through a series of judicial decisions. The next question, which arose soon after and which required definitive answers, was whether Jews were to be accepted as witnesses in a court of law, and whether they could appear as parties and give evidence even on their own behalf. The matter came to light on 29 January 1667 in the case of Robeley v Langston and continued to do so with a regular occurrence for many years. In that case the barristers and judge undertook considerable research to determine whether chief justice Sir Edward Coke was correct when he stated in the early 17th century: 'An infidel cannot be a witness'. According to Coke, Jews were infidels by 'shutting their eyes against light', and whenever he mentioned Jews, he called them 'infidel Jews'. His opinion and the effect of his wording led, therefore, to crucial doubts whether a non-Christian could give evidence. However, records that survived from Norman times showed precedents that proved that Jews gave evidence in court. What's more, they were sworn in according to Jewish custom and upon the Scroll of the Law. That evidence enabled Charles II's judges to accept the Jewish oath as being consistent with Common Law. In effect, they overruled Coke.[22]

In 1677 the venue of a case was altered so that a Jewish witness did not need to appear on a Saturday. Another far-reaching decision took place in 1684, when Judge George Jeffreys — whose would become infamous for his part in the 'bloody assizes' that tried the Monmouth rebels in 1685 — refused the plea that because the Jews were 'perpetual enemies' in law, the religion of a Jewish plaintiff made it impossible for him to bring an action for the recovery of a debt. There was judicial opposition, too. The Bishop of St Asaph called for steps to vindicate the honour of the Christian religion and the English nation and was joined by Sir Peter Pett, the eminent lawyer and a kinsman of the Pett family, who for several generations were master shipwrights at Chatham Dockyard. Pett and the bishop drew up a plan suggesting that the Jews in England should be segregated on pre-expulsion lines, under the control of their own justiciar, who was to be responsible for the collection of taxes and to supervise their relations with the Crown. Pett offered himself as the first justiciar.[23]

As for Rochester, officially Jews did not reside in the city and had not visited there since their expulsion in 1290. However, it would be reasonable to presume that as Jews lived in London, some would have passed through the area or even lived in the city since the Reformation. Watling Street has been the main thoroughfare connecting London with the Continent since Roman times. There are simply no records that could shed light on the matter. The only surviving information we have is about a Jewish musician from Italy, originally invited to court by Henry VIII. Thomas Lupo, a violinist and composer, seems to have lived in Gillingham after 1620 until his death at the end of 1627. His son, Theophilus, who replaced him as court violinist from 16 February 1628 probably also lived within the manor of Gillingham. On 6 June 1629 he wrote a letter from Cooling on assigning arrears to pay debts.[24]

However, the inhabitants of Rochester and the surrounding area were probably familiar with the stories and plays about the Jew as a bogeyman. As if to confirm their fears, the first official newspaper story, published shortly after their readmission, was about a murder.

'On Tuesday, 15 October 1661, a prince of Transylvania, Cossuma Albertus, who had been on a visit to King Charles II, was approaching Rochester in his chariot. The vehicle got stuck fast in the mire near Gads Hill, within a mile from Strood. The Prince resolved to sleep in his coach. According to the report of Mercurius Publicus newspaper for October, 1661, while the Prince was fast asleep, his coachman, Isaac Jacob, a Jew, about midnight takes the Prince's hanger from under his head, and stabs him to the heart; and calling to his aid his companion—whose name was Casimirus Karsagi — they both completed the tragedy by dragging him out of the carriage, cutting off his head and throwing the mutilated remains into a ditch near at hand. The two men having possessed themselves of

a large sum of money which the Prince had about his person, then took back the carriage and horses to Greenhithe, where they left them "to be called for". On the following Saturday, an arm of the murdered Prince was brought by a dog belonging to a Doctor of Physic of Rochester, who was riding by the spot, whereupon search being made, the other remains were discovered. Not long afterwards the Jew and the footboy were both taken in London, and being brought before the Lord Mayor, the footboy confessed the whole murder. They were tried at Maidstone Assizes before Sir Orlando Bridgman and were sentenced to be executed.'

The prince was buried with great solemnity in Rochester Cathedral.[25] Rochesterians' worst fears were confirmed. But if the city could not construct physical walls against the Jews, they could build political and corporate ones. On 6 September 1673, Rochester Corporation passed by-laws, which included:

❖ *That no person shall sell or put to sale any Victuals or Merchandize upon the River Medway at any place but the Town key [quay], till the duties are paid, on pain (after warning) of forfeiting the value of the goods.*
❖ *No Foreigner shall use the trade of a Taylor, Shoe-maker, Barber, Joiner, Carpenter, Mason, Glover, or the occupation of a Hackneyman, or letting Horses or Coaches to hire, or any other trade, mystery, or occupation, for hire, gain or sale, within the said City and Liberties, or sell or utter, by retail any wares or goods (except at Fairs, and except victual and such like provisions as hath been or may be lawfully sold on Market Days) on pain of forfeiting 10s. And that no Foreigner shall keep any Shop or Place to put to sale any Merchandize by retail on pain of 20s a week.*
❖ *No Freeman shall employ in his house a Foreigner, to use any other trade than his own, on pain of 10s a week.*
❖ *No person shall on any Lord's Day, in his house, shop, or chamber, exercise his trade. No Tradesman shall, upon Sunday, open his shop or shop windows, save only so much as is necessary for the entrance into his house. And no Tradesman (except Apothecaries and others in case of sickness, or urgent necessity) shall sell or expose to sale upon Sunday, any merchandizes, on pain of 5s.[26]*

The last prohibition, intended to preserve the sanctity of Sunday, put Jews at great disadvantage, as they were unable to trade on the Sabbath.

Jews were permitted to settle in England without any restrictions, but it would be an exaggeration to say that they were welcomed by many. Having fled from persecution in their countries, and hopeful of a peaceful life, Jews were nevertheless fearful of their new surroundings. Hostility of local populations only reminded them of the countries they left. Conversion was viewed by some as a pragmatic solution for survival.

The first reference to Jews in the area appears already on 19 February 1674. Rochester Cathedral's officer records the alms given: [one shilling] 'to a poor Jew lately made a Christian, by order of Dr Dixon'[27] It was further seven years before another reference to Jews, on 24 June 1681, stated: 'To the relief of a Jew turned Christian.'[28] It seems the record-keeping was lax, as the names of the Jews are not known. The next year brings us the first names. On 17 January 1682 one shilling was 'given to Thomas Abraham a Jew newly converted'[29] and a 4 April record states: 'Paid 2s to John Alexander a converted Jew by the Dean's order and the Vice Dean.'[30]

Each record appears in the long list of people who received alms. Some were passing through Rochester, as the description next to their names stated. Others lived in the vicinity. Nothing in the above records hints that those Jews were mere travellers, passing through the area. The absence of any description next to their names tells us that they were the first Jewish residents of Rochester, and their poverty suggests their Ashkenazi origin.

By 1663 the city, with its suburbs, extended about a mile and a half along the Medway and, according to a French physician who visited Rochester that year, it was much larger than Canterbury. Another traveller, writing in 1669, stated that Rochester was justly reckoned among the most considerable places in Kent, and among the best in England. He estimated that its population was between 16,000 and 18,000, which probably included the city and all surrounding areas, whose people devoted themselves to craft or to the sea service, especially to imports from the Baltics.[31] Opinions differed, though. In 1697, another French writer claimed that Rochester was a long, straggling city, dirty and ill-built.[32]

By the end of the 17th century, Rochester had acquired a commercial rival.

The neighbouring small settlement of Chatham, which had only 200 people living within its boundaries in 1568,[33] developed into an important governmental town with an estimated population of 2,100. Its rapidly expanding royal dockyard offered numerous opportunities for making a living and, as a result, the poverty levels were much lower than in many other Kentish towns.[34]

While the citizens of Rochester 'basked in their winter sunshine of tradition, enjoying the advantages and suffering the ills pertaining to antiquity, Chatham possessed no traditions, and no local precedents impeded its development.'[34] Its occupants spoke a different tongue alien to the Kentish natives. As the historian James Presnail writes: 'Chatham was a colony of the New England set down in the midst of the Old, a pioneer township separated from the long-established by the forbidding barriers of change.'[36] It raised expectations for toleration, opportunities for work and a possibility for Jews to blend in with the environment.

No synagogue existed in the area, and there was no possibility of registering a birth of a child. However, a registration was necessary for legal purposes. The heirs of the property were required to prove their legitimate descent. To do so they needed to procure depositions from midwives who had attended their mother's confinement, from other family members and from the neighbours and attested by a notary. So, it became quite a common practice for Jews to pay the local clergy for the entry of their births and marriages in the registers of the local parish church.[37] Indeed, the registers of St Mary's Church in Chatham record the baptisms of the children of a certain Moses in September 1677, April 1683 and June 1687, and the children of Moise in April 1678, May 1680, December 1684 and February 1688. We also find the marriages of William Levy in 1694 and Isaac Raphuen — probably a garbling of the Sephardi name Raphael — in 1695. It is Chatham, not Rochester, that would become the main player in the coming centuries.

Chapter 4

Settling in the Area:
From the 18th to the early 19th century, part 1

The military campaigns of the early 18th century dominated public discourse, detracting attention away from Jewish aliens, though the relationship between the Jews and the English was tense under the surface. The situation erupted in 1753 with the introduction of a parliamentary bill that would have allowed any Jew who had continuously lived in the country for at least three years to be naturalised by parliament without taking the Sacrament.[1] The arguments in favour stated the economic, social and religious benefits, such as the introduction of capital into the country, and the notion that Jews never attempted to make converts. To the contrary, allowing Jewish immigrants to settle in the country would present an opportunity for their conversion. An additional bonus was the tradition of Jews to provide for their own poor, which meant there would be no recourse or drain on parishes.

And immediate backlash ensued with the familiar arguments under the banner "No Jews, No Wooden Shoes!" — a reference to the Jews from Amsterdam. William Northey, MP for Calne in Wiltshire (1747-61) and for Maidstone (1761-68), claimed that 'the Bill was an attempt to rob them of their birthright as Christians' and that swarms of Jews would come and settle in the country. Others argued that Jewish merchants were a threat to the English ones; that Jews would force the Protestants out of all offices, trades and professions; that Jews were a threat to the female population, as the daughters would be forced to marry rich Jews. The previous wild rumour of the conversion of

St Paul's Cathedral into a synagogue was revived as well as the well-trodden path of blood libels. A novel argument claimed that the eventual act would reduce the consumption of ham and bacon.[2] The situation was so intense that the Archbishop of Canterbury, being sympathetic to the Jews, feared a general massacre.[3]

There are no absolute figures for population in the first half of the 18th century, but the best estimates suggest that there were between five-and-a-half and six million people in England and Wales.[4] By 1750 the Jewish population of England was about 8,000, according to the consensus among academics.[5]

Despite the opposition, the bill passed into law by 96 to 55 votes in June 1753, only to be repealed six months later after a well-orchestrated anti-Jewish campaign. In addition to speeches and sermons by the clergy, there were many caricatures and numerous epistles attacking and lampooning Jews. One of these literary examples was a satirical piece published by the *London Evening Post*, prophesying public circumcisions and celebrations marking the anniversary of the Crucifixion to appear in *The London Gazette* — the official, and arguably the most important, governmental periodical, which published statutory notices. It was to be renamed *The Hebrew Journal*, following the establishment of Jews in the country.[6]

The great majority of Anglo-Jewry were desperately poor, and academics agree that there were no more than 20 prosperous families. There also were another 40 brokers and their families, relatively comfortable financially, and apart from a few physicians, the rest were hawkers and peddlers. The last two were scraping a living by travelling around the country; some settling in the provinces, others returning to London for restocking and to attend the Sabbath prayers in the synagogue. *Kent's London Directory* for 1753 — the directory for London, but published in Kent — gives us only 108 Jewish names, out of the 3,800 listed, who carried on a business successful enough to merit an entry, confirming this view.[7]

The popular image of a wealthy Sephardi stockbroker and of a ragged Ashkenazi was also a myth. It mattered not if the immigrants arrived from the Iberian Peninsula, Germany or Poland: they arrived penniless and unskilled. Those immigrants were mainly young men with no opportunity to learn a craft in their country of origin. And if the box of a Sephardi peddler included cuckoo

The Dreadful Consequence of Naturalising Jews — one of the images during the campaign of anti-Jewish agitation in 1753, when parliament was debating whether to allow Jews to be naturalised

clocks, sealing wax, spices, thimbles, penknives and pencils, Ashkenazi peddlers tended to specialise in inexpensive jewellery.[8] The latter were a common sight at Strood Fair, as recorded in the poem written in 1756 by the Rev Thomas Austen, Vicar of Allhallows, and published the same year:

> *Here Jews, with pencils, seals, and gaudy rings,*
> *Convert your money into needless things.*[9]

It is not clear from the poem whether those were travelling Jews or those who had settled in the area. However, the parish records provide us with a glimpse into the numbers and geographical distribution of the Jewish population who did settle in the Medway Towns, and who resorted to the churches to register marriage or births of their children. From the beginning of the 18th century until 1780 there are 81 birth registrations, *ie* baptisms (the separation of birth registration and baptism would come only in 1836 with the introduction of the civil registration and the establishment of the General Records Office), seven marriages and eight burials recorded in St Mary's Church in Chatham, while St Margaret's parish registers record 19 baptisms and one marriage; St Nicholas of Rochester had merely two baptisms (see Appendix 1). Chatham, with its cosmopolitan population, proved to be at least on the surface a more hospitable and accepting place.

The peak of the baptisms fell during the 1740s with a total of 27 baptisms recorded — 25 baptisms for St Mary's, Chatham and two for St Nicholas, Rochester (see Appendix 1). The number of Jewish immigrants would have been very small in comparison with the overall population of both Rochester and Chatham. However, there is no doubt that their presence was noticeable, mainly by their appearance. This was especially true for those who had recently arrived into the country — Jews wore beards, which were not fashionable in England until the 19th century: they wore a long garment and later some would also have sidelocks and a wide-brimmed hat.

As for the attitudes of the communities towards them, they are best described through contemporary poems. The earliest example is the above poem (see Appendix 11). The vicar's hostile attitude comes through as he employs the long-standing adage about Jews and money — the lines describing Jewish stalls imply that Jewish peddlers are interested only in getting as much money from the innocent locals as possible by selling them some useless items of jewellery. However, his tone changes when he describes a similar stall with probably a similar kind of jewellery, but of a Christian seller. It is indulging and patronisingly sympathetic towards the necessity of female adornments:

> *Here ribbons, ear-rings, grace a lady's stall;*
> *There other fancies do the eyes enthral.* [10]

Fifteen years later, in 1771 Jews feature in an anonymous poem published in the *Kentish Gazette*. This time the narrative relates to Chatham, confirming the existence of the Jewish community in the town with its diverse population (see Appendix 11). The words were based on a famous tune of *Nancy Dawson*, a contemporary London dancer and actress, and the melody was popular the previous decade. The title *The Chathamites* is self-explanatory. Written from a perspective of a respectable Church of England Englishman, the poet does not hold back:

> *Here drunken soldiers and ship crews,*
> *Whores, Baptists, Methodists, and Jews,*
> *Swarm ev'ry part of Chatham.*

We get the drift — the town is rowdy, violent, and very diverse. The author continues:

> *Proud Rochester and Strood may talk*
> *Of pavements smooth, and roads of chalk,*
> *For those who chuse to ride or walk:*
> *Not so the folks of Chatham.*
>
> *Contented in their dirty hole,*
> *They hobble on with meaner soul …*

No doubt, the poet is familiar with the arguments and differences between Rochester and Chatham — the above lines are the reference to Chatham's refusal to join Rochester and Strood in 1770 — to obtain the act for the High Street improvement. The Court Leet, which governed the town, was not prepared to spend the money. The same issue of the *Kentish Gazette*, which published the poem, declares: 'The town has almost as many stenches as Cologne, its streets are narrow and squalid; and its only productions are soldiers, sailors, marines, and shell-fish. The shops are filled with those commodities peculiarly favoured by seafaring people; and 'the children of Israel' are here established in the various capacities of salesmen, outfitters, tailors, old clothesmen, army and navy accoutrement makers, and bill discounters.' The description is used almost word by word by Charles Dickens in 1851 in his *One Man in a Dockyard*.[11] In 1777, to ease the traffic from the narrow High Street, Chatham obtained a separate act to build a New Road, which probably pleased the poet.[12]

Another poem mentioning Jews, this time by the dockyard workers, published in the *Canterbury Journal* in the same year of 1771 and entitled *A Tour through Kent by a West Country Party; an Irregular Ode* was written under the pseudonym of Richard Ranger (see Appendix 11). On 10 May a group of three men and two women, probably the 'country bumpkins', as the poet implies, decided to have an outing through Kent. It must be noted though that quite a few from the West Country settled in the area — no doubt, the Medway Towns held an attraction for the opportunities the area provided.

At some point, the group arrived at Rochester. Clearly the party is not impressed by the antiquities of the city, its castle and cathedral. Out of 72 lines, the *Ode* dismisses Rochester in four lines as 'Where we zaw naught worth minding To grace a tale or ditty.' The cosmopolitan Chatham, on the other hand, deserves the party's full attention, providing them with the utmost excitement with its hustle and bustle produced by people of different occupations and crafts:

> *But when we came to Chatham, Zure ! how we wonder'd at 'um!*
> *There was zuch a racket With trouser and jacket,*
> *With zhipwrights, and blackzmiths, and ropers,*
> *We thought we were got in A place vull of zotting,*
> *'Mongst mariners, mermaids, and topers.*

The exploration of the town, no doubt the part of the High Street later known as the Golden Mile for its variety of shops and eateries, followed the trip to the dockyard, during which the company is given a tour of a ship fitted for the future military operation:

> *They zhow'd us cannons zmall and great, With grape-zhot, bombs, and mortars,*
> *And zed that these were made to kill The heathen Jews and Tartars.*

Whoever was providing the tour and explanation was referring to the *Book of Common Prayer* and undoubtedly expressing the common viewpoint,

'The West Prospect of His Majestys Dock-Yard at Chatham, 1738'

including that of the dockyard force. However, one of the visitors expressed sadness at the idea of destruction, which in his opinion, benefited only the Crown but not a common man:

Joe thought it was a burning shame, With those destructive things,
To murder Martyrs, Turks, and Jews, And all to pleasure Kings.

Joe, that 'country bumpkin' is echoing the same line from the *Book of Common Prayer* and 'mirroring' the dockyard guide but utters the words of compassion. One cannot help but think that the poet hiding behind the 'Richard Ranger' nom de plume was poking fun at officialdom and was firmly on the side of empathy and tolerance.

Combined, both of the above poems give us a glimpse into the atmosphere and the attitudes of Chatham in the early 1770s. Despite the diverse population, it does not look a welcoming and tolerant environment. To be fair, hostility and xenophobia were common features of the English working class of the time. Almost 40 years since the end of the 17th century were occupied with military operations — including the War of the Spanish Succession (1701-14); the Great Northern War (1700-21); conflict with Scotland (ended after the battle of Culloden in 1746); the War of Austrian Succession (1740-48); and the Seven Years War (1755-63). Even though England had done nothing to ease the despicable conditions in which people lived, the poorest of the poor had learnt that by being English, they were better than anyone. An immigrant Jew from Germany or Eastern Europe, a peddler or a destitute beggar with his foreign looks, would have been an easy target for an uninhibited population.

With such attitudes as the backdrop, Rochester Corporation's attitude towards the Jews seems an anomaly. In the 1740s and 1750s the corporation was frequently alarmed at the prospect of foreign merchants trading in England. On 16 March 1750 the city's aldermen submitted a petition to parliament objecting to the naturalisation of, as they coyly put, foreign Protestants, and warning parliament of the dangers of allowing them (and some Roman Catholics, who might be able to slip through the net) to settle in the country. The rhetoric and arguments were precisely the same as the ones employed during the discussions of the Jewish Naturalisation Bill three years later.[13]

However, on 21 January 1788 Rochester Corporation admitted Israel Levi, shopkeeper, as a freeman of the city.[14] The admission was in full contrast to the City of London, which in 1785 ordered that even baptised Jews could not be admitted. The prohibition of the City of London against Jews lasted till 1831.[15]

In Rochester one became a freeman by service, by inheritance or birth, by purchase or by gift. Israel Levi paid £20 for the right to trade in the city. It was the same price as the price requested from Christian merchants wishing to obtain the privilege, in contrast to the common practice in the country where any sums requested from a Jew would have been much higher those requested from a Christian.

However, the most puzzling phenomenon is the oath undertaken on admission to the corporation. Until 1858, when all the disabilities relating to Jews in the country were lifted, admission to the city, taking office, etc, demanded the candidate to swear an oath, which contained the words 'On true faith of a Christian'. Israel Levi never converted. He was a practising Jew — only a year before, in 1787, his name appeared on the list of Jews renting premises for the synagogue. How did he take the oath then?

Frederick Smith, in his *History of Rochester* quotes the oath:

> *Ye shall swear that ye shall be true and faithful to our Sovereign Lord King ... and to the heirs of our said Sovereign King; obeysant and obedient shall ye be to the mayor and Ministers of the City; the Franchises and Customs*

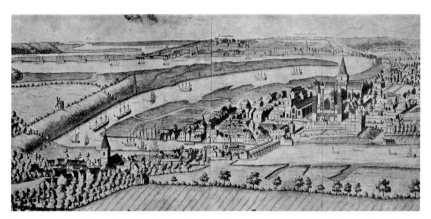

Rochester, 1720, where citizens 'basked in their winter sunshine of tradition, enjoying the advantages and suffering the ills pertaining to antiquity', but some visitors 'zaw naught worth minding to grace a tale or ditty'

thereof ye shall maintain and this City keep harmless in that in you is [sic]. Ye shall be contributory to all manner of charges within this City, as summons, watches, contributions, lot and scot, and to all other charges, bearing your part as a Freeman ought to do. Ye shall implead or sue no Freeman out of this City, while ye have right and law within the said City. Ye shall also keep the King's peace in your own person: ye shall know no gatherings, conventicles or conspiracies made against the King's peace; but ye shall warn the Mayor thereof, to let it, to your power. All these points and articles ye shall well and truly keep, according to the laws and customs of this City, to your power. So help you God.[16]

The phrase 'on true faith of a Christian' is nowhere to be seen. Could it be that Rochester aldermen omitted the phrase for the benefit of Jews? Furthermore, the *Alphabetical List of Freemen* for 1807 gives us two additional Jewish names who pay for the privilege to trade in the city — Solomon Mordecai, jeweller, and a shopkeeper Cohan (Cohen).[17] Both of them were professing Jews and were on the same list of the synagogue founders. They would have taken the same oath on admission to the corporation. It appears the city's aldermen omitted the phrase to allow Levi, Mordecai and Cohan to join the corporation. What ensured such a rapid transformation within less than 40 years? Toleration and pragmatism unexpectedly came to the fore, in stark contrast to the official position of the government.

In 1766, John Roberts, a house carpenter originally of Chatham, acquired a 40-year lease for two tenements in St Margaret's parish from St Bartholomew's Hospital. One of the cottages was on the bank of Bull's Head Alley, tucked away from the main thoroughfare of the High Street and nearly opposite the Bull's Head.[18] By 1770 the property was adapted for Jewish worship.[19] On 14 August 1780 Roberts renewed the lease and continued to sublet the cottage, now described as 'lately rebuilt', to the Jews — this time the document provides us with one name, though it is silent about the others: Levi Israel, who is not to be confused with Israel Levi.[20] On 6 January 1787 the carpenter obtained a licence to alienate two adjacent premises and the alleyway to Levi Israel and others, making the arrangement legally more solid and more permanent for the Jewish community. As a result, the subsequent renewal in 1794 allowed the parties to deal with the trustees of St Bartholomew's Hospital directly and rent the properties in their own right. Those responsible for the 40-year lease were:

- ❖ Levi Israel of Chatham, silversmith
- ❖ Solomon Mordecai (Rochester), silversmith
- ❖ Israel Levi (Rochester), chapman
- ❖ Humphrey Solomon (Rochester) salesman
- ❖ Isaac Abraham (St Margaret), tobacconist
- ❖ Hart Cohen (Chatham), salesman
- ❖ Michael Abraham (Chatham), salesman
- ❖ Abraham Moses (Chatham), salesman[21, 22]

The above records allow us to deduce several facts about the Jewish community of the Medway Towns at the time.

Judaism puts especial importance on collective worship. The minimum quorum, 10 adult men (over the age of 13), does not require the worship to take place in a purpose-built structure: any can be adapted for the collective prayer and it can even be in the open air. An enclosed place, such as a room adapted accordingly, is required only to house a *Sefer Torah* (Torah scroll), needed for public reading of the Jewish Law. This style of worship is compatible with the history of exile and wandering. It is also reminiscent of *Mishkan*, the biblical tent. The need for a dedicated building signifies the size and the permanency of the Jewish community in the Medway Towns. A room in a private home was not enough to accommodate all the members of the congregation. The increasing number of entries in the parish records, from five at the turn of the century to more than 20 in the 1740s, makes it obvious that the community expanded dramatically, and required a dedicated synagogue.

The place was a substantial distance from the city of Rochester and away from direct view from the High Street, chosen as if not to offend the hosts. The area of extreme west end of Chatham High Street on the border with Rochester also had a notorious reputation; in the 1820s it was referred to as the Khyber Pass — narrow and dangerous, but essential for getting from Chatham to Rochester and vice-versa. The proximity to the river, the dockyard and the barracks ensured the existence of many drinking establishments, frequently troubled by bouts of violence, spilling over into the streets.

Jews were classed as aliens and therefore forbidden to own freehold land for any purpose until the change in legislation in 1844. Aliens were permitted to take leases on domestic dwellings for a fixed term of years; legally it was a moot point if a lease could be taken to build a synagogue or open a burial ground. Discretion was exercised, and initially the Jewish community worshipped in private houses and looked for a sympathetic Christian landowner, like John Roberts in Chatham, who was willing to grant a lease.[23] It was also unusual to obtain the lease for such a long term, 40 years; typically, the leases granted to Jews were short-term, similar to the annual lease in Plymouth. A clue as to why Roberts acted differently can be found in his will — his close friend was Jewish. Lewis Wolfe of London is mentioned several times in Roberts's will as his 'dear friend' and one of the beneficiaries.

Eight people collaborated to establish a synagogue in the area to allow the community to practise their worship. Their financial position was rather precarious. Thefts and burglaries were a frequent occurrence; one unsuccessful investment would throw the family into destitution. This would have rendered the rent price prohibitive. It required eight people to chip in to afford the rent and maintain the building. It also tells us that only eight people from the community, however big it was, were wealthy enough to contribute.

But what about those who died? In Hebrew there are several names that can refer to a burial ground: *Beth Kevarot* (House of Graves), *Beth Hayim* (House of Life) or *Beth Olam* (House of Eternity). According to Jewish Law, to disturb the physical remains of the dead is forbidden; a burial ground is considered a sacred place in perpetuity. The concept of *Tehi'at HaMetim* (the resurrection of the dead) is the essential doctrine. A Jewish burial ground is a consecrated ground, and ought never be disturbed by archaeological investigation or redevelopment.[24]

A burial ground is essential for a permanent settlement. A Jewish community cannot put down roots without a dedicated burial ground, while a synagogue, in essence, is secondary to the community's needs. As a result, a burial ground is usually acquired soon after the first arrivals settle in a place. So far, no record has surfaced to show when the burial ground was acquired by the Chatham Jewish community. Taking into account the Jewish entries in the parish churches of the 18th century and that the community established a synagogue in the 1760s, the Jewish burials would have taken place about two decades before that. However, the first gravestone there is dated 1782. Either earlier gravestones did not survive, or there was no sympathetic Christian before John Roberts to grant a lease to open a burial ground. Travel to London or Canterbury would have taken at least a day and resulted in unacceptable delay in burial — it was essential to bury the body within 24 hours, according to Jewish Law. And so, the Jews were buried in the church graveyards like Sarah Honniker, wife of Moses, who was interred in St Mary's Church graveyard in November 1751 (see Appendix 1).

Furthermore, unlike churchyards, Jewish burial grounds are only extremely rarely found next to a synagogue. The tradition goes back to the Temple times. The Book of Leviticus 21:6-7 stipulates that HaKohenim (priests) and members of their families, including descendants, are forbidden to come into contact or be in close proximity to the dead.[25] The Chatham synagogue is the exception to the rule. The position of the burial ground is fully compliant with the Jewish Law, being physically separated from the synagogue by a steep bank. However, it is doubtful if that were the case when originally established.

It may have been that this particular plot presented the only option available and for pragmatic reasons the rules were relaxed. Later, the Bull's Head was demolished allowing the burial ground to expand. The combination of flat stones characteristic of Sephardi graves and upright stones of the Ashkenazim points out to the mixed nature of the community.

Several years later, for the first time, the Chatham Jewish community was mentioned in the national press, or to be more precise, a strange incident, that occurred on 23 June 1786 and reported in *The Times* a couple of days later:

> 'Friday last a box was sent from London by the Chatham stage, directed to Mr Levi Israel (a Jew). On opening the box, it was found to contain a coffin with a dead male Jew child in it supposed to be about a week or ten days old. A letter accompanied it, desiring Mr Israel to bury the child, which was done in the Jewish synagogue ground here, in the presence of the constable, etc.'

If a report about burials was rather a common feature in the newspapers, its content was not. The sender was clearly familiar with the Chatham Jewish community and Levi Israel, as the grim box was addressed to him. The sender also knew that Chatham community had an established burial ground. So, it is reasonable to suppose that the sender was a member of the Chatham community before moving to London. However, it is highly unusual to receive a coffin for burial from London, which had several well-established Jewish cemeteries. That it arrived unaccompanied by any members of the family only adds to the mystery.

According to Edwin Harris, an early 20th-century local printer and enthusiastic local historian, the synagogue was a turreted and castellated wooden edifice — small and quaint. The picturesque building was refurbished to resemble synagogues in Poland. The community followed the Ashkenazi *minhag* (tradition) with most of its members coming from Germany and Poland, though immigrants from the Iberian Peninsula or even as far afield as Iraq were also welcome — names like Raphael and Sison, a corrupt version of Sassoon — tell us about their Sephardi origin. Nineteenth-century directories over the years, in addition to Harris's reminiscences, state that the synagogue was established in the first decade of reign of George III (1760-70). This firmly places the establishment of the organised Jewish community of Chatham in the decade of 1760, contemporary with the establishment of the earliest provincial synagogues in the country — Canterbury, Plymouth and Exeter.

Jews, with Quakers, were exempt from the 1753 Hardwicke Marriage Act, which stipulated that all marriages were to take place in an Anglican church and only after the publication of banns. They were allowed to conduct their marriages in the synagogues and keep their own registers. Jewish communities of the 18th century had a rather haphazard method of record-keeping, and the first surviving local record appears only in 1777. It was a wedding conducted in Chatham, either in a private house or in the synagogue, by an itinerant minister, Rabbi Ash of Dover, who was operating in the southeast between 1765 and 1818. The only information available is the name of the bridegroom, Judah. The wedding took place on 1 Iyyar 5537, or 8 May 1777.[26]

Those marrying under the Orthodox Jewish Law had to undergo an interview with the *Beth Din* (rabbinical court), which in 1793 was recognised as the authority on validity of Jewish marriages. If the court was satisfied that both parties were halachically Jewish or had an acceptable certificate of conversion, a permission to marry was granted by the Office of the Chief Rabbi.[27] However, apart from the elite, many Jews had quite a casual attitude to matrimony. As a Jewish marriage can be solemnised without a presence or consent of an ordained rabbi, many Jews entered into relationships frowned upon by the Jewish authorities. Couples often lived together as husband and wife without any religious ceremony intended to ensure the purity of family life. Jacob Nunes Martines (known as Jacob Martin) and Fanny Solomon had several children and had been living together in Chatham for several years when the community persuaded them to get married properly in 1822.[28] It might have been that Jews were simply copying the habits of Gentile couples — the wrongly perceived concept of 'common-law marriage' goes back to time

Facing page: map showing the position of the synagogue and the burial ground (OS map XIX.7, 1866)

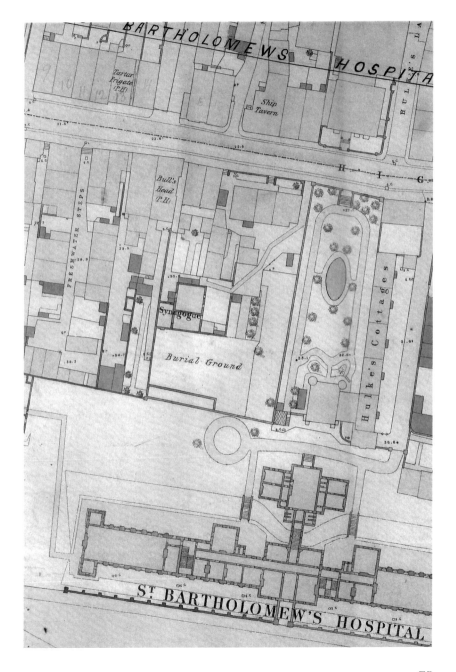

immemorial. Furthermore, frequently the relationships were mixed, with only one partner being Jewish, such as marriage between Samson Levi and Sarah Dadd, which took place in St Margaret's Church, Rochester, on 10 September 1764. Many such marriages typically resulted in the baptism of the Jewish partner, or baptism of his or her children. Levi arrived at Chatham in the 1750s from Midlenbourg, today's Middelburg, Netherlands, as an unskilled labourer, later enlisting in the Royal Marines. The couple had three children — Thomas, Maryann and Sarah, the elder two were baptised at St Mary's Church in Chatham, the youngest at St Margaret's, Rochester (see Appendix 1).

The intense hostility towards Jews as a group was no doubt a strong contributing factor in the desire to escape the stigma. Baptisms were considered the most convincing way of gaining social acceptability, even though the area was not an Anglican stronghold. Since the Restoration, the bishops tended to be absent, and nonconformity flourished. It was estimated that in the four parishes of the towns — city of Rochester, Chatham, Strood and St Margaret — there were 504 dissenters over the age of 16 against 3,810 conformists.[29]

The Christian population dictated the customs and rejected anyone who did not fit the mould. Unless the Jewish minority was prepared to live on the margins of society and lead a precarious existence relying on the whims of the ruling majority, it had no choice but to adapt. Ultimately, Jewish integration was dependent not on Jewish achievements but on the attitudes of those with whom they wanted and needed to mix.

The beards, which were not fashionable till the 19th century, and the traditional dress code were the first to go. So when Lord George Gordon converted to Judaism and started growing a beard, many of his contemporaries decided that he was insane.[30] Wives in the better-off families abandoned the regulation of wearing wigs in public and were eager to follow fashion. Jews frequented coffee houses — Rochester had its first one by 1711[31] — and abandoned Yiddish as another distinctive feature setting them apart from the local population. In keeping with the national trend, by 1815 the language of the records of Rochester and Chatham Jewish community had switched from the combination of Hebrew and Yiddish to be exclusively English. The process of acculturation began, and it preceded social integration and political emancipation.

Chapter 5

Settling in the Area:
From the 18th to the early 19th century, part 2

The French Revolution of 1789 and its consequences were observed with increasing alarm by the Tory government of William Pitt the Younger. Worried that the French uprising might spread over the Channel, they began suppressing works that embraced radical philosophies along with the activities of societies who favoured a radical change in Britain.

In February 1793 a war broke out with France that was to last, with two short intervals, until 1815. Concerned by the anti-government agitation and propaganda, the state intensified the suppression of organisations such as the London Corresponding Society[1], whose main mission was universal suffrage and annual parliaments. However, anti-government feelings grew, especially in the port towns. Food shortages were reported and prices rose steeply.

In February 1796 John Gale-Jones, a member of the society, visited the area. He described the mood at the time:

'We stopt a while to rest ourselves at Brompton — numerous barracks and fortifications which every where surrounded us, lamented their enormous expences, and ridiculed the idea of their being useful either to prevent an invasion from without, or quell a general insurrection within …

'[From several gentlemen] I learned, that the general sentiment of the inhabitants of Rochester, Chatham, and even all Kent, was decidedly against the present Minister and the present war. The strenuous opposition

*shewn by the Whig Club to the two late extraordinary Bills introduced
into Parliament by Mr Pitt and Lord Grenville, seems to have raised that
association very high in their estimation …'*[2]

He stayed at Bull's Head in Rochester, and one morning witnessed a solemn
procession carrying the effigy of the bishop of Rochester.'A label was fixed upon
his breast with the following words, which he is said to have delivered in the
House of Lords, *'The People have nothing to do with the Laws but to obey them!'*
In one of his hands was placed a Bible, and in the other a lighted taper; and in
this manner, after having been shewn to the minor canons, every one of whom
was obliged to open his door and contemplate the curious sight, he was led into
a large field, and committed to the flames, amidst the loud acclamations of the
surrounding multitude!'[3]

Some clerics viewed the French Revolution as a divine intervention and
fulfilment of the prophecy able to complete the conversion of the Jews. But in
1799, Samuel Horsley, the Bishop of Rochester, attacked this interpretation
of purely secular events. He thought it was highly improbable that the conversion of the Jews would be performed by the 'atheistical democracy'. On the
contrary, he considered 'the French democracy, from its infancy to the present
moment, has been a conspicuous and principal branch at least of the Western
Antichrist.'[4]

As a minority group, Jews came under suspicion due to their familial links
with France. They were perceived as enemy agents coming into the country
under the 'refugee' cover. By the winter of 1792 the situation had become so
serious that the rabbis of Bevis Marks Synagogue and the Great Synagogue
in London delivered a sermon emphasising the virtues of loyalty to king and
country. The next year both congregations printed a special prayer for the
success of the British Army.[5]

In January 1793 the House of Commons passed the Aliens Act, which gave
the government total control over foreigners' movement. Legally, Jews were
viewed as aliens. They may have considered England their home, with many
having been born here, but they still had to prove their loyalty.

From Roman times Jews were excluded from the career in the military.
The career bestowed privileges, and the church ensured that the profession

was barred to non-believers. Subsequently, the development of the feudal system and the close correlation between the king's service and owning land, strengthened the prohibition. However, that did not preclude baptised Jews from joining the forces. After the readmission, the Test Act of 1673 confirmed the requirement of taking the Sacrament according to the rites of the Church of England for any person wishing to hold a civil or military commission under the Crown. Effectively, this prohibited any professing Jew from pursuing a military career.

On the other hand, there were no objections to them joining as volunteers. It is in this category we find local Jews joining the navy from the middle of the 18th century. Samson Levi, 22, enlisted to the Royal Marines in Chatham on 22 September 1758, and was promoted sergeant in May 1766.

His son, Thomas, followed his father's steps. Born in Chatham and baptised at St Mary's Church in September 1765, he joined the navy at the age of 14. In 1806 Thomas Levi served on *HMS Blanche* as master at arms, later moving to *HMS Prince*, and probably taking part in the Battle of Trafalgar. Having served for 37 years in the navy, possibly the longest-serving Jew, he was discharged in 1814 with a leg injury but with no pension. The lack of pension for a wounded man was unusual. Levi returned to Chatham, and having found lodgings at Lord Hood's Arms, appealed. He was clearly successful because he was admitted to Greenwich Hospital, home for retired Royal Navy seamen, on 22 July 1815, aged 50.[6]

An additional record shows David Jacobs, 17, a landsman (somebody with no experience at sea), discharged at Chatham as a servant to Lieutenant Hewitt on *HMS Sandwich* on 20 October 1787[7].

On 28 September 1797, another landsman, 22-year-old Richard Barnett, future uncle of literary critic and essayist Samuel Phillips (1814-54), was drafted aboard *HMS Vanguard*. The ship was being fitted at Chatham and would become Nelson's flagship in the Battle of the Nile the next August.

Barnett, the son of a German Jewish immigrant, came from Berwick Street, Soho, London. To be accepted to serve, he had to change his name from Abraham to Richard to avoid being treated with suspicion and aversion. His *Journal of Remarkable Occurrences on Board HMS Vanguard, commencing December 24 1797, ending January 31, 1800* provides us with a rare and compelling insight into the seamen's lives.[8] His mate aboard *Vanguard* was another Jewish volunteer — a Chathamite, Isaac Samuel, who joined the ship on 4 October 1797, having volunteered four years before, at the age of 19.[9]

From the middle of the 18th century, Chatham's prominence was growing. The increasing importance of maritime operations that century saw Chatham gaining more and more significance as England's principal military and naval base. It was to Chatham Dockyard where the fleets were put for repair, and it was here where the privateers brought their prizes. The town, with the dockyard at its apex, expanded, especially in the latter decades of the century. Its prosperity and the opportunities to earn a living attracted more and more Jewish settlers: soldiers and sailors required supplies. They moved here from London and from as far as Norfolk and Devon.

These jewellers and silversmiths, slopsellers and salesmen, were termed navy agents, because it was compulsory for every captain to appoint a ship's agent. In reality they were pawnbrokers, providing cash to the lower ranks and ordinary seamen, thus playing a vital role in maintaining peace and quiet below decks.

Petty officers and seamen were paid at least six months in arrears. It was also common for them to wait for their wages and the prize money due to them, an average of £1 per month, for years. Fearing potential capture either by enemy or by pirates, the ships did not carry large sums of coins. As a result, the seamen would receive a wage ticket cashable at the pay office at Chatham, Portsmouth, Sheerness, or other office close to the sailor's home. Officially, they were to be cashed in person only, but for a small sum the pay clerks could be willing to process the tickets presented by a third party. The men, never sure how long they were going to be ashore — for many times they were kept on board for fear of desertion — the sailors preferred to sign their tickets over to the 'ticket buyer', who would acquire them at a discount. Inevitably, malpractice occurred. In 1809 the first attempts to regulate the activities of the navy agents were made.

Non-Jews, too, were acting and licensed as navy agents, though in the port towns, the majority were Jews. It was a way of making a living, especially as they were still excluded from joining the guilds.

By 1809 at Chatham out of a total of seven agents, five were members of the Jewish community:

- ❖ Joseph Aaron
- ❖ Joel Barnett
- ❖ Mark Cohen
- ❖ Lazarus Magnus
- ❖ Elias Moss (see Appendix 6)

Most of them were slopsellers — selling ready-made clothing worn by the seamen. They had to be willing to defer payments and to gratify personal tastes, as dress regulations were rather vague. The slopsellers were the first to know when the ships were anchored at Chatham; they would board the ship and trade in return for prize orders. That allowed captains to keep discipline on board. The hawkers and petty traders boarded on payday only.[10]

If the sailors had clothing in exchange for a 'wage ticket', some of the agents had difficulty cashing the tickets in. They also faced other risks: until 1819 a seaman could revoke his prize order with no consequence, or some seamen gave their orders to the second navy agent after they received some advance from the first agent. The agent also faced the risk of seamen deserting, which happened to Elias Moss. On 1 April 1814 Moss wrote to the principal officers and commissioners of HM Navy in London:

> *Honourable Sirs,*
> *I beg leave to acquaint you that being Agent for William Cliff late Boatswain of His Majesty's Sloop Ranger I advanced him upwards of one hundred pounds during the time of that brig being in the Baltic, since which the Ranger arrived at Sheerness, and in the month of January last the said William Cliff had leave of absence and came to Chatham but did not afterwards join his Brig or has he ever since been heard of. I have at very great expense, and trouble in getting his accounts papers which I have accomplished and obtained a certificate for his pay between 19 march 1812 and 8 August 1813 but refused payment on account of his being marked R on his books of the Ranger.*
> *I therefore humbly beg leave for payment to your Honours that I shall be a very considerable loser unless you will be so good to take my case into consideration and be pleased to order the R to be taken off that I may be*

enabled to receive the pay due to the said William Cliff.
  I have the honour to be with great respect Honourable Sirs
  Your most obedient and very humble servant
E Moss — Navy Agent

Moss never recovered his £100.[11]

Being a licensed navy agent provided a title, and a perceived advancement in a status from a common slopseller or a second-hand clothes-man. It did not mean carrying on a lucrative business, though some prospered, but the title made them look respectable, and respectability, the desire to blend in and to be accepted were important.

The community continued to expand, and in 1808 they renewed the lease for the synagogue for another 40 years, received acknowledgement as the Orthodox Jewish community from the Office of the Chief Rabbi, had their own approved residential rabbi — a certain Barlin, whose surname points to his native town of Berlin, and hosted a visit by Solomon Hirschell, Chief Rabbi of Ashkenazi Jews (1802-42).[12]

By that time Israel Levi and Levi Israel had died, and additional members appeared on the document:

- ❖ Simon Davis, shopkeeper
- ❖ Lazarus Magnus, Chatham, shopkeeper
- ❖ Joshua Alexander, Chatham, shopkeeper
- ❖ Samuel Simons, Frindsbury, shopkeeper
- ❖ Lion Benjamin, Chatham, shopkeeper
- ❖ Aaron Moss, Sheerness, shopkeeper[13]

In 1818 synagogue became recognised as a legal establishment, but the courts' doctrine of Jews as perpetual enemies persisted 'for between them, as with the devils, whose subjects they are, and the Christian there can be no peace'. Public life was barred. Jews were excluded from office under the Crown, civic government and any employment relating to the administration of justice or education. The compulsory requirement to take the Sacrament disqualified Jews from the universities, guilds and many professions.[14]

By 1821, the community had been through a change of three rabbis. Barlin was succeeded by Lyon Benjamin, and then Henry Levy (see Appendix 5).

Lazarus Magnus, another new name on the lease, moved to Chatham from Portsmouth. According to family research, Lazarus's parents, Pinchas (Phineas, Philip) Simon Gross and Anna Eleazar née Cohen, came from Kassel in Germany via Holland, and settled in the English seaport and market town of King's Lynn in the middle of the 18th century, having translated their surname into Latin: Magnus. Lazarus was born in 1776 in Zwolle, Netherlands, where the family might have lived for a while. In the 1790s young Magnus, seeking ways to establish himself, moved to Portsmouth, another seaport town, where in 1798 he married Sarah Moses (born 1774), a daughter of one of the prominent members of the Jewish community. Their first child, Phoebe, was born in 1800 followed by 12 more children, including two sons, Simon, born in 1801 and Jacob in 1805. The prosperity of Chatham and the growing Jewish community were alluring and, between the birth of Phoebe and 1808, the family settled in Chatham. This time it was for good.

In 1825, Phoebe moved to America. By that time, she was married to a watchmaker Abraham David Cohen (born *c.* 1791) and had two daughters, Esther (born 1816) and Elizabeth (born 1820). They settled in New York.[15] As a young adult, Jacob moved to Dover, and then to London. His son Philip, who was created a baronet in 1917 for his works as a British educational reformer and politician, retained his Chatham family links throughout his life. Simon stayed in Chatham, becoming one of the prominent local businessmen and benefactors. Like his father he also played an important role in the Jewish community, locally and nationally.

Lazarus maintained his status as one of the leading members of the Chatham Jewish community till his death on 21 July 1821. He was buried at the synagogue's graveyard.

The *Beth Din* (rabbinical court) was recognised as the authority to regulate *kosher* (ritual) food from 1788. The community had a kosher butcher, though the first name, Lewis Alexander appears only in 1823.[16] However, the Chathamites were rather lax in their observance of *kashrut* laws relating to the slaughter of the animals. On 25 July 1823 the Chief Rabbi sent a stern letter to the *shochet* (ritual butcher) for not obeying the rules.[17]

Propriety and acceptance were the main drives for the Chatham Jewish community. Gentry did not form a large element in the Medway Towns, which were both too far away from the capital to be a fashionable outskirt of the city, as Greenwich and Eltham were, and not far enough to be considered a provincial capital, a status that had been awarded to Canterbury centuries before.[18] At the turn of the 19th century the population of Rochester, Chatham, Gillingham and Strood was 25,000, and the area was rife with criminal elements[19] — a sign of poverty. 'Rochester was quite a lawless place!' — exclaimed Gale-Jones during his visit in 1796.

'Old Chatham's a place,
That's the nation's disgrace,
Where the club and the fist prove the law, sir;' — observed another
tourist.

The lack of newspaper criminal reports relating to the Jewish community suggests there were no Chatham or Rochester 'fences' (traders dealing with stolen goods), as there were in London. And though Chatham was a very convenient place for criminals as an escape route, there are no reports about Jewish criminals there. One of a very few stories was reported in the *Kentish Weekly Post* on 7 March 1823. Three hawkers, professing to be Dutch Jews, appeared in Rochester. They were passing off inferior produce as high-quality products, and were soon apprehended in Maidstone, where they moved after Rochester. This type of business behaviour was not exclusive to Jews, though it was a biased perception. Luckily for the Chatham community, the hawkers were not locals.

Community members were eager to present themselves to the natives as hard-working respectable men. They were fighting to maintain a friendly relationship with the locals, especially with the military and the navy, who were providing them with the main source of income. They rejected anyone who did not fit the mould, who presented a threat to respectability, who could taint the community. When, in 1819, the notorious case of Abraham Abrahams resulted in him being sentenced to death, the members of the Chatham Jewish community refused to allow the body to be buried in the synagogue graveyard.

'The most daring robbery committed on the premises of Messrs Abrahams and Myers, pawnbrokers, of Mile Town, Sheerness,' the *Maidstone Gazette* reported on 2 February 1819. Very soon, three culprits were apprehended. Their first escape stop was supposed to be in Chatham, but due to the bad weather, the boat in which they were travelling had to anchor on the Isle of Grain. The fugitives decided to walk to Chatham. A walk from the Isle of Grain to Chatham is just under 14 miles. By the time they reached Strood, which was on the same side of the river as Grain, they were tired, and it was late. They abandoned the idea of reaching Chatham, for which they would have needed to cross the river. Having stayed overnight in the Duke of Gloucester Inn, at half past seven next morning they took the Nelson coach to Gravesend. Very soon the robbers were apprehended and sentenced to death. Later, two of them had their sentences commuted to transportation for life; the third one received his pardon.

On 2 July 1819 three more men were arrested, one of whom was 24-year-old Abraham Abrahams (full namesake but no relation with the burglary victim). The charges were: 'feloniously and maliciously, procuring, counselling, inciting and hiring' the above burglars to break into the premises of Abrahams and Myers. They were duly tried and condemned. Requests for pardon were sent to the Home Office. The convicted, being an accessory to burglary, expected a reprieve. Their appeals were refused and reduced to transportation only at the last moment — except Abraham Abrahams, whose name, originally on the list for commutation, was crossed out.[20] He was hanged at Penenden Heath, near Maidstone, on 19 August 1819.

Jewish Law requires the body to be interred within 24 hours.[21] The body of Abrahams was taken down and a hearse was to take it to Chatham. But before the body was taken down, a letter written in Hebrew was received. It was from Dr Marcus (Mordecai) Hyman, an apothecary and a surgeon, of Chatham, who said it should be taken to Sheerness. The hearse, however, proceeded to Chatham, where permission to inter the body in the burial ground was denied by Dr Hyman and others. Officers were employed to prevent the body being buried by force. A 'disgraceful altercation' took place, and eventually the corpse was conveyed by water to Sheerness, where it was buried the next day.[22]

The same newspaper article also reported rumours circulating at the time.

Jewish community. If they were to be talked about, it had to be for something other than crime. The precarious peace where they were tolerated had to be preserved.

Hyman was originally a member of Bevis Marks Synagogue in London. He joined the Chatham community at the beginning of the century. His daughter Rebecca was born there *c.*1813. Hyman resided with his family at Rome Lane (now Railway Street) in Chatham, later moving to King Street in Troy Town, Rochester.

The *Ipswich Journal* of 30 December 1797 reports a prosecution against Hyman, then living in London, for recovery of the penalty of £500, for offering bribe to an officer in His Majesty's Customs. Hyman offered four guineas to a customs officials called Cook to assist him in getting from on board ship a quantity of plate glass upon which the duty was 60 per cent. When the attempted fraud was detected, Hyman offered Cook £100, if he would make an affidavit that the glass was intended for Liverpool. A clerk at Staunton wharf, Ralph Carr, informed on Hyman, because Hyman did not pay him money he owed for helping to smuggle other goods. Carr had been involved in dealings with Hyman for the past 12 months and had landed him about 30 cases of plate glass. Hyman was committed for trial by the King's Bench on 8 February 1798 where he was found guilty. He was freed three years later.

It was probable that Hyman then decided to start afresh, moving to Chatham. It is not clear where he trained as an apothecary and a surgeon, as he does not appear on any professional register in London. This is, however, is no surprise: to be admitted, he would have been required to take the Sacrament, unacceptable to a professing Jew. It seems Hyman's training was completed by 1817, the year he took out an insurance policy for premises in Chatham High Street. By 1819 he was clearly an esteemed member of the community and by 1823 he had become one of the synagogue's trustees, appearing on the renewal of the lease together with Isaac Abraham, Michael Abraham, Lion Benjamin, Lewis Alexander, and Jonathan Zacharia, whose son Issachar was to become the friend and chiropodist of Abraham Lincoln.[23]

Hard times followed, and Hyman filed for bankruptcy on 4 April 1829, but on 29 September his insurance as a surgeon was renewed, this time for 211 High Street Rochester. Dr Mordecai Hyman died, aged 95, 'from natural

Rabbi Solomon Hirschell, Chief Rabbi of the Ashkenazi Jews in England (1802-42). Portrait by the Chatham artist Frederick Benjamin Barlin, 1802

decay' on 2 July 1846 and was buried at the synagogue's cemetery.

With higher education, and apprenticeships for trades and crafts prohibited, it was hard for the Jews to secure employment that could provide a steady income. When one trade went bust, they simply switched to another — from slop-selling to pawnbroking to general dealing (see Appendix 9). Even if the family was not in dire straits, for most shopkeepers and salesmen it was rare to educate their children beyond the age of 11 and 12.

One of the more specialised occupations was dealing in precious metals and jewellery. Another one included seal-cutting, and illuminating Hebrew manuscripts and marriage contracts. From there, it is a very short leap to painting. The only known artist who came from the Chatham Jewish community was Frederick Benjamin Barlin, a son of the rabbi. The family originated from Berlin, but it is not known when they moved to England and settled at Chatham. A member and an honorary exhibitor of the Royal Academy of Art, Barlin was active between 1802 and 1807, having moved from Chatham and settling at 38 Beech Street, Barbican, London. One of his most notable portraits is of Solomon Hirschell, Chief Rabbi of the Ashkenazi Jews in England, in the collection of the National Portrait Gallery in London.[24]

From Shakespeare and Marlowe, between 1584 and 1820 there were 80 plays published in England that contained at least one Jewish character, suggests the historian Alfred Rubens. Playwrights continued to stereotype the Jew with his imaginary wealth, or as a threat to English females due to some mythical erotic tendencies. Sometimes they were inspired by caricatures, such as Hogarth's series *The Harlot's Progress*, produced in 1731, which triggered the production of further anti-Jewish caricatures and plays for decades.

Jewish women were not exempt either, as was the case with Thomas Dibdin's opera *Family Quarrels*, premiered at Covent Garden on 18 December 1802. John Fawcett played a leading role of a peddler, Proteus. At one point Proteus disguises himself as 'Aaron the Jew' and in a song entitled *I Courted Miss Levi* tells the audience about his woes in courting Miss Levi, Miss Abrams and Miss Moses — not 'three Jewish whores', as suggested by one researcher[25], but not shrinking violets either. Miss Moses's boxing lessons that she was taking from her brother scared Aaron away, for 'I shouldn't like a Vife to knock me down'. The Jewish audience, who were present at the premiere protested. Dibdin recalled in his memoirs that 'a lady of Hebrew race from Rochester' informed him that the Jews strongly objected to the song, which they saw was specifically written to insult Jewish women. Even after a public apology, the protests were so strong that, after a couple of more nights, Dibdin was obliged to remove the song to save the opera.[26]

However, as the music historian David Conway suggests, the audience's wrath probably had nothing to do with the lyrics of the offending song, but with its music. The jog-like tune breaks off for a section where the singer delivers a punchline. The notes of that particular section precisely replicate the rhythms and the cadence commonly used in the *kaddish*, the mourning prayer for the dead.[27]

Among all those fun-poking plays at the expense of Jews, the most notable one that signified the beginning of a new development in portraying Jews was Richard Cumberland's *The Jew* premiered at Drury Lane Theatre on 8 May 1794, which for the first time attempted to introduce a benevolent Jew in its title role of Sheva. The play was a great success, revived and produced for many years, though the character of Sheva was regarded as unrealistic. Originally performed by a non-Jewish thespian, it was later, on many occasions reprised by a Jewish actor, Henry Sherenbeck from Chatham.

Sherenbeck, born in 1762, moved to Chatham from Plymouth, where his father, Joseph Jacob Sherenbeck, a goldsmith, was the founder of the Jewish community. Henry had certainly settled in Chatham by 1794, as in April that year when registered as a candidate for the masonic Lodge of Israel, he gave Chatham as his place of residence.[28]

Henry continued the family trade as a jeweller and silversmith, later on adding 'optician' to his list of occupations. But it looks as if theatre was his main passion and he frequently performed as an amateur at Canterbury Theatre, the Little Theatre in Haymarket and Covent Garden at the beginning of the 19th century. He specialised in Jewish characters, adding 'authenticity' and 'realism' to the portrayal of Shylock from *The Merchant of Venice* and Sheva from Cumberland's *The Jew*. The earliest review of Cumberland's play with Sherenbeck as Sheva appears in the *Kentish Weekly Post* on 3 June 1806 when the favourable reviewer says Sheva is portrayed by 'a true descendant from the flock of Abraham' with 'here and there a slight variation between the Hebrew and the German, supported the dialect and the part with the great feeling and effect, and deservedly obtained the applause of his audience.'

In May 1814, the play, condensed from five acts to three, was revived in Covent Garden with Sherenbeck reprising his Sheva. This time, opinions were divided. The *Theatrical Inquisitor* found the actor 'worth many qualifications for the stage, his person manly, his intonation vigorous and distinct and his manner impressive'. However, a monthly magazine, *The Scourge*, commented: 'Report says that he is by birth and religious persuasion one of that class of people whose benevolence Cumberland sought to propitiate when he delineated a philanthropic Jew', and continued: 'The house indeed contained no small proportion of circumcised auditors who were inordinately clamorous in supporting their representative.'[29] Meanwhile, the *Morning Post*, acknowledged the actor's 'very favourable reception and … considerable applause all through the play. Mr Sherenbeck's voice is strong, and this in some instances, enabled him to give the author's meaning tolerable effect.' But it added: 'Generally speaking, he was by no means very successful. He could not give that dignity, interest, and importance to the character of Sheva, which had heretofore attached to it.'[30]

His other talked-about role was Shylock from Shakespeare's *The Merchant of Venice*. The *Kentish Weekly Post* of 6 March 1810 commented on his performance at the Little Theatre at Canterbury the previous first night: 'Mr Sherenbeck, a gentleman of Jewish persuasion (not unknown to the dramatic world), undertook to perform the part of the obdurate Israelite, in the peculiar accent of that Sect. His conception of the character was perfectly unique — his delineation just and proper — his figure and features correctly corresponding with the arduous part allotted to him. The House was crowded to the excess; and never, we believe, did an audience vie with each other more than on this occasion, to testify their applause, so justly merited by this chaste and astonishing performer.'[31]

In 1817 Sherenbeck gave his Shylock again 'in the lisping dialect of the stage Jew', this time at Covent Garden. As with his Sheva, his Covent Garden performance was not too favourable. The *Theatrical Inquisitor* observed: 'Mr Sherenbeck's exposition of Shylock was neither sound nor orthodox and the equipment of this Jew in the dialect of his tribe seemed equally absurd and ineffective. His enunciation was painfully correct and divested of every claim to professional merit.'[32]

However uneven his acting career was, Sherenbeck definitely made his mark and was remembered long after his death. The *Dundee Evening Telegraph* of 9 May 1901 describes the journalist's earlier interview with an actress, when she recalled her visit to the Rochester Theatre (the Theatre Royal) in January 1805 'when Mr Sherenbeck … with a pronounced Yiddish delivery, appeared as the malignant usurer, and made a great hit, particularly in a trial scene.'

Henry Sherenbeck died in 1832. He never married. In his will he left his estate to be divided between his housekeeper, Mary Ann Field, and her daughter Caroline Field.[33] Mary Field continued to reside in the same High Street property, a woman of independent means, according to the 1841 census.

The Sloman, or originally Solomon, family from Rochester produced several performers. If nothing is known about John Sloman's career as a comedian, apart from his rather successful stint in America in 1827, we know a little bit more about his brothers Henry (1793-1873) and Charles (1808-70), who also specialised in comedy.

Henry — an actor and singer, was popular at London's Coburg Theatre (now the Old Vic). He became a celebrity in the pantomimes and melodramas produced by Joseph Glossop. Henry was especially well known as Watty Wagstaff in *Edward the Black Prince*.

Though both brothers lived in London, they retained their connections with their home area. After Glossop's death in 1835, Henry Sloman left the Coburg and together with Charles became the proprietor of the Theatre Royal in Rochester. Henry died in August 1873 and was interred in West Ham Cemetery.[34]

Charles was a prolific composer and a singer. He had an incredible ability to improvise, and his immensely successful performances included improvisations in the Italianate style, on subjects proposed by the audience. Charles composed *Sacred Strains and Hymns* (1860) among many other songs, including *Daughters of Israel, Maid of Judah, Promised Land*; but only one of them was to survive — *Pop Goes the Weasel*, written in the 1830s and sung by him at the Cole Hole, the prime song-and-supper room in the Strand, and the Cyder Cellars in Maiden Lane in London.

Interactions between Jews and non-Jews occurred on a daily basis, but that did not mean that they mingled much socially. Aside from occasional inter-marriages, originally, two completely segregated groups, they co-existed side by side. Very few Christians were interested in the Jews unless there was a matter at hand that affected them personally. On the other hand, Jews felt insecure in their new environment, and as long as they were allowed to continue with their traditions, customs and worship without being hassled, they were content to satisfy their social needs within their own community. However, within the passage of time, the inspirations grew, the natural psychological need to feel at home emerged and developed. Those who wanted for their children a life with no limitations, converted, and their children were baptised; others were not prepared to sever their connections with the faith of their fathers. They had acquired the tastes and the habits of the hosts, such as visiting theatres and drinking coffee in the coffee-houses; though this did not necessarily guarantee unrestricted admission to English social circles or voluntary associations. However, one place where Jews and non-Jews were able to meet, where religion and politics were not discussed, was the brotherhood of Freemasons.

According to the legend, the first grand masters of the brotherhood were Abraham, Moses and King Solomon, who built the Temple — the key object in masonry. The masonic tales are permeated with references to familiar biblical characters and stories are peppered with Hebrew words and phrases. Another Jewish connection to Freemasonry is the design of the original coat of arms of the Antients. It included four Hebrew biblical symbols — man, ox, lion and eagle. As time passed more and more Christian concepts and symbols have developed, but the Hebrew ones were retained.[35]

There is no definitive answer as to how and when the fraternity of Freemasons was formed, but the general consensus is that from medieval times skilled stone masons and other craftsmen, involved in construction of build-ings, formed guilds. The nature of their work, frequently far from home, meant they were compelled to live in communal huts — lodging together, hence the term 'lodge'. Most of the time, people would not know each other, but thrown together on the building site of a cathedral, or a church, they would enjoy the opportunity of regular jovial eating and drinking and a friendly talk.[36]

If it were to be true to its belief — 'we are all brethren' — and aims,

Henry Sloman (1793-1873) as Watty Wagstaff in *Edward the Black Prince*, the role that first brought him to notice, 1822. Henry was an actor, singer and proprietor of Theatre Royal in Rochester

Freemasonry could not prohibit Jews to join. Its emphasis was on equal dignity of man irrespective of his creed, colour or race, under the protection of the Creator; its ceremonies were built around the Old Testament and the biblical figures; the principle of *rachmanut* (benevolence, righteousness) — masonic charities were established early on — is fundamental to the principles of Jewish Law. All this appealed and drew Jews to join. In addition, it was a rare opportunity for building business connections on equal footing, or to put it in today's parlance, networking. Freemasonry offered a rare opening to much desired friendliness and integration denied in other aspects of life in England.[37]

In general, the admission of immigrants into the brotherhood was quite a feature. Apart from Jews, one can spot Huguenot and other foreign names, including probably the earliest Muslim — His Excellency Mirza Abdul Khan, the Persian Ambassador to England, who was initiated in, but did not become a member, of the Lodge of Friendship No 6 in June 1810.[38]

There were five lodges in Chatham and one in neighbouring Brompton that operated from the 18th century under the umbrella of the Grand Lodge:

- ❖ The Kentish Lodge of Antiquity
- ❖ Lodge No 243, meeting at the Globe Inn
- ❖ Globe Lodge, which merged in 1825 with Lodge No 306
- ❖ Royal Marine Lodge
- ❖ Royal Kent Lodge of Antiquity No 20
- ❖ Brompton Lodge

Rochester had no established lodges. The lists of admission provide a fascinating insight into their diverse membership — their ages, occupations, and places of residence (see Appendix 4). The earliest one, the Kentish Lodge of Antiquity, gives us the first possible Jewish name of George Meuris, a gunner, who appears in the list as early as January 1764. Out of five Jewish names, all of them young men up to the age of 30, the most interesting admission is of John Solomon, an attorney from Rochester, who joined the lodge on 4 January 1808. This is the first time we encounter a specific Jewish attorney within the community. The register stops in 1810.

In addition to the usual occupations, such as tailors, slopsellers, jewellers and navy agents, we also find surgeons in His Majesty's service, such as Hugh Moises, John Gideon Millingen, or Mellingen, as he is recorded in the list[39] and Richard Morris; Moses Aarons, a hatter; Lyon Aaron, a draper; Thomas Levi, a musician and drummer; Jacob Schnebbelie, a pastry cook and confectioner; his brother John Schnebelie, professor of music; and John Sloman, a comedian from the Sloman (Solomon) family of entertainers. Over the years, being part of the Freemason brotherhood became more or less a compulsory requirement if one wanted to succeed.[40] The acceptance into Freemasonry became the first step on the long journey of emancipation.

Left: Charles Sloman (1808-70): composer and proprietor of Theatre Royal in Rochester, and his brother John Sloman singing S*weet Kitty Clover,* during his American tour, *c. 1828.* Lithograph by D.C. Johnston

Chapter 6

The Road to Emancipation
1830-1858

By the mid-1820s the character of the Jewish community in England had changed. By then, most English Jews had been born in England. They considered it their home, and saw participation in the country's legislative affairs as their birthright. However, they were still excluded from taking any official post. The first attempt to remedy the situation and remove Jewish disabilities was a petition presented to the House of Lords by the Philo-Judean Society, an evangelical group comprising Jews and Gentiles, on 29 June 1826. It did not succeed. The next attempt in 1828 was the introduction of a bill to repeal the Test and Corporation Act.[1] This succeeded in 1829, resulting in emancipation of Roman Catholics and Protestant Dissenters.

However, the hope that the Roman Catholic Relief Act 1829 would also put an end to Jewish disabilities were dashed when the House of Lords introduced the words 'On the true faith of a Christian' into the oath as a prerequisite upon taking public office. The wording left Jews as the only section of the English population excluded from politics by their faith. Some of the Jewish leaders felt that it was not a mere disability but a slight.[2] A campaign for equal rights, which was to last for decades, began.

On 5 April 1830, Sir Robert Grant, a Whig stalwart, introduced into the Commons a bill to repeal all Jewish disabilities. He was supported by some peers, among them Duke of Norfolk, who presented petitions by Jews from west London and Rochester and Chatham. The attempt failed. The Great

Reform Act of 1832, which introduced wide-ranging changes to the electoral system and increased significantly the number of men entitled to vote, did not extend this entitlement to Jews.

Another attempt was made in 1833 but was again thrown out, with the Archbishop of Canterbury leading the opposition. The third unsuccessful attempt was made the next year, after which the subject was dropped for another 11 years.[3] In 1844 the struggle was transferred to the municipal constituencies. The following year, having received the Royal Assent on 31 July, the Municipal Act 1845 established the principle of religious liberty. Jews were now allowed to participate in local affairs.[4]

The city of Rochester had been governed by the corporation for centuries. Following the Municipal Corporation Act 1835, its governing body comprised 18 councillors elected by the burgesses — the city citizens, freemen who had a right to vote. The councillors then elected six aldermen — high-ranking members of the corporation, who possessed judicial, administrative or military functions — between themselves, and a mayor, elected by both councillors and aldermen. Upon taking office, each councillor, alderman and mayor were to take oath. The original declaration, before the 1835 act contained the following:

> I _____ do solemnly and sincerely in the presence of God profess, testify and declare, upon the True faith of a Christian, That I will never exercise any power authority or influence which I may possess by virtue of my office to injure or weaken the protestant Church as it is by law established in England, or to disturb the said Church or the Bishops and Clergy of the said Church, in the possession of any Rights or Privileges to which such Church or the said Bishops and Clergy, are or may be by Law entitled.

It looked like a typical oath of the time. What is fascinating to note though, is the dramatic change of the wording of the oath following the act:

> I _____ having been elected Mayor and as such Mayor, Justice of the Peace of the City, and Borough of Rochester, in the County of Kent, do hereby declare that I take the said office upon myself, and will duly and faithfully fulfil the duties thereof according to the best of my judgment and ability.[5]

It is understandable that the councillors wanted to modernise the original oath, allowing Catholics and nonconformists to participate in the municipal affairs. However, it is highly unusual to remove the phrase "upon the true faith of a Christian" completely, ultimately paving way for non-Christians to take office. As with the freeman's oath previously, it is hard to imagine that the councillors and aldermen were not aware of the state's position on the subject. The only plausible explanation seems that it was a deliberate act; though it would take another five years for the first Jew to become part of the establishment following the 1845 Act for the Relief of Persons of the Jewish Religion elected to municipal offices. In December 1850 John Lewis Levy, with John Foord, Stephen Steele and Edwards Robert Coles, was appointed magistrate to the city — the first Jewish magistrate in the country.[6]

In comparison with Rochester, Chatham was governed by Court Leet — a remnant form of governance from feudal days. Operating together with the churchwardens and overseers, the Court Leet administered the old 'watch and ward' customs and appointed part-time constables (borsholders) under the overall authority of the Lord of the Manor. Annually, 24 men of good repute and standing were chosen out of the freeholders of the town to serve as jurors of the Court Leet. The jurors then elected a high constable, whose privileges included reading royal proclamations.[7]

It would be Chatham, with its antiquated form of governance, with its rather hostile environment, with its filthy streets and perpetually drunk soldiers and sailors — described by the historian R. G. Hobbes as 'the wickedest place in the world'[8] — that would prove to be the pioneer of Jewish emancipation in the whole country. Indeed, the competition between two towns, Rochester and Chatham, never took on a more interesting form, not even when they competed for the supremacy of their markets.

On 10 November 1854, the *Morning Chronicle* reported the results of the elections in both towns. R. Clements, a high Tory, was elected Mayor of Rochester. In the neighbouring town of Chatham, Charles Isaacs, a Liberal, then in his early thirties, was elected High Constable of the borough for the ensuing year. 'Mr Isaacs belongs to the Jewish persuasion. We believe this to be almost the first instance on record of a gentleman of Mr Isaacs's faith having been elected to fill the principal office in any borough,' the *Chronicle* said. It was

The Mitre Hotel, meeting place of Court Leet, which governed Chatham

indeed the first instance in England for a Jew to fill a principal office. David Salomons, who until now was thought to be the first Jewish mayor in the country, was elected Lord Mayor of London in 1855.

Isaacs was born in Chatham about 1821. He was the eldest child of six, of Isaac Isaacs, a navy agent and army clothier, and his wife Katherine. Katherine died in December 1848 during the national cholera outbreak — the epidemic that led to creation of local boards of health and the first Public Health Act in 1848. Isaac Isaacs died in 1850, leaving Charles in charge of his younger siblings and of the outfitter's business. On 14 May 1854, six months before his election, Charles married Julia, the youngest daughter of the late John Samuel, a prominent member of the Richmond Jewish community.

It was the time when England was involved in yet another war, this time against Russia. Chatham was swollen with troops getting ready for the Crimean front or coming back on leave. Local hospitals were full of the wounded and the convalescing. On 6 March 1855 Queen Victoria visited the town and public hospitals in Chatham and its vicinity, and inspected the patients who had recently arrived from the Crimea.

The queen was hosted by the High Constable Charles Isaacs and the members of Court Leet, Messrs Dunford, Ruck, Wilkins, Ralph, Marks, Lott, Budden and Austin. At Fort Pitt Hospital, Her Majesty was presented with the following dutiful address:

> 'To the Queen's Most Excellent Majesty, — We, the High Constable and Court Sect of the ancient town of Chatham, humbly venture to approach your Majesty with the most profound feelings of duty and loyalty, at this time when your Majesty has graciously condescended to visit our town and manifest your Royal sympathy for the unfortunate inmates of our Public Hospitals, who have lately returned from the war in the Crimea.
>
> While we heartly appreciate such an act of charitable condescension on the part of your Majesty and His Royal Highness Prince Albert, and while we entertain the deepest concern for our noble fellow-countrymen in the East, we humbly trust, through the blessings of Providence, by the firm and vigorous efforts of this nation, and the great powers with which it is allied, the peace of the world may soon once more safely and honourably established.
>
> 'And we will, as in duty bound, ever pray, etc.
> 'Charles Isaacs,
> 'March 3rd, 1855 For Self and Sect.'

Her Majesty graciously condescended to receive the address from the hands of the high constable, and replied, 'I have much pleasure in receiving it.'[9]

The significance and the irony of this event is hard to overestimate — the first Jewish high constable hosting the English monarch — the monarch of the country, which still excluded Jews from parliament on grounds of their faith.

A year later, on 12 November 1856, another annual meeting of Chatham Court Leet was held by the outgoing High Constable Mr Charles Lott in the chair. It took place at Mitre Hotel — the regular place of Court Leet meetings. Having disposed of the usual business, the court proceeded to elect a high constable for the ensuing year, when the choice unanimously fell on John

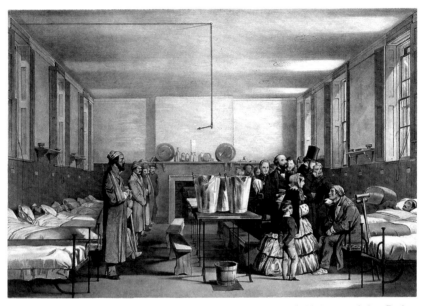

Queen Victoria and Prince Albert, with the Prince of Wales and the Duke of Coburg, visiting soldiers wounded in the Crimean War at Brompton Hospital, Chatham, March 1855

Montagu Marks — another member of Chatham Jewish community. Marks, about the same age as Charles Isaacs, had also a similar background. Born in Chatham, a son of Montagu (Mordecai) Marks, outfitter, and his wife Hannah, née Moses, John was the eldest of six children. Mordecai died in 1833 at the age of 47, and the 13-year-old John took over his father's business. He was considered a prudent and intelligent young man. By his zeal, integrity, untiring energy, and perseverance, he had also achieved for himself a most respectable position among his fellow townsmen. The congratulatory speech was made by Mr Budden, one of the chief officers of Court Leet, who also congratulated Marks on his election as the representative for the Chatham Jewish community to the Board of Deputies. The high constable elect replied that he felt proud of the positions and looked upon that as the most distinguished honour. The election to civic office showed to the country at large that a Jew was just as well suited to take high office as another subject of Her Majesty. It had shown also that a Jew could pay respect to the established religion of his country, and yet have regard to the principles of his own religion.[10]

During his tenure as high constable, John Montagu Marks led the opposition to the Admiralty's decision to reduce the dockyard workers' pay to 12 shillings a week. He considered the proposed pay to be almost lower than that of a soldier. The latter received 7s 7d per week with fuel and no rent, as a result being better off than a labourer. Marks's suggestion was to write to other dockyard towns, to induce them to take part in the movement, as Chatham alone would not have an effect on the Lords of the Admiralty.[11]

He was also instrumental in installing a wall letter-box in the Chatham High Street — an accomplishment of not much significance today, but of great importance for the people of Chatham in the 1850s.[12] The innovation, introduced in the country in 1857, allowed people to deposit their stamped mail day or night. John Montagu Marks died on 21 December 1863 in his early forties and was buried at the Chatham synagogue burial ground.

In 1862, Daniel Barnard would become the third Jewish high constable for the town. Born in 1825, Daniel — Dan as he was known — was the second generation of Jews born in England. His grandfather, Rabbi Daniel Segal from Prague, arrived in England in the 1780s, probably following the expulsion of the entire Jewish population from Bohemia and Moravia in 1745. Segal settled in the borough of Staplegate, on the outskirts of Canterbury. In time he married and, according to the family legend, took the surname of his wife Tzippy, becoming Daniel Barnard. As with so many European Jewish immigrants, Dan was a watchmaker and a silversmith, supplementing his income by selling slops and pawnbroking. The couple had seven sons and three daughters. On Daniel's death in July 1815, Tzippy took over the second-hand clothing business.

Soon after the father's death, two brothers — Bearman and Samuel — joined the growing Jewish community of Chatham. They settled in the High Street, establishing themselves as general dealers. In time, Samuel married Louisa, née Benjamin, a niece and a ward of the community stalwart Lyon Benjamin and his wife Hannah. Samuel died in 1837 at the age of 42, leaving Louisa with five children in charge of the business. For the 12-year-old Daniel, the eldest of the children, helping his mother was the start of his working life.

In early 1846 Dan, then 21, married Amelia, née Levy, from London. The couple settled at 333 Chatham High Street. During the first three years of the marriage, Dan tried various trades — clothier, general dealer, newsagent, and tobacconist. A small inheritance from his aunt, Hannah Benjamin, who died in 1843, and which was held on trust for him and his sister Sarah by his mother, proved handy in 1849. A public house came up on the market at an affordable price. The Granby Head, near Sun Pier, which had just changed its name to Railway Saloon, to celebrate the arrival of the novel mode of transport to the Medway Towns, was for sale. To improve its unsavoury reputation, Barnard demolished the pub's adjoining skittle-alley and built a music hall in its place. But more of that in the next chapter.[13]

Fires were the curse of Chatham, with its many wood-clad houses. They occurred on a regular basis, especially in the overcrowded area of Chatham Intra, with its wharves, warehouses and slums. The town did not have its own fire brigade, and had to rely on its neighbours. During his tenure as high constable, Dan devoted his time and energy to establish one, but in vain. He called two or three meetings to discuss the subject during that year, but they were not well attended, and nothing came out of them.[14] Fire became Dan's obsession. The meetings' failure only made him more determined. Several years later, at a meeting on 13 November 1866, 'it was resolved that a volunteer Fire Brigade be formed in Chatham under the authority of the local Board of Health and that such Brigade consists of 14 members — 1 captain, 1 Lieutenant and 12 firemen. Officers and members elected annually. Members sworn as special constables.'[15] The next two meetings were devoted to the development of rules and regulations.

On 25 November 1866, Daniel Barnard was appointed captain of the newly formed Chatham Volunteer Fire Brigade. The first drill took place on 17 December 1866 under the leadership of their captain. The next day the fire brigade attended their first fire … at Barnard's music hall. Fire would become the curse of the Barnard family for generations to come.

Rochester followed Chatham's lead. On 9 November 1859 three Liberals — John Lewis Levy, John Foord and John Saxelby Cobb with 16 votes each — were elected aldermen. The next year, 1860, witnessed the city electing its first

Jewish mayor — Alderman Levy, a 53-year-old merchant.[16] Levy was the third generation of a Jewish family who made the Medway Towns their permanent home. His grandfather, Naphtali ben Judah settled in the area in the late 18th century. He died in 1815 and was interred in the synagogue's burial ground. Naphtali's son, Isaac, born in 1781, was a successful merchant and general dealer, who died on 5 November 1840, on his way back to Rochester. He was about to board a steam packet when he collapsed at the entrance to the London Bridge Pier. He was buried next to his father at Chatham.[17]

John (his Hebrew name was Judah, after his great grandfather) was born in Rochester in 1807, eldest son of Isaac and his wife Sarah. Their other children were Charles, Hester and Hannah. As tradition went, from an early age John helped his father to run the business, eventually becoming a successful merchant in his own right. As early as 1820 he was the owner of a warehouse behind 240 High Street Rochester, at the foot of Star Hill. The contents of the warehouse ranged from coffins to oranges and Levy's trade is commemorated still in Orange Terrace.[18] His sister Hester's marriage, and her subsequent move across the Channel to Boulogne, helped to enhance the network of business contacts and expand the business.

When later John built the Upper Nile Terrace, today's 5, 6 and 7 New Road, it was thought that nobody would ever like to live there as they were deemed to be too far out of town. The properties were nicknamed 'Levy's Folly', and John with his family had to move into one of the properties himself. One Sunday burglars broke in and made off with a large haul. The crime was reported in the local newspaper, which stated that the thieves had overlooked a handsome pair of antique silver candelabra. The next Sunday, the house was burgled again, the silver removed and a note left on the table: 'Thanks for the information. We have now taken the silver candelabra.'[19]

In December 1850 John Lewis Levy was appointed a magistrate to the city of Rochester, a position he held until 31 December 1870. In April 1853 he was nominated by opposing parties for the office of guardian of the borough of Chatham. However, his name was removed from the Chatham list at the request of some of his friends, because Rochester wanted to return him as a guardian for the city.[20] He was elected mayor twice — in 1860, and in 1865 after the death of the incumbent, Mr Boucher.

Dan Barnard (1825-79) later in life. As well as being High Constable of Chatham and founder of Chatham Volunteer Fire Brigade, Barnard was also proprietor of one of the first music halls in the country and the founder of dynasty of showbiz entertainers

John Lewis Levy died at his Upper Nile Terrace residence from what was described in the press as 'fatty degeneration of the heart' just after 8pm on Sunday, 29 January 1871. He was 64. His extensive obituary, published in local and the national newspapers, celebrated his achievements and personality in glowing terms.

He was, the obituarists said, an active member of nearly every public body in the towns and was most diligent in the numerous duties devolved upon him. As senior magistrate in the city he was assiduous in his attendance on the bench and was known to temper justice with mercy, where he invariably displayed great aptitude and ability, and was held in the highest esteem by other magistrates. He was one of the directors of the Rochester, Chatham and Strood Gaslight Company, a member of the Medway Board of Guardians, Chatham Local Board of Health, St Margaret's Highway Board and Burial Board, and Rochester and Chatham Paving Commissions — working tirelessly on the maintenance of the roads, which he found almost impassable after the frost in early spring; governor of Rochester Savings Bank and Sir Joseph Williamson's Mathematical School; trustee of the Rochester Building Society, and director of the Kent Fire Office.

He was the leader of the Liberal Party in Rochester, but 'he never permitted the slightest bitterness of spirit to exist within himself towards those whose feelings were opposed to his own.' As a result, he was held in esteem by Conservatives. 'Mr Levy was of the Jewish creed; he was thoroughly liberal and tolerant man, as we believe most of his creed in our country are', the local newspaper obituary said. Levy's charitable generosity, coupled with humility, was widely known.

As soon as the news of his death spread through the city, many shops closed, as a mark of respect. On the day of his funeral, the Rochester Castle flag was flown half-mast. The funeral was attended by the mayor and the corporation, the city officers, the whole city police force, Medway Board of Guardians, Chatham Local Board of Heath, High Constable of Chatham, and numerous citizens. The procession, of 15 carriages and many on foot, arrived at the synagogue's burial ground. Levy's remains were interred in the vault beside those of his parents. After the burial the Rev Lazarus Polack, assisted by Simon Magnus and Asher Lyons conducted the service at the newly built synagogue.[21]

John Lewis Levy left a widow, Mary Ann, née Coles, sons John and Lewis and three daughters, Elizabeth, Sophia and Mary Ann. Throughout his life John Lewis Levy retained strong connections to the Jewish community, being one of the trustees of the synagogue. But in line with those, who were wary of their precarious position and wishing to ensure life without limitations for their children, saw the only way forward as accepting Christianity. As a result, the children were baptised, according to their mother's faith. One of the couple's sons, Lewis Levy, was baptised at his birth in 1848. He attended a school at Crouch Street in Colchester, Essex, run by a Methodist preacher, Francis Truscott. Following his father's steps, Lewis took great interest in the local affairs. He was elected Mayor of Rochester in 1874, 1885 and 1886. His mayoral regalia — chain and badges — are on permanent display in the Grand Chamber at the Guildhall Museum, Rochester.

Having secured equal rights to participate in politics on the municipal level in 1845, it was important to achieve and secure similar equality in parliament. However, this last and the most important bastion of English identity was to be defended by those who perceived any changes as their personal threats, for well over a decade longer.

A familiar trope of 'un-Christianising', this time of the legislature, raised its head again. It was acceptable for the laws of a Christian country to be managed by Jews, but the country would be in great jeopardy if non-Christians were permitted to be part of the making of the laws.[22] The anti-Jewish campaign was gathering pace.

John Bull, a weekly periodical, which was described as 'admirably adapted to country gentlemen' and had on its masthead the crown and sceptre lying on the Holy Bible accompanied by the text 'For God, the Sovereign, and the People', pursued a long-term campaign against Jews. They were often portrayed — with Catholics, dissenters and Muslims — as deadly opponents of Protestant Christianity. Every attempt to admit Jews to parliament inflamed *John Bull*. For example, in 1845 it stated that 'to do so, will, in our judgment, be virtually to un-Christianise the British legislature, and thereby to invite the displeasure of Almighty God'. According to *John Bull*, Jews, if allowed any political power, then might be admitted to the ancient universities, which will result in the ban of pork and the New Testament.[23]

The public opinion was also influenced by the works of some authors, adding more colour to the campaign. The best-known and best-received were the works of Charles Dickens, who spent some of his childhood in Chatham. The writer would retain his connections to the area while living in London, returning to live in Gad's Hill in Higham in March 1856. His first novel, *The Posthumous Papers of the Pickwick Club*, published in 1837, features a description of Chatham and Rochester.

> *'The principal productions of these towns', says Mr Pickwick, 'appear to be soldiers, sailors, Jews, chalk, shrimps, officers, and dockyard men. The commodities chiefly exposed for sale in the public streets are marine stores, hardbake, apples, flat-fish, and oysters. The streets present a lively and animated appearance, occasioned chiefly by the conviviality of the military.*[24]

The 1831 census return for Rochester and Chatham shows a population of 32,122, excluding soldiers and sailors.[25] The Jewish community, the fourth-largest provincial community in the country — behind only Birmingham, Liverpool and Plymouth, according to the survey conducted by the *Jewish Chronicle* in 1847 — was recorded as 189 individuals, out of total estimate of 9,000 in the whole country, excluding London.

Dickens's attitude towards the community is subtle, but distinct and decipherable. Soldiers, sailors, officers, dockyard men who come to the Medway Towns from Wales, Scotland and every corner of England are treated en masse. Their origin does not matter: they are defined by their occupation. By comparison, no matter what the occupation of a Jew is, he is first and foremost a Jew. They were a tiny minority, but they were perceived by Dickens as a non-Christian thorn to be singled out.

The author's attitude is clearer in *The Mudfog Papers*, a Pickwickian parody on the British Association for the Advancement of Science, published after the *Pickwick Papers*, in 1837-38 in *Bentley's Miscellany*. The Mudfog Association for the Advancement of Everything is based in Rochester, and one of the chapters supplies the reader with the full report of the association's first meeting. The audience of the *'section on Zoology and Botany' were particularly delighted by '… a most interesting and valuable paper 'on the last moments of a learned pig' … [and which] stated in the most emphatic terms that the animal's name was … Solomon'* — an explicitly distasteful remark, eliciting a distinct emotional response from the reader who undoubtedly knew about a strong Jewish aversion to pigs.

The next Dickens novel, *Oliver Twist; or, the Parish Boy's Progress* was serialised in *Bentley's Miscellany* from February 1837 to April 1839, and also published in November 1838 before the serialisation was complete. It would become one of the 'authoritative' works of English literature in the depiction of Jews in England. The novel is a Christian fable: the story of an innocent Christian boy, who finds himself in a workhouse, leaves it, goes through various dangerous adventures, progressing 'through all the wickedness of London before his eventual rescue and redemption' from the Jewish captor, Fagin. It is a new version of an old theme, which connects children, Jews and danger, very similar to Chaucer's *Prioress's Tale*.[26]

Almost immediately on his arrival in London, Oliver is befriended by a young pickpocket and is taken by him to Fagin, a Jew, notorious for running a gang of child pickpockets. On seeing Oliver, Fagin begins 'slowly instilling in his soul the poison which he hoped would blacken it.'[27] Fagin corrupts and contaminates the boys, polluting their morals. Like a vampire, drinking fresh life, he destroys this young generation of children, denying them any hope, draining them of life. His forceful and hypnotic personality subdues his captives and denies them any future. To Oliver, Fagin 'looked like death.'[28]

Fagin is not only a soul poisoner. Demanding liquor from the Jew, the violent criminal Bill Sikes warns him, 'And mind you don't poison it.' Fagin is described as 'some loathsome reptile', gliding 'stealthily along, creeping beneath the shelter of walls and doorways'; seeking out at night 'some rich offal for a meal'. He is 'some hideous phantom, moist from the grave, and worried by an evil spirit'. The threat posed by this malevolent, shape-shifting Jew registers in 'little Oliver's blood'.

As in other stories, where the Jews are dragged off and executed, be it physically, like in the *Prioress's Tale* or spiritually, by conversion, like in the *Merchant of Venice*, Fagin is hanged. There is no description of Fagin's trial, but when the death sentence was pronounced, 'The [court] building rang with the tremendous shout, and another, and another, and then it echoed deep loud groans that gathered strength as they swelled out, like angry thunder. It was a peal of joy from the populace outside, greeting the news that he would die on Monday.' Like in melodrama, there is no ambiguity in the novel, it compels the readers to confront and expel the evil.[29]

In sharp opposition to *John Bull* and Dickens's works was the liberal *Nonconformist* edited by a Congregational minister. Despite some dissenters still wishing to see the conversion of all the Jews, they nevertheless advocated for equality which included the admission of Jews to parliament. In one of its editorials, the editor argued that Jews presented no threat to the state, and that despite some citing religion as the reason for discriminating against Jews, he found no biblical justification for such prejudice.[30]

Locally, *The Reformer and Chatham Literary Gazette*, under the editorship of Frederick William Chesson, declared themselves progressionists and were fighting the same battle. 'Oppression whether practised by Lord Derby or Lord John Russell, shall find us among its bitterest foes and its most uncompromising opponents,' stated its editorial in September 1852. 'The phalanx of priestcraft and Toryism, the bench of bishops has successfully opposed the full emancipation of our Jewish fellow-countrymen, just as it has almost invariably fought against every other measure which tended to improve our political institutions, and to grant to the people their just rights. Our 'right reverend fathers' in the Upper House ... have always been the deadliest foes of religious freedom, under the garb of Christianity.' Chesson called for the radical move to remove 'the whole batch of the 'Lords Spiritual' from the House of Lords to give way to the law of progress — the law, which demands that men of all creeds should stand on an equality.'

In the next issue, in October 1853, Chesson published a letter, addressed to the Jewish inhabitants of Chatham, Rochester, and the vicinity, calling for co-operation between Jews and Christians in the fight for the removal of disabilities:

> 'Fellow-Townsmen, — *The exclusion of members of your faith — a faith so closely allied to the Christian religion — from the legislature, is a blot upon the boasted justice of this country, and a barrier in the path of progress. Reformers must not lose sight of this great question, so intimately connected as it is with the watchword of the age, 'Equal Rights'. We must agitate this subject unceasingly until the Jewish Disabilities are entirely removed. Parliament will soon meet. Let us be up and doing. Let us arouse the right feeling of the country, and deluge the House of Commons with petitions. Let me earnestly invite you to consider the propriety of forming in these towns a committee of Jews and Christians, to organise the friends of religious freedom into a party, having for its sole object the bursting asunder of the last legal fetter which binds you.'*

The same issue reported that Sir Frederick Smith, the newly elected Conservative MP for Chatham, pledged himself to vote for the entire emancipation of the Jews, only to renege on his promise two months later.[31]

The Jewish community in Rochester and Chatham were not going to give up upon what they considered their birthright. On 7 March 1853 they submitted a petition to the House of Lords asking it to pass the bill 'for the relief of Her Majesty's subjects professing the Jewish religion.' In the petition they stated that they have always been faithful subjects to Her Majesty, that they truly believed that the difference in faith could not prevent them in executing their duties in office, as they have already proven over the years. 'That no valid grounds exist for their being disqualified from admission to seats in the legislature' the petition concluded.[32] The bill was postponed until 11 April.

Press attacks on Jews continued. The same accusations were made of perceived wealth and greediness and the imagined propensity to treachery. In essence, however, these were attacks on their inability to be Englishmen, irrespective of the time spent in the country, ignoring that most Jews by that time were English-born. A leading article of the *Morning Herald* on 18 March 1853 accused Jews of being mere traders who did not contribute to the country as soldiers or husbandmen, and therefore could not be Englishmen. The editor suggested that if the English required new allies, they had better 'take the Mahommedan, the Hindoo, the Buddhist,' who, according to some convoluted and contradictory editorial argument, respected and venerated Christianity.[33] In short, anyone was better than a Jew.

This particular insult provoked a strong reaction from a 28-year-old Chathamite and member of the Jewish community Lazarus Simon Magnus. In his letter to the *Jewish Chronicle* — the only newspaper that considered it worthy of publication — Magnus dismantled the allegations one by one, pointing out the absurdity of the accusations regarding the absence of Jews in the military and their inability of being Englishmen while remaining a Jew. He reminded readers about the law of economy that required the existence of merchants, and appealed to many Christian clergymen, who were readers of the *Jewish Chronicle* 'to undertake a mission and attempt to convert the editor of the *Morning Herald* to Christianity'.[34]

In the same issue, Magnus stated that petitions from the Portsmouth and Brighton communities requesting the removal of Jewish disabilities, signed by both Jews and Gentiles, were sent to the House of Lords. A petition from Chatham, also containing signatures of many Gentiles and supporting the cause, was on its way.

The same day that Lazarus Simon Magnus sent his letter to the *Jewish Chronicle*, 22 March 1853, another petition was submitted to parliament. This

one was from 29 clergymen led by the Archdeacon of Rochester Cathedral, the
Venerable Walker King:

> *To the Right Honourable the Lords Spiritual and Temporal of the United*
> *Kingdom of Great Britain and Ireland in Parliament assembled.*
> *The humble petition of the Archdeacon and Clergy of the Archdeaconry of*
> *Rochester*
> > *Sheweth,*
> > *We regard with apprehension and deep concern the Bill lately*
> *introduced into You Honourable Lordships' House for the admission of*
> *Jews into parliament.*
> > *We believe that the sanction of all Laws is their resting upon a*
> *Religious Foundation, and that in this Country, a conscientious obedience*
> *on the part of the people and cheerful assent to the authority of the Law,*
> *mainly depend upon its being founded on Christian principles.*
> > *We consider therefore that any circumstance which tends to throw*
> *discredit on the sanction and authority of the Law, by divesting the*
> *legislature of its Christian character, or by raising doubts as to the religious*
> *truth of those by whom the Law may be enacted, is alike injuries to the*
> *State and detrimental to the best interests of the Community at large –*
> > *As Christian Ministers therefore we respectfully but earnestly call upon*
> *Your Honourable Lordships' House, not indeed to persecute the Jews, or*
> *deprive them of those civil rights, which consist in them participating in the*
> *execution of the Laws, but to withhold from them the power of making the*
> *Laws, which in a Christian Country we submit ought to be the privilege of*
> *Christians only.*
> > *And Your Lordships' Petitioners as in duly bound will ever pray*
> *[undersigned]*
> *Walker King, Archdeacon of Rochester*
> *Rᵗ Stevens, Dean of Rochester*
> *John Griffith, Canon of Rochester*
> *E. G. March, Vicar of Aylesford*
> *Revᵈ Dʳ Irving, Canon of Rochester*
> *Joshᵃ Nalson, Vicar of Halling*

W. H. Drage, Vicar of St Margaret's next Rochester
Daniel Cooke, Incumbent of Brompton
William Conway, Vicar of St Nicholas Rochester
John Darby Birt MA, Curate of St Bartholomew's Chapel Chatham
Daniel Francis Warner, Vicar of Hoo St Warburgh [sic]
George Chambers, Curate of Chatham
H. Dampier Phelps, Rector of Snodland
G. E. Nash, Vicar of Allhallows Hoo
Robt Burt, Rector of St Mary's High Halstow
Edward Henry Lee, Curate of Cliffe at Hoo
J Page DD, Vicar of Gillingham
Robt O. Lernan AM, Curate of Gillingham
Joseph Hindle, Vicar of Higham
Geo Davies, Vicar of St James, Grayne
Richard Jones, Curate of Chatham
J. Formby, Vicar of Frindsbury
J. W. Sheringham, Vicar of Strood
J. H. Fairbanks, Incumbent of Luton
H. L. Wingfield, Curate of Strood
Henry Meeres, Rochester
L. B. Larking, Vicar of Burham
Jacob J. Marsham, Vicar of Shorne
Ed . J. Shepherd, Rector of Luddesdown[35]

Similar petitions were submitted from other parishes around Kent:

'To the Lords Spiritual and temporal in Parliament assembled — the
humble petition of the undersigned Inhabitants of the Parish of
Horsmonden sheweth

That your Lordships Petitioners have seen with grief and dismay the
introduction of a Bill by one of her Majesty's Ministers for the alteration of
the Parliamentary oath — enabling JEWS to be admitted to Parliament,
and thereby UNCHRISTIANISING the Legislature and at the same
time throwing off that SECURITY — which on the admission of Roman

113

*Catholics to Parliament was wisely provided for the protection of the
PROTESTANT FAITH, and the resistance of further attempts of
PAPAL AGGRESSION. Your Petitioners — humbly pray that should
such a Bill be introduced to your Lordships' House — Your Lordships will
forthaith and summarily eject it — and your Petitioners will forever pray.'[36]*

On 13 April 1853 a circular was distributed in Chatham, Rochester and
Maidstone calling on the Christians of those places to affix their signatures
to the petition to the House of Lords in favour of the removal of Jewish
disabilities:

*'Every Englishman is called on to sign it, on the ground that it is the
inherent right of every other Englishman to enjoy his own opinion, more
especially on religious subjects.*

*'And every Christian is called on to sign it, on the ground that it is said
'Render therefore unto Caesar the things which are Caesar's and unto God
the things that are God's' (Matt. Xxii.21)*

*'And therefore, any disqualification on religious grounds is a
presumptuous defiance of Divine authority.'[37]*

The bill failed. The fierce opposition was led by the Earl Lord Stanhope
and Lord Derby. The political posters circulated around bragging:

*'No! No! my brave Tories,
We'll stick to our glories;
Nor yield up a tittle of right:
Let the renegade Blues
Fraternise with the Jews;
But the Ballot, we'll choke the first night.*

*The Jews are all fretting,
The Commons to get in;
The Whigs give them courage and hope;
But I'll take jolly care*

They shall never get there …'[38]

In May 1854 another attempt by Lord John Russell to pass the bill failed. The same happened in 1856 and 1857. On that occasion the government accepted an amendment providing that no Jew should hold the office of regent of the kingdom, prime minister, lord chancellor, lord lieutenant of Ireland, or commissioner to the General Assembly of the Church of Scotland.[39]

Early 1858 the bill was again presented to parliament. On Tuesday night, 4 May 1858, the Archbishop of Canterbury with the bishops of Bangor, Cashel, Chichester, Exeter, Llandaff, Oxford, Ripon, Rochester, St Asaph and Winchester, voted for the omission of the fifth clause, which would have admitted the Jews, while the bishops of Carlisle, Hereford and St David's voted for its retention. The strength of the opposition laid among the earls.[40] But this time the bill passed through both houses, and in July 1858 received Royal Assent:

> *'An Act to provide for the Relief of Her Majesty's Subjects professing the Jewish Religion. [23rd July 1858]*
>
> *Power to either House of Parliament to modify the Form of Oath to be taken instead of the Oaths of Allegiance, etc by a Person professing the Jewish Religion, to entitle him to sit and vote in such House.*
>
> *…Any Person professing the Jewish Religion, in taking the said Oath to entitle him to sit and vote as aforesaid, may omit the Words "and I make this Declaration upon the true Faith of a Christian'…*

Jews were now fully emancipated. Legally, at least.

Chapter 7

The Reforms
1830-1870

The struggle for emancipation, which started in 1829, was closely inter-twined with the history of the United Deputies of the British Jews, a communal organisation established in London in 1760. In 1835 London synagogues for the first time offered the provincial congregations the opportunity to join the Board of the United Deputies. However, the proposal met little success. Another attempt to entice the provincial congregations to join the board and strengthen the Jewish representative body was made in 1838. Again, the uptake was disappointing, with Chatham refusing to do so. The reasons for the refusal are not recorded.[1] Eventually, the community joined the board, but for decades the relationship remained turbulent.

Until then, Sephardi and Ashkenazi communities differed in their communal structure and in their worship, with each community following its own rituals. Both congregations adhered to Orthodox Jewish practice, but they did not attend each other's events; intermarriages were frowned upon and required special dispensation from each community's spiritual leaders.

On 15 April 1840 a group of 24 Sephardi and Ashkenazi Jews announced their secession from their congregations and declared their intention to form a group, which allowed them to worship together. The new group became known as the West London Synagogue, or the Margaret Street Congregation, named after the street where the new synagogue was. The secessionists also intended to modernise the rituals and introduce some decorum into the services. In 1841 the publication of a new prayer book of the reformers, edited by the minister of the congregation, the Rev (later Professor) David Woolf Marks, omitted many prayers and altered the text of the others, creating a great stir in Orthodox circles. The wrath of the ecclesiastical authorities was immediate. Dr Solomon Hirschell, Chief Rabbi of the Ashkenazi Jews, issued a 'caution', followed by a 'declaration', in essence constituting *herem* (a bull of excommunication).[2] It was countersigned by the *Beth Din* (rabbinical court) of the Sephardi congregation.[3]

The Chatham Jewish community was firmly on the side of the reformers — they had numerous friends and associates within the group, and Dr Marks was a friend of Simon Magnus, treasurer of the Chatham community.

The controversy was at its peak when, in October 1842, Dr Hirschell died. The Ashkenazi Jewish community of England needed to elect another chief rabbi. During the interregnum, truce was announced, and all parties expressed hope that the new chief rabbi would bring reconciliation.[4] In 1845, in the first election involving the participation of provincial communities, Dr Nathan Marcus Adler, Rabbi of Hanover, was elected Chief Rabbi of the Ashkenazi Jews in England.[5] He was installed in office on 9 July. Many congregations sent their representatives to see the ceremony; among them was Mr Isaacs from Chatham.[6]

The Chief Rabbinate was the most important single authority holding together the Ashkenazi community in the country. The provincial congregations were able to refer for rabbinical guidance on issues such as ritual, the authorisation of marriage and the licensing of *shochetim* (ritual butchers). In some cases, the rabbi would seek the formal allegiance of the provincial community.[7] This had happened in the late 18th century, when Chatham supported Tevele Schiff, who subsequently became chief rabbi in December 1791.

The Chatham Jews welcomed the appointment of the new chief rabbi. On the 2 August 1845, the congregation's deputy, the Rev Jehiel Phillips, delivered Chatham's address to Dr Adler, congratulating him on the post and acknowledging his authority. Several days later the community received a courteous reply, expressing the chief rabbi's gratitude.

However, the much-hoped-for reconciliation between the reformers and the orthodox communities did not come to fruition. Adler continued to enforce the ban imposed by his predecessor. The Board of Deputies, under the leadership of Sir Moses Montefiore, refused to recognise the West London Synagogue and its representatives or certify the secretary of the congregation as the secretary of the congregation of people professing the Jewish religion under the Registration Act 1837. The ban was lifted by the Sephardi congregation in 1849, after which the social separation between communities dwindled and even interchange of religious courtesies became possible.[8] It was not, however, a full reconciliation, and in 1853 the differences between the Reform and the Orthodox erupted into a full-blown conflict yet again.

Moving with the times, the Board of Deputies remodelled its constitution. This resulted in an increased number of the congregations qualified to send their representatives to the board. Four provincial congregations — Sunderland, Portsea, Norwich and Chatham — elected their deputies, who were members of their respective communities, but also members of the West London Synagogue. Samuel Ellis was the elected representative for the Chatham Orthodox community.

On 18 August 1853 the Board of Deputies with Montefiore in the chair passed the resolution that any member or seat-holder of a place of worship that did not conform in religious matters to the rabbinical authorities was not qualified to fill the office of deputy at the board. The resolution divided the English Jewish community with many sending pro and contra letters to the editor of the *Jewish Chronicle*.

The next meeting took place a week later. Three out of four deputies, including the Chatham deputy, entered the meeting room and took their seats. Montefiore, chairman of the board, ordered them to withdraw. His order was ignored even after the threat to call the police. Montefiore's demand for support from other members met a great division of opinions. The meeting descended into chaos and ended.

As a result, letters from the four affected congregations of Chatham, Portsmouth, Sunderland and Norwich were not discussed. Subsequently, the *Jewish Chronicle* published one of the letters — a joint protest from the congregations. The communities objected to the resolution that created a new qualification for the office of deputy and argued against any exclusion of members of the board, which may be founded on this resolution. They reasoned that the board had no power to question and reject the elected members. Neither had the board the power to interfere in the matters of religion.[9]

It is not clear whether the protest had any effect on the board. However, at the next meeting, in early September, the deputies decided to postpone for two months the decision about the elected deputies from Sunderland, Norwich, Portsmouth and Chatham.[10]

According to academic estimates, because no precise data exists, the Jewish community of England by that time numbered 30,000 to 35,000 with the London Jewish population between 18,000 to 25,000.[11] It was not a homogeneous community any more. The relative freedom in England, which Jews did not enjoy in their countries of origins — Germany, Poland, Russia — opened up the horizons and the desire to explore and change. Acculturation, which started in the 18th century, and increasing secularisation split the community into three factions.

There was what the *Jewish Chronicle* termed as the Ultra-Orthodox Party. Its members were terrified at the prospect of departing from ancient customs. They managed to preserve the faith of their ancestors over the centuries, despite the expulsions, despite the massacres, despite the numerous attempts at conversion. The strict adherence to those ancient customs defined them as Jews. For them, even the most trivial reforms were innovations of the dreadful nature and had to be opposed, as an assault on their essence. This party did not recognise the members of the West London Synagogue as brethren and as Jews.

The Liberal Conservative Orthodox Party wished to preserve orthodoxy but were firm supporters and advocates of liturgical and ceremonial improvements. They wanted to create a more spiritualised form of Judaism, but only if reforms were initiated, sanctioned and supervised by the authorised and acknowledged ecclesiastical authority. However, in accordance with high authority and in the spirit of universal love, they looked on reformers as brethren and treated them as such.

The third party were the Reformers, the members of the West London Synagogue and their supporters. They identified themselves as Jews, but having lived in England for years, and gone through the process of acculturation, they were now eager to challenge the traditions and revise the customs.[12]

The meeting to decide the fate of the four representatives took place at the beginning of December 1853. This time the Chatham congregation sent a petition to the board expressing their deep concern at the expulsion of Samuel Ellis, 'a gentleman possessing the confidence of the Chatham congregation, and unanimously elected to represent them' at the board, and requesting to admit him without delay. The petition was signed by Joseph Sloman and Reuben Alexander, wardens of the community; Solomon Abrahams, the third officer; Simon Magnus, treasurer; and the following trustees and members of the community — Charles Solomon, Morris Goldsmith, Charles Isaacs, John Montagu Marks, Samuel Solomon, Lewis Solomon, J.J. Solomon, L.S. Magnus, Joseph Pyke, Charles Sloman, Barnett Harris, John Solomon, Asher Lyons, Simon Lyons and Daniel Barnard.

The fate of the four deputies was to be decided by open voting, where each representative stated his reasons. The arguments against the admission questioned the identities of the four deputies as Jews. To those members of the board, the Reform congregation formed a separate religion contrary to the customs of Israel. They also referred to the excommunication of the Margaret Street Congregation by the chief rabbi.

The arguments of the members for the admission pointed out the hypocrisy of the excommunication argument, bringing as evidence a recent marriage between the nephew of the chairman, Sir Moses Montefiore, and the daughter of the founding member of the Reform synagogue. They also referred to the recent religious ceremony at Chatham, which was attended by both the chief rabbi and the minister of the Margaret Street Synagogue, and where both had a friendly conversation.

In the end, the votes were divided equally: 23 deputies, including Lazarus Simon Magnus, deputy for Sheerness, and J. Hart, deputy for Dover, for the admission, with 23 deputies against, including H. Guedallia, deputy for Canterbury. The final word was to be cast by the president, Sir Moses Montefiore. He voted against the admission.[13]

The final decision of the board outraged members of various communities across the country who saw it as unfair and illegal. The most vocal critic was Lazarus Simon Magnus, the founding member of the new Sheerness congregation and their deputy at the board. Lazarus was son of Simon Magnus, treasurer of the Chatham congregation, and also a member of the Chatham community. On 8 December he wrote a strongly worded open letter to Sir Moses Montefiore, admonishing him for his decision. 'The ecclesiastical authorities', Magnus wrote, 'have not declared that Mr Ellis is not a member of Chatham congregation, and I very much doubt that they would have the power in doing so.' As for the *herem* [excommunication], the notion of it was repudiated at the meeting. In any case, ' … as Jews we have the right to discuss its merits and the grounds given for its conclusions, and if the premises be untrue, or the decision unjust, we have the most perfect right to reject it … The power of the Jewish ecclesiastics are entirely the gift of the congregation — the congregation creates the Rabbi, installs him, follows his advice, or rejects it, as seems in accordance with the congregational interests; deposes the Rabbi, if such a course be deemed necessary; so that he who was Rabbi yesterday, may today be a Rabbi no more. The decision of the Rabbis must in all case be based on the acknowledged principles of right and law; and when they're found wanting in this respect, they must be rejected.'[14]

Meanwhile, following the decision of the board, on 12 December 1853 Samuel Ellis tendered his resignation to the wardens, treasurer and members of the Chatham congregation. However, Chatham Jews were not to be easily defeated. They were going to fight the board's decision. Six days later, on the 18 December at the synagogue's meeting, Ellis was unanimously re-elected deputy for the Chatham community.[15]

The Chatham congregation was so outraged by the Board of Deputies' decision to exclude Ellis that in January 1854 withheld their portion of the chief rabbi's stipend until Ellis was permitted to take his seat.[16] It was all in vain. In September 1854, the Board of Deputies declared the election of the deputies for Portsmouth, Norwich, Chatham and Sunderland void.[17]

The schism within the Jewish community of England was, much to its anxiety, widely reported by newspapers across the country. On 28 February 1854, the *Maidstone Journal* published a gleeful editorial, savouring details of the dispute. In the end of his long article, the editor compared the current dispute to the ancient split of Karaite Judaism from the mainstream Rabbinic Judaism in the second and first centuries BCE, stating that the mainstream

Jews hated Karaites more than they hated Gentiles.[18] In doing so he unsubtly implied that members of the Margaret Street Congregation were not only hated by the Jews, but that they were also hated more than Gentiles.

The article did not go unnoticed. Lazarus Simon Magnus, who had become the mouthpiece for the Jewish communities of Chatham and Sheerness, immediately sent a strongly worded reply to the *Journal*. He candidly explained the nature of the current conflict engulfing the Board of Deputies, and the decision to exclude the deputies, which rested in the casting voice of Sir Moses Montefiore. Taking a dig at the editor's inflammatory language, Magnus wrote that he had 'no means of ascertaining whether that gentleman's [Montefiore's] repugnance amounts to hatred, but if it does, there's no reason why that feeling should be attributed to the whole of the other [Orthodox]Jews in England, and thus cast a slur on the whole community, because one influential man happens to be a bigot'.

He then continued to address the long-standing stereotype of Jewish antagonism to Christianity. Pointing a finger at the priests, the very men who should have eradicated the fallacy, Magnus said that instead of finding common ground and thus bring Jews and Gentiles to reconciliation, the priests busied themselves discovering the differences in men's religious opinions; the moment they found a slight breach, they widened it. The Bible was the religion of the Jews, he said, and an appeal to its pages would discover whether they were taught to hate Gentiles.

Magnus pointed out the generosity with which Jews subscribed to Christian charities, Christian schools, and even to Christian churches, and that without distinction or question as to which of the fifty denominations of Christians it was to benefit. Drawing on various passages from the Old Testament, he candidly explained the attitude of Jews towards different religions and concluded with a sublime passage that the Talmud had declared to be the fountain of every other law: 'Thou shalt love thy neighbour as thyself.'[19] The editor of the *Maidstone Journal* had been taught a lesson and had no choice but to publish a humble apology in the same issue. It was not, however, a particularly sincere apology. The editor blamed the *Christian Times* from which, he said, the bulk of the article was taken. 'These days Christians have no hatred to the Jews', the editor added, 'and Magnus's reflection was unjust.'[20]

In 1855, the Chatham community finally accepted Ellis's resignation, and over the following years the congregation was represented by Samuel Isaacs of St James Street, London, and John Montagu Marks, a Chatham outfitter.[21] In 1859, the community elected John Isaac Solomon, a solicitor, of Coleman Street, London, as their representative at the Board of Deputies of British Jews.[22] John, born in Chatham in 1834, was the son of a navy agent, Samuel Solomon, and as a young man John had been articled to Mr Hill, a local solicitor, eventually moving to London.[23] Solomon would represent the community for 21 years, until 1880.[24]

The rift between the Orthodox and the Reform rumbled on for another 20 years. Only in January 1874 when a member of the Reform synagogue was sent as their representative to the Board of Deputies, was he accepted as its rightful member.[25] It was finally full reconciliation and the recognition of the Reform movement in Judaism.

In the early 1850s, a regular sight in Chatham was a recruiting sergeant bringing to town a long procession of recruits from all over the country — those whom he persuaded to take 'the Queen's shilling'. The recruits came from all walks of life: agricultural labourers, clerks, broken-down tradesmen, a gentleman's runaway son, or a rogue of some kind. They were mainly those who were in trouble, either financially or with the law, and had nothing to lose.[26]

> *'Men were only noticeable here by scores, by hundreds, by thousands, rank and file, companies, regiments, detachments, vessels full for exportation. They walked about the streets in rows or bodies, carrying their heads in exactly the same way, and doing exactly the same thing with their limbs.'*[27]

Another scene took place in the early mornings. Departing soldiers assembled at the barrack square for inspection and the last words of counsel and good wishes from the general of the division. The brass band accompanied their departure by playing folk tunes, including the compulsory *The Girl I Left Behind Me*. They would be followed by a crowd of onlookers, including weeping sweethearts and anxious mothers and fathers. Marching in well-ordered columns and ranks, the soldiers would leave the town on their way to Gravesend — the port of embarkation. Or the military might be seen coming into Chatham, returning from abroad, '... embrowned by the suns of Africa or India, worn and thin, and some of them, crippled and wounded ... Their arrival had been anticipated; the band went out to meet them, and they came marching through the streets, all soiled with dust and fatigued. Cheer after cheer greeted them, as the men of the garrison and the people gathered around.'[28]

After half a century of peace, England found itself again joining the war in Europe. This time it was an alliance with its past foe, France, and against its former ally, Russia. In February 1854, England sent troops as well as ships to the Black Sea to help the Turks. According to the newspapers, the enthusiasm that prevailed was extraordinary, and the excitement was intense.[29] But like all other military campaigns, the Crimean War, brought many casualties. When army medical staff were sent to the front line, Fort Pitt Hospital was left in the charge of an alien, a Jewish surgeon, Dr Jacob Solomon, originally from Cracow, who had settled in Chatham by 1840.[30]

The conflict also brought prisoners of war. No records of any Russian prisoners held at Chatham have been discovered, but there were several vessels containing Russian prisoners of war at neighbouring Sheerness. In September 1854 two of those ships — *Devonshire* and *Beubo* — contained about 60 Russo-Jewish prisoners: conscripted men, their wives and children.[31]

They were visited by Sir Moses Montefiore, his wife Lady Montefiore, and Lazarus Simon Magnus. The Sheerness deputy then persuaded the Board of Deputies to petition the government to provide the Jewish prisoners of war with an opportunity to observe Jewish custom. A temporary synagogue was set up on board one of the vessels and kosher meat was procured — English Jews raised funds to pay the difference between the contract meat and kosher meat. When the authorities permitted the POWs to land, the prisoners were allowed to accept service in the English merchant navy or exercise their handicraft under the surveillance of the police. The Sheerness congregation was enriched by eight shoemakers, four locksmiths, two smiths, two carpenters, eight tailors, one doctor's assistant, one bookbinder, eight masons, three oven-builders and one tinman.[32]

View of Chatham
from Fort Pitt,
*c.*1830 and (left)
Russo-Jewish
prisoners on
The Devonshire,
September 1854

In Chatham, those connected to the military operation were doing well — the numbers of the dockyard workers swelled — by 1855 the dockyard had six dry docks building slips, three of the latter were large enough for the construction of first-rate line-of-battle ships and 27 auxiliary workshops.[33]

However, others not connected to the military and naval machine could find themselves on the brink of destitution — sauch as a young couple, both in their early twenties, where the husband was unable to find employment for five months and whose wife was in the final months of pregnancy. An appeal, published on their behalf in the *Jewish Chronicle* in February 1855, highlighted the couple's trustworthiness and faithfulness, especially the wife's, who used to work as a 'shop person':

> *'A destitute family with three children, oldest under three, youngest three months, lying with the mother on the bare floor scarcely a thing to cover them, or any article of the furniture. Husband — a watchmaker and jeweller by trade; he and his wife both natives of London, highly respectable, have been living in Chatham … They lost everything … Husband and wife not older than 23. Appeal to raise some money to start some business …*

The increasing working-class population of the Medway Towns — mainly the military and the navy — were demanding something to do in the leisure time and that usually meant pub entertainment. In the season of 1848-49 James Atkins, proprietor of the Railway Saloon, introduced a pantomime on the premises.[34] The full-scale production, however, was contrary to the Theatre Act of 1843, which forbade alcohol consumption in the auditorium. Atkins was prosecuted for infringing this law, paid his fine and pledged not to reoffend. According to the rumour, though, he was unable to make the Railway Saloon pay without allowing drink and, in desperation, hanged himself from a beam in the skittle alley adjoining the pub.

The pub had a scandalous reputation, not least for its geographical position, and its second-rate beer, and came onto the market at a knock-down price, to be snapped up by 24-year-old Daniel Barnard who demolished the ill-famed skittle alley and built a music hall in its place. He also worked on bringing respectability to the establishment — the chairman, prominently seated in the hall, was to ensure order among the din that accompanied each artiste's performance. The location of the pub ensured a wide presence of uniformed servicemen in addition to the young men and women in their teens and twenties who tended to frequent the place.

The Railway Saloon became the first music hall in the country to introduce a twice-nightly system of performances, according to Daniel's son Sam, who was said to have pioneered this system. Sam, the eldest child, usually deputised for his father when he was away on business. The observant teenager noticed that the military tattoo — return to barracks — was sounded at 9pm. One day Sam decided to move the first house for servicemen to 5pm. It was followed by the 8pm second performance for the civilians.

According to stories recalled by Dan's sons, the pub became extremely popular during the Crimean War of 1854-56. The departing soldiers, marching past the hall on their way to the Strood railway station (Chatham railway line would open only two years after the war, in 1858), shouted 'Good old Barnard's!' On the battlefield, during one of the attacks against the Russians, troops yelled, 'Down 'em, boys, and let's get back to Barnard's!'

On one occasion, just after the war, a bewildered waiter approached the bar and asked for a ten-shilling bowl of punch. A sailor had just returned from the Black Sea service. While at the front, in a moment of depression he bet his mate that they would never see Barnard's again. The sailor lost his bet and was paying up!

Over the next 40 years, Barnard's welcomed many important music hall and silent cinema stars, including Dan Leno, Vesta Tilley, Marie Lloyd, Charlie Chaplin and Harry Houdini.[35]

Chatham, 'the wickedest place in the world', according to Hobbes's reminiscences, lacked no public houses frequented by soldiers and sailors. The very words, sailor and soldier, were identified with drunkenness and debauchery. Men had nowhere to go but to the canteen or a pub. Street arguments and midnight brawls were a frequent occurrence.[36] The need for healthy recreation was evident.

The Mechanics Institute in Chatham, established in the early 1850s, aimed to furnish the aspiring tradesmen with a possibility of social advancement through its lectures. The foundation and the initial maintenance of the institute were secured by Joseph Pyke, then in his twenties, and a member of the Chatham Jewish community. As he recalled later, it was started from one morning visit of some 'respectable men' to his house on Chatham Hill. The men requested Pyke's help in obtaining books for their Philosophical Institution, which they were circulating between themselves — free libraries and public education did not yet exist — and help with the running of the institution, as it was in financial trouble. Instead, Pyke suggested that the men paid off the debt they owed to the landowner and establish a Mechanics Institution, as was the up-and-coming trend nationally. The same morning, Pyke obtained the money to pay off the debt, of about £90.

He then bought the lease of a disused market-place and building, not far from the dockyard, from Messrs Vennell and Whitehead, strict Calvinists whom Pyke had to convince that the wide scope of lectures envisaged for the institution was more beneficial for working men than dull prayer meetings. After that, he secured a meeting with Charles Dickens at Gad's Hill, intending to ask him to become the president of the institution. According to Pyke's recollections, 'He was seated in his morning room … After the animated conversation about what can be done for the workers, in which he was most interested, I proposed to him he should become president of the Rochester and Chatham Mechanics' Institution, and after much persuasion, he said, "Well, Mr Pyke, I become president on one understanding, and that is that you are vice-president, and do all the work." To this I willingly acceded. Then with characteristic courage I asked him if he could do anything for the opening day, and he said, "No, I don't think I can." I said, "Cannot you give us a reading from one of your famous books?" and to the best of my recollection, he said, "I do not think I am capable of doing what you ask." After much pressing, and my telling him he could be sure to have a sympathetic audience, he said "Very well, I will try." This he did gratuitously, which brought in a very large sum of money on the opening night.'

The Railway Saloon in Chatham, one of the first music halls in the country

He read *A Christmas Carol*. It was a huge success, scarcely a dry eye in the house when he pictured Tiny Tim on his father's shoulder.[37] It was Dickens's first public reading.

Soon after Dickens's death in 1870, his friend John Forster published the first biography of him, but omitted the Chatham public reading. Pyke wrote to him, asking to rectify the issue. Forster sent a word by messenger, with the promise to do so in the next edition — an omission that still has not been remedied. [38]

Pyke was vice-president of the institute until March 1858. In reply to the testimonial upon his retirement from the office, Pyke replied that 'he hoped to see the time when the young tradesman, instead of asking and begging political influence and patronage to obtain for him a government appointment, should by joining their institution, which was in union with the Society of Arts, and by studying, became capable of undergoing the usual examination, and obtaining the coveted appointment, if successful.'[39]

So, who was the energetic Joseph Pyke? His grandfather, Moses Snoek, was born in Amsterdam on 3 January 1724. In 1762 Moses moved to London in pursuit of a better life, and settled in Houndsditch, having translated his name Snoek to Pike. One of his sons altered the spelling to Pyke.

Joseph's father, Louis (or Lewis) Eleazar, the eldest of five children, married Charlotte, a daughter of Dr Abraham Wolff, originally from Frankfurt. Unable to find enough patients to sustain his family, Dr Wolff reinvented himself as a podiatrist, believed to be the first in England. The change proved a success. Schooling was held in high regard and four daughters and two sons were well educated. One of Charlotte's sisters, Sara, moved to Chatham, having married Simon Magnus.

Joseph, the sixth of eight children, was born on 3 March 1824 in Houndsditch, within the 'borders of ghetto', according to the unpublished recollections left to his daughter Cordelia. About four years later, the family moved to Cree Church Lane, Leadenhall Street, a few doors from the Bevis Marks Synagogue. From the earliest age Joseph eagerly engaged himself in communal work. His involvement was not unnoticed — and as a 21-year-old, he was appointed chairman of the committee to welcome the newly elected chief rabbi, Dr Nathan Marcus Adler.[40]

In 1849, Joseph, then 25, moved to Chatham to marry his cousin Sara Magnus, one of the daughters of Simon and Sara Magnus; the wedding took place on 16 January the next year.[41] The Magnus family, like the Pykes, put great importance on learning; the girls were educated on a par with their brother, and Sara had attended Rebecca Norton's school for girls at Eastgate House in Rochester.

In the early years of marriage, Joseph

Joseph Pyke (1824-1902), photographed in his later years, founded the Mechanics' Institute at Chatham and persuaded Charles Dickens to give public readings

supplemented his income of a silversmith by conducting business with his brother, Eliezar (Lizer), who had moved to America. Joseph shipped goods to California — clothes, weapons and food — receiving in return tortoiseshell, coffee, arrowroot and novelty items.

The charismatic Joseph promptly established his place in the community, becoming a warden in 1851. As a successful jeweller, he soon built Beacon Lodge, a family home on Chatham Hill, while operating his business from Simon Magnus's premises in Chatham High Street.

The family home was in the countryside next to Luton village, but occasionally they stayed in the rooms above the business at 302 High Street. Crime was rife in the area, and shop-breaking was a regular occurrence, but the burglary of Joseph's premises on 8 February 1859 was clearly out of ordinary even by the mid-19th century standards — it was reported by 27 newspapers across the country.

That night, burglars scaled the wall at the rear of the shop leading from the New Road. At first, they attempted to break open the kitchen door, but it was reinforced with iron and so that idea was abandoned . Then, using a crowbar to break away the door post and the brickwork, they prised the door open and gained access to the kitchen.

Now the criminals had to get into the shop and started cutting away the ceiling but that proved too complicated. Eventually, they cut through a door panels, and stole nearly every article of stock, including 40 gold watches, three dozen diamond rings, a tray of gold 'charms' valued £150, several trays of signet and other rings, a tray of 50 wedding rings, nearly 100 gold pins, bracelets, a dozen silver watches, three sets of silver salts and a bowl of gold and silver coins.

A neighbour's dog barked furiously, but the family stayed sound asleep. However, about four o'clock in the morning Police Constable Baker, 24, observed a man leave the side of Pyke's building carrying a carpetbag. On seeing the officer, he threw the bag down and fled up Hamond Hill, managing to escape. The bag contained much of the stolen property. The accomplices got away by a different route. The total value stolen was about £1,500.[42]

The family stayed in the area until 1870, and eight out of the 13 children were born in Chatham and educated locally. Having moved to London, the

Pykes retained the connection with the Medway Jewish community for generations as wardens and trustees of the synagogue.[43]

By 1841 the population of Rochester city and Chatham town expanded to 11,026 and 17,123 respectively, and the overall population of the area, including Strood and Gillingham, plus the navy and the military, were just under 50,000. Most residents were in their twenties or children under five.[44] It was a diverse community — by 1851 almost one-third of the population of Rochester and more than half of Chatham did not worship in Anglican parish churches. The spiritual needs of others were catered for at a Roman Catholic church or in the chapels of the Baptists, Presbyterians, Calvinists, Unitarians, Methodists, and the Latter-Day Saints (see Appendix 7).[45] The synagogue was the only non-Christian establishment in the area.

Of the estimated 189 Jewish population of the area in the 1840s (see Appendix 8),[46] 30 people attended service on eve of Sabbath, and an average of 20 on Saturday mornings. In 1847 there were 16 free members and 40 seat-holders, rising to 54 appropriated seats in 1851.[47]

Most of the community were engaged in commerce. Inspection of the directories over the years shows a steady rise in the numbers of Jewish trades with Chatham as its hub, up from nine traders in 1792 to 70 in the 1840s. However, the Crimean War and the economic crisis of the 1850s were the main contributing factors in the sharp slump to 38 traders eligible for an entry in the directory in 1858. One can speculate on the reasons. Either by the end of the 1850s the community was much poorer, or the number of the community members shrank through death and moving out of the area (see Appendix 9). Chatham Jewish businesses were mainly concentrated along the portion of the High Street near the synagogue. Closeness to the barracks and the dockyard was also a contributing factor in the location.

In comparison with Chatham, Rochester — where a licence was necessary to conduct business within the city walls — had very few Jewish traders. There were two salesmen in 1792, Israel Levi and Solomon Mordecai. By 1807 they were joined by a third name, Cohan, a shopkeeper. After the demise of Israel Levi, Solomon Mordecai remained the only Jewish business in Rochester in the 1810s; nothing is known about the fate of Cohan. In 1826 Rochester still had only one Jewish trader, Berman J. Barnard, a hardware man; by 1832 he had moved out of the city. Only the 1840s saw the rise in the numbers of Jewish traders in the city of Rochester, when eight businesses were recorded.

Eastgate and St Margaret's Banks, on the other hand, provided a slightly easier opportunity to conduct one's business being outside the city. Both areas combined formed a buffer zone between the city of Rochester with its antiquities and perceived gentility and the noise and rowdiness of Chatham High Street.

From the 1830s the Jewish businesses started spreading beyond Rochester and Chatham towards Brompton and Strood. By 1838 Lewis Isaac, an army outfitter and a furniture broker moved his business from Chatham High Street to Garden Street, Brompton. He continued to trade from the same premises throughout the 1840s. In 1848-49 Nathan Charles Levy, a dealer in marine stores, moved his business from Rochester to Strood High Street.

We need to keep in mind that the number of entries does not directly correspond to the number of individuals. To make a living many had to move from one occupation to the next in case of need, like Solomon Mordecai who switched from salesman in 1792 to being a silversmith by the 1810s, or Jacob Alexander from being a tailor in 1826 to furniture broker in the 1830s. Others simply diversified, adding additional trade, meriting several entries in the directory, such as Lewis Cohan, who was listed in *Pigot's Directory* for 1826 as a furniture broker, a slopseller and salesman and a dealer in marine stores. Some traders operated their various businesses from the same premises, such as Samuel Isaacs, a bookseller and stationer, outfitter, tailor, draper and tobacconist, who conducted all his businesses from the premises at 79 Chatham High Street in 1840.

As for the range of the occupations, the starting trades for the overwhelming majority of Jewish immigrants who settled in the Medway Towns were: slopseller, salesman, navy agent, clothier, clothes dealer, clothes broker or outfitter. At its peak in the 1840s there were 28 Jewish traders dealing with second-hand clothing. The Jewish peddler of the 18th and 19th centuries was always eager to better himself, aiming to rise from the travelling vendor to a settled stallkeeper. Progressing from that he would aspire to a small shop, expanding to a larger one, or to manufacturing goods for street sellers, or as a wholesaler with a warehouse.[48] Other common trades were watch and clockmaker, usually combined with the trade as a silversmith, goldsmith and jeweller: there were two of them in 1792, increasing to six in the 1840s; and furniture broker — from four in 1826 to seven in the 1840s, followed by tobacconist and pawnbroker.

Alternatively, we can turn again to Charles Dickens, and his description of the Chatham Jewish community. It is hard to ignore his strong anti-Jewish attitude, which no doubt influenced many: 'The children of Israel were established in Chatham, as salesmen, outfitters, tailors, old clothesmen, army and navy accoutrement makers, bill discounters, and general despoilers of the Christian world, in tribes, rather than in families.'[49] He wrote that in 1851, quoting almost word for word a description by an anonymous writer in the *Kentish Gazette* in 1771, but adding his own punchline — the 'general despoilers' phrase. Dickens's attitude towards the community is clear enough. His subsequent denial, in the 1860s, of any anti-Jewish feeling and his lame attempt to portray a positive Jewish character — Riah in *Our Mutual Friend* — somehow ring hollow.

With acculturation, which started in the 18th century and was gathering pace in the 19th, religious scruples were relaxed. For some, wishing to remove every possible barrier in the society and achieve the full degree of acceptance, the only possible way was conversion, either of himself or his children. This was the case of John Levy. His children were baptised at birth, though he retained strong connections to the Jewish community: he was fully involved in the congregation's affairs and was interred in the Chatham burial ground.

Sometimes, the eldest boy was baptised, while the rest of the family retained steady links with their Jewish community. Joseph Maas, a famous tenor, born in Dartford on 30 January 1847 to Joseph and Frances Maas, was baptised at birth. In 1851 his family moved to Chatham. Between 1856 and 1861, Joseph was a chorister at Rochester Cathedral, later on going to study opera in Milan.[50] The family, however, retained their Jewish roots. On several occasions Joseph performed at the Chatham synagogue. In March 1877 Joseph's sister Joyce married Maurice De Solla in Paris; the ceremony was performed by the Chief Rabbi of France.[51]

After full emancipation and the Jewish Disabilities Act of 1858, the level of baptisms tailed off, though it did not mean that the attempts to 'save' Jewish souls stopped. Periodically, the Medway Towns were visited by missionaries, such as members of a very prominent London Society for the Promotion of

This watch, made by Lyon Benjamin before 1825, remains in the family

Christianity among Jews preaching for conversion of all Jews. Established in 1809, the society focused its efforts on Jews in Britain. Its supporters included nobility and MPs. During their visit in April 1869 the missionaries of the society preached at St Paul's Church in Luton, Chatham, Holy Trinity in Brompton and St Nicholas in Rochester, attempting to raise funds for the society.[52] However, some Christian leaders adopted the principle of 'live and let live' in relation to the Jewish communities in their midst.

In April 1867, Dr Joseph Wigram, the Bishop of Rochester, died. He was succeeded by a high church clergyman, the Rev Thomas Cloughton, Vicar of Kidderminster. According to the editorial in the *Jewish Chronicle*, it was a promising appointment for the Jewish community of England, and that of Medway in particular: members of the high church were less disposed to intrude upon Jews than evangelicals, of which the deceased prelate had been a member. Both wished to save Jewish souls from perdition, but high church clergymen were perceived to be more reasonable and realised that damage resulted from conversions far outweighed any benefit that could accrue from them to the church. The desire to convert created a corrupt market system of buyers and sellers. The buyer, a Christian clergyman, eager to obtain as many converts as possible, could not be diligent and pedantic in the examination of the articles offered to him — after all, his position, promotion and consequently, income depend on the number of converts. The seller, a Jew willing to convert, eager to make the best of the bargain, would set himself to the greatest advantage in the potential transaction. As a result, this market system produced hypocrites, rogues, vagabonds or paupers, dependant on the charity of the converters, and ready to relapse should Jews come forward to bid against Christians in this kind of auction market.[53] With appointment of the new bishop, the system of Jewish conversions pursued by Dr Wigram, seems to have come to an end.

Before the Elementary Education Act of 1870 established compulsory education for all children between the ages of five and twelve, tuition for children was provided by two means — Jewish charities or private academies, such as the academy run by Caroline and Anne Morris, which operated in 1840 in Rome Lane (now Military Road), Chatham, and May Place Academy, established by Fanny Crawcour in 1839 in Northfleet. Lazarus Simon Magnus was educated at Neumegen Academy at Highgate, London. Alternatively, Jewish children attended local non-Jewish schools: Lazarus's sister Sara was a pupil of Rebecca Norton's Academy, based in Eastgate House, and James Polack, a son of Rabbi Lazarus Polack, was a pupil of Sir Joseph Williamson's Mathematical School.

The middle-class girl's education was aimed at obtaining a husband. If a marriage did not materialise, the only socially approved route for a girl to earn her own living was to become a governess,[54] or establish her own school. And this what Fanny Crawcour (née Alexander) from Gravesend, and originally from

A memorial dedicated to tenor Joseph Maas (1847-86) can be seen in Rochester Cathedral

Sampler made by Sara Pyke (née Magnus) at Rebecca Norton's
Academy, Eastgate House, Rochester, 1839

Chatham, did. After the death of her husband in 1834, Fanny and her seven
daughters returned to her family in Chatham. There was no prospect of a
husband, and a widow had to find a way to earn her own living. In 1839 Fanny
Crawcour opened May Place Academy on the old London and Dover Road in
Northfleet. In 1841 there were 24 pupils, studying French and German, Bible
studies, mathematics, English, geography and history, in addition to Hebrew.[55]
Her daughters were pupils, later on becoming teachers there. In 1859, one of
Fanny's daughters, Eliza, by then married to Samuel Barczinsky, took over the
establishment. The academy was attended by boys from the age of six, and girls
from the age of seven; both genders graduated at the age of 15.[56] Both families
attended Chatham synagogue and took part in community affairs.

One of the main principles in Judaism relates to *tzedakah* — charity. It is
an obligation for every Jew to do what is right and just. The root of the word
'tzedek', from which tzedakah derives, means justice or righteousness. The
Talmud in *Tractate Baba Bathra* 9a states: 'Charity is equal in importance to all
other commandments combined.' Unlike voluntary philanthropy, *tzedakah* is a
religious obligation to be performed regardless of one's financial position. It is
mandatory even for those of limited financial means. 'For the poor shall never
cease out of the land; therefore I command thee, saying: "Though shall surely

open thy hand unto thy poor and needy brother, in thy land.'"[57] *Tzedakah* may be fulfilled in various ways — giving money to the poor, contributing to a worthy cause, such as healthcare or educational institutions or by assisting and helping others. It is not a sin to do well, but having good income brings bigger obligations, to do more to support the poor and wider community.

There are numerous examples throughout the years of the Chatham community contributing to various worthy causes, Jewish and non-Jewish alike — raising funds to alleviate sufferings of Jews abroad, helping workers during the Lancashire Cotton Famine in the 1860s, contributing to the education of the poor, subscribing to a charity for the blind, or building a lodging house for young women, to name just a few.

The internal structure of the Chatham Jewish congregation remodelled their constitution in 1844 along the lines of the Great Synagogue in London and formalised its membership. Typically, the congregations consisted of three categories of members — *ba'ale batim*, 'free' or privileged members, enjoying the full membership of the community. They were entitled to communal honours, which included saying *kaddish*[58] and helping the rabbi to read the weekday weekly service, or the right to elect and be eligible for communal office. The second category were the yearly renters of the seats and the rest were occasional visitors who attended the community services from time to time.

The congregations elected honorary officers from the *ba'ale batim* (in ascending order):

❖ *Gabbai tzedakah* (the overseer of the poor);
❖ *Goveh* (treasurer);
❖ *Parnassim* (wardens).

Usually there were two wardens, one of them acting as president. Sometimes there was a third officer.[59]

It is impossible to ascertain if the Chatham community adhered strictly to the above structure, as the record-keeping was rather lax; also, as mentioned earlier, the Chathamites liked conducting their affairs in their own style. However, there is a record of the elected *parnassim* (wardens) of the newly adopted constitution. The record also provides us with the names of those who were possibly trustees of the synagogue. The Laws were signed on the 28 April 1844 by the following:

> *Jehiel Phillips, Samuel Isaacs, senior wardens; John Sloman, junior*
> *warden; Samuel Simons, Simon Magnus, Simeon ben Asher Dov, Reuben*
> *Alexander, Coleman Abrahams, Lewis Casper, B. S. Barnard, D. L.*
> *Davis, Chas Sloman, Saul Isaacs.*[60]

The elected rabbi was Jehiel Phillips, senior warden of the congregation as well as the secretary. In addition, he was also the registrar of the community, certified to register births, marriages and deaths in accordance with the Marriage Act of 1836. The act specified that marriage was to be recorded by the registrar appointed for that purpose. Couples wishing to marry were legally obliged to notify the registrar of their forthcoming marriage. The act also required the registration to take place only at the venues licensed for that purpose. Jewish congregations required to meet additional conditions for marriages to take place in the synagogues — it had to be defined as a 'place of worship'. To be defined so, the synagogue had to be used for regular public worship by minimum 20 heads of households for at least 12 months before the licence application.

The act came into power on 30 June 1837 with Sir Moses Montefiore responsible for certifying the appointments of registrars for Jewish communities. By the end of June 1839, the first certificates were issued to three synagogues in London and the provincial synagogues of Bedford, Chatham, Cheltenham, Hull, Plymouth and Ramsgate.[61] The powers given to the communities to register births, marriages and deaths meant travel to London was no longer needed to make a record.

The first marriage under the provision of the act took place on 6 June 1838 between Samuel Magnus, a tailor, of full age, residing at 76 Margate Street Dover, and Miriam Isaacs, of full age, daughter of Lewis Isaacs, a broker of Garden Street, Brompton. The marriage was solemnised by Jehiel Phillips in the presence of Samuel Isaacs and Nathaniel Isaacs, witnesses.[62]

Rabbi Jehiel Phillips was born in 1799 in Berlin, Germany. As a young man he moved to Warsaw, Poland, probably to study Judaism under the instruction of one of the prominent rabbis. Soon he married Rosa. The twins David and Jane were born in 1826, and shortly after, the family moved to England, settling in Chatham. Phillips quickly established himself as a prominent member of the congregation and in 1831 was elected rabbi.[63] With the position, came accommodation — the family resided in the Minister's House, which was under the same roof as the synagogue, in what was described in directories of the time as the Synagogue's Yard.

In December 1846 Phillips solemnised the marriage of his daughter Jane to Barnett Lyons, a pawnbroker from Glamorganshire, and in the early 1850s the family moved to Wales to become part of the small Jewish community in Cardiff. There is no doubt that the knowledgeable Phillips was welcomed by the new community — he was the celebrant at the first Jewish wedding, which took place on 26 February 1854.

However, the family retained their connections with the Chatham community — Jehiel even tried to take part in elections in 1856. At the time the law required the lists of electors to be posted on the church and chapel doors within the borough. The lists had to be placed on a specified day, so that every person entitled to be registered could ascertain that his name had been duly enrolled. In his attempt to verify that he was enrolled, Phillips, a Liberal, stated he could not recollect where he was born, but he had been in England for many years. However, his name was struck off — the court assumed that without a title of proof, he was an alien.[64]

After the Phillips family's departure, the Chatham congregation needed a new rabbi. They chose the 41-year-old Lazarus Polack. Born in 1813 in Hamburg, then under the Napoleonic rule, Lazarus was the son of a well-to-do bookseller and antiquarian, David Polack, by his second wife. David Polack's bookshop was frequented by many scholars and notables of the time, including the poet Heinrich Heine. On several occasions Lazarus witnessed his father asking the young and high-spirited poet to leave the library and the shop because of his irrepressible jokes.[65]

At the age of 37 Lazarus Polack decided to see England, and his father gave him a letter of recommendation to Martin Grünwald, a bookseller from Hamburg who lived in Dover. On 17 June 1850, Lazarus arrived in England and settled in the same town, teaching German and French at the school of the Rev R.I. Cohen. In 1854 he was appointed simultaneously rabbi to Hull and Chatham synagogues. Polack favoured Chatham. Shortly after, he married Mindela, a daughter of Isaac Berlin, a famed Rabbi of Hamburg. Twenty-three-year-old Mindela arrived from Hamburg on 2 June 1853 on board the *John Bull* and stayed with her family at Portsmouth before the marriage on 10 September 1854.

Polack's appointment as rabbi provided an annual salary of £75 plus a house. The salary never increased for the next 30 years. The couple had nine children, and to provide for the family Lazarus supplemented his income by teaching German, French, and Hebrew. In one instance he taught Latin, of which he knew nothing, but was persuaded despite all his protestation. Two eager women were convinced that 'being so clever a linguist' he must know enough Latin to teach them 'the elements of so simple a field of learning'. According to the recollections of his son James, the children never learnt about the progress those ladies made in studying Latin. Among Polack's students were Herbert Kitchener (later the 1st Earl Kitchener), who was taking the engineering course at Chatham Barracks, and the composer Edward Elgar, who at the time was living in Rochester.

The children attended the local schools, with the boys being educated at Sir Joseph Williamson's Mathematical School, where they, children of naturalised German parents (the Polacks naturalised in 1866), were frequently held up as models of correct English. James recalled that the teachers' frequent rebuke to the pupils was: 'Why don't you read and do your composition like the Polacks?' In 1875 James's younger brother, Emmanuel, the only Jewish pupil in the school, was awarded the first prize in his class for French and Latin.[66] James remained silent, however, on how the rest of the pupils reacted to the masters' rebukes and the brothers' success in English. Some years later James would become the principal of Craufurd College in Maidenhead, and his elder brother, the Rev Joseph Polack, BA, the housemaster of Clifton College, Bristol.

The Chatham community received a terrible blow in the new year of 1865. On Friday, 6 January, Lazarus Simon Magnus finished his business for the week in his offices at 3 Adelaide Place near London Bridge. During the day he had developed toothache — a recurrent problem, but that day it troubled him more than usual. He even complained about it to his brother-in-law, Manuel

Castello, the husband of his younger sister Lizzy. Manuel suggested Lazarus should come home with him, to Sydenham, where Lizzy could treat it, but Lazarus declined. He didn't feel like travelling and decided to stay for the Sabbath in the rooms next to his offices.

At 10pm he chatted to his housekeeper, Mrs Thurgood and asked for the best remedy for his toothache. She suggested some laudanum on a piece of lint, but Lazarus had another idea: chloroform. He knew he had to take precautions — the anaesthetic had to be carefully measured and administered while sitting. This way, when its effect took place, the arm would drop, stopping the inhalation. The pain was becoming unbearable, and Lazarus decided to let chloroform flow freely on the sponge. Also, he thought, perhaps the pain might disappear more quickly if he lay down.

He was found lifeless the next morning by Mrs Thurgood. He was 39.

Born in April 1825 and named after his grandfather Lazarus, one of the early trustees of the synagogue, Lazarus Simon was the firstborn child and only son of Simon Magnus and his wife Sara, née Wolff, whose sister Charlotte married Lewis Eleazar Pyke, father of Joseph. Lazarus was schooled in the well-established Leopold Neumegen Academy in Highgate, London. He was well versed in Hebrew and biblical studies, as well as being accomplished in other disciplines, aimed to help young Jewish students to succeed in English society.

His three-year relationship with Rosa Levy had ended acrimoniously in 1844[67] and that put him entirely off the idea of marriage. Instead, Lazarus threw himself into the business and public life. He was proud to be born in Britain and considered himself an Englishman. He identified himself with the national spirit, while preserving his Jewishness, which to him meant adhering to the principles of Jewish Law.

He was instrumental in the opening of the new Sheerness Synagogue in 1853[68] and for years he served as their deputy for Sheerness at the Board of Deputies of British Jews, having been elected the same year.[69] During the conflict when the Chatham deputy, Samuel Ellis, and three others, were refused their seat at the board, Magnus fought the decision. He battled fairly — and publicly. He sent letters to the editor of the *Jewish Chronicle* and argued his case, neither mincing his words nor shying away from exposing Montefiore's bigotry.

The Rev Lazarus Polack with his wife Mindela and their children (from left): Joseph (born 1856), Emmanuel (born 1864), Isaac (born 1861), David (born 1855), James (born 1859) and Cecily (born 1855). To deter the expansion of Reform Judaism and to appeal to English-born Jews, chief rabbis had to concede some ground. The concessions allowed to develop *minhag angli* (the Anglo-Jewish rite) in the custom of English Jewry. It reconciled traditional Jewish content with English decorum: rabbis wore top hats and dog collars, and professional chazanim (cantors), if the congregation was able to afford them, led choral services

Lazarus Simon was also the driving force behind the development of the Isle of Sheppey, particularly in the 1840s and 1850s, when railways were all the rage. The first railway connecting London with the Medway Towns reached the area in 1848 — Strood, being on the same side of the river as the capital, was a comparatively easy link. A line to Sheppey would have also made the connection between Sheerness and Chatham dockyards more efficient, less time-consuming, and less dependent on the weather. However, the opposition to the change was fierce, and by the time the Sittingbourne and Sheerness Railway company was formed, it only had 10 days to prepare a bill for incorporation.[70] Despite the rush and the resistance, the act was passed in July 1856.

The line, which would include a bridge to link the island and the mainland, would start at a junction with the East Kent line at Sittingbourne, passing through Milton over the Swale, continue through Queenborough and terminate near Sheerness Dockyard. This was the final link between all the great government dockyards and arsenals, and the line would supply a ready access to the Thames and Medway fortifications and additionally connect the fertile Isle of Sheppey with the rest of Kent, opening an easy communication between Sheerness and Canterbury, Deal and Dover on one hand, and London, Chatham, Maidstone, Woolwich, Aldershot, Portsmouth and Plymouth on the other. In addition, it would form part of a direct route to the Continent from Southend and the counties of Norfolk, Suffolk, and Essex.

The main figures in the company were Stephen Rumbold Lushington, of Norton Court, Teynham, a former governor of Madras, as chairman; and Lazarus Simon Magnus the company's vice-chairman and managing director.[71]

The railway directors encountered numerous problems. First, summer 1857 brought a worldwide financial crisis, caused in part by a panic on the banks in the United States. Then, there was a constant struggle against robust opposition: was there enough money to finish the line? And was the line ever going to make any profit? But by September 1859 the works were almost completed. The impressive bridge was about 600ft long, had 10 brick piers, which were supported by iron piling. The arches were made of iron, and the fifth one from the mainland had a swing roadway, which could be raised to admit the vessels going through. The works connected with this part of the structure, were not, however, completed, and the rails were not yet laid upon the bridge. It was expected that the bridge and the line would be open for traffic the next month.[72]

However, the railway did not open that October, or in the following months. The raised expectations were frustrated so many times, that the *Sheerness Guardian* commented in May 1860: 'It is now stated by the directors that the railway will be formally opened on Friday next, but whether any credence attached to the statement, the newspaper cannot say. Seeing will be believing. The "hope" and expectation of the opening has been so often "deferred" that the heart is "sick" of promises.'[73]

The line, seven-and-a-quarter miles long, successfully passed its final government inspection on 13 July 1860 and officially opened five days later,[74] connecting Sheerness with Woolwich, Deptford, Portsmouth, and the whole of the coast from Margate to Weymouth.[75] The day was declared a public holiday locally,[76] and the great crowds at Queenborough and Sheerness enthusiastically cheered welcoming the train's arrival.

The launch did not pass without incident. The 13th Corps of Kent Artillery Volunteers were in readiness to fire a salute as the train approached the Sheerness terminus, but one of the gunners fired point blank into the carriages. Four passengers were injured and many others were exceedingly annoyed. However, this incident did not dampen the feelings of public elation at having a railway line, and numerous guests were treated to an excellent dinner.

During the dinner the company secretary, S.J. Breeze, gave a speech in which he recalled the struggles during the construction, including the problem with money. 'But,' he concluded with unfailing optimism, 'whether we have got the money or not, we have got the railway! … Sheerness had been a place cut off from the rest of the world, and only held to it by a rope — now it is joined to the rest of the world.'[77]

Lazarus Magnus remained vice-chairman of the railway until his death. He was a successful businessman, who, in accordance with the Jewish principle of justice and righteousness, engaged in projects that promoted public interest.

In 1858, no doubt in appreciation of Lazarus Magnus's contribution to the development of the railway line, he was unanimously elected Mayor of Queenborough.[78] Lazarus was one of the first Jewish officials taking office and the first Jewish mayor in the country, following the elections of Charles

Isaacs and John Montagu Marks as high constables of Chatham in 1854 and 1856. His mayoralty preceded the 1860 election as Mayor of Rochester of John Lewis Levy, who had always been considered to be the first Jewish mayor outside London. Magnus was re-elected mayor in 1859 and again in 1862.[79] His responsibilities included duties as justice of the peace, and Magnus attended to this commitment with diligence, recalled by his contemporaries as enlightened and conscientious magistrate.

If Lazarus considered that it was his birthright to participate in civic affairs of the country, he also knew that this birthright brought responsibilities and obligations. One of them was national security and the protection of England from invasion. Out of concern for home defence, the War Office on 12 May 1859 gave the sanction to form volunteer corps. Volunteer Artillery Corps were formed to man the batteries of the coastal towns. On 9 January 1860 Lazarus Simon Magnus received a military commission signed by Lord Lieutenant of Kent, Viscount Sydney, later the 1st Earl Sydney, to raise the 4th Kent Artillery Corps.[80] He was the first openly Jewish person in the country to receive such a commission. During that January Captain Magnus raised 80 men — the full capacity of the corps. For him the protection of the Queen, and the safety of home and property, was also duty imposed by God.[81] There were frequent inspections; each of them complimented the 4th Volunteer Corps' efficiency and expertise.[82] Incidentally, all Jewish men in Chatham joined the 9th Kent Volunteer Rifle Corps, with Charles Isaacs as their lieutenant.[83]

On the day of Lazarus Simon's funeral many shops were closed as a mark of respect. Six mourning coaches carried family and friends, including Professor Neumegen, Lazarus's former teacher, now in his eighties. Sixty members of the 4th Kent Artillery Corps marched in the procession.

The stone-setting ceremony took place a year later, in January 1866. It was attended by the whole Jewish community of the Medway Towns and many Gentiles, including Mayor of Rochester John Boucher. Edward James Physick, from a known London family of sculptors, created a monument nearly 14ft high, from blocks of Sicilian marble. The centre point of the monument, produced in Carrara marble, featured an oak tree split by a lightning. The inscription designed in letters of solid lead was unique. The technique, used by the Romans, was unknown in England. Physick learnt it when he had lived in

Rome, and this monument was the first of its kind in Chatham.

During the ceremony Professor the Rev David Woolf Marks of the West London Synagogue gave a sermon. Referring to *tzedakah*, the highest obligation of every Jew, he appealed to the bereaved father to contemplate on ensuring a permanent legacy to the memory of his son by building a new synagogue for the community. The purpose of the new building would be twofold. It would ensure that Jews settled in the area permanently. No more would they need to be the transitory sojourners of the community, but rightfully ensure their equality in the area. The new building would also improve the façade of the street and provide the much-needed decorum to Chatham Intra.[84]

The words resonated with the grieving Simon Magnus. The synagogue's lease was due to expire in 1876; it would need to be renegotiated. The current wooden synagogue building, quaint as it was with its turret and a clock,[85] was small and dilapidated. The improvements, made from time to time, such as a new wall to the burial ground and gas lighting,[86] were not enough. The building simply did not answer the community's needs. He would bear all the costs of the task.

In August 1866 Simon Magnus sent a letter to the trustees of St Bartholomew's Hospital outlining his proposal to purchase the freehold of the Jews Tabernacle Synagogue messuages or tenements piece or parcel of ground, known as the 'Synagogue estate' for the purpose of building a permanent synagogue for the community. Two months later, the trustees of the hospital unanimously agreed to the proposal to sell the freehold upon the following conditions:

❖ The land was to be sold exclusively for the purpose of building a synagogue and a rabbi's house;
❖ Magnus to widen High Street pavement 10ft from the current gutter and properly level the ground.

In April 1867 the agreement received the seal of approval from the Charity Commissioners. The indenture of the new synagogue trust stated that Jewish strangers, *ie* not permanent members of the Chatham community, could be buried there, too. In addition, in case of excess of income, the trustees of the new synagogue were to buy a site in Chatham or Rochester and build alms-houses for poor Jews, men and women, and pay the inmates a weekly allowance. The indenture also stipulated that the appointment and dismissal of the rabbi was vested in the congregation. It further stated that the congregation was to keep in repair the tombs of Captain Lazarus Simon Magnus, Simon Magnus, his wife Sara, Simon's parents — Lazarus and Sarah, Simon's sister Cordelia, Permilia Hart, Simon's grandparents — Abraham and Elizabeth Moses, his brother Philip and his niece Permilia Magnus.[87]

In July 1867, the Chatham congregation welcomed a pastoral visit from the Chief Rabbi Dr Nathan Marcus Adler. He was received by Simon Magnus, president of the congregation, the minister the Rev Lazarus Polack, and several members of the community. The chief rabbi examined the children's classes, inspected the piece of land on which the synagogue was to be built, and the adjoining burial ground, which was also secured in perpetuity for the congregation. In the afternoon Dr Adler attended the service at the synagogue; for the occasion the entire congregation was present. After the service, the chief rabbi delivered a sermon. He expressed the earnest hope that the new synagogue's services would be conducted on Orthodox principles — referring to the Chatham congregation's stance during the rift between the Orthodox and Reform.[88]

The building commenced in June 1868. Magnus employed the services of Hyman Henry Collins from the City of London, one of the most prolific Jewish architects in England; the builders were a Rochester firm led by Alderman James Gouge Naylar. Before the beginning of the 19th century there were no notable Jewish architects in England. Not that Jews lacked the skills or aptitude required for the profession; there were simply no building opportunities. To enter the profession required an immigrant family to be adequately settled and financially comfortable to afford the necessary training and attain a certain level of social acceptance, which took one or two generations.[89]

Architecture also requires permanent settlement. The precarious situation of a Jewish congregation, when the community was uncertain in the legality of holding a property or unsure when they would leave the place if the lease were not renewed, had little attraction in building. The nervousness and awareness of the community to the feelings and wishes of the hosts prompted it to settle

Lazarus Simon Magnus (1825-65) and his grave memorial, sculpted by Edward James Physick

and establish their synagogues away from the main roads, so as not to offend or intrude. This fettered their architectural expression.[90] Like many other synagogues in the country, Chatham's was in a maze of shops and tenements, away from the public eye. Besides, Chatham Intra was in the cheapest part of the High Street, and one of the most notorious.

In addition, architecture needs a property-owing community. It required the community to be wealthy enough, as Jews could appeal only to their own congregation to subscribe for the cost. Only after full Jewish emancipation could synagogue design try to compete with the churches in their glory.[91]

On Tuesday, 5 October 1868, Simon Magnus laid a foundation stone for the new synagogue — a ceremony reported by local and national papers. In the cavity of the stone he deposited a glass jar, containing a scroll, the photographs of Simon Magnus and Captain Lazarus Simon Magnus, copies of *The*

Times, Illustrated London News, Standard, Telegraph, Jewish Record and *Jewish Chronicle*, reporting the interment of Captain Magnus and uncovering of his monument, and coins — sovereign, half-sovereign, florin, shilling, sixpence, threepenny piece, halfpenny and a farthing. The parchment scroll explained that the land was a freehold bought from the trustees of St Bartholomew's Hospital in Rochester.

The inscription on the foundation stone read:

'This foundation stone was laid by Simon Magnus for a memorial synagogue in affectionate remembrance of his much lamented and only son, Lazarus Simon Magnus, Esq, on the 19th day of Tishri, A. M. 5629; 5th day of October, 1868. H. H. Collins, Architect. J. G. Naylar, Builder.'

During the ceremony the Rev Philip Magnus gave a speech praising his uncle for the donation and expressed hope that the worship would be in harmony with the beautiful building. 'There will be no place for religious bigotry in the new synagogue,' he said — a nod to the decades-long confrontation with the Board of Deputies and the Office of Chief Rabbi.[92]

The building works finished in May 1870. The new synagogue became a striking addition to the public structures of the town. It was separated from the main road by an ornamental screen and was placed on a terrace. A broad flight of steps led to a pedimented position, supported by semi-circular arches. A marble tablet stating the origin and the object of the structure was placed in this portion. A handsome 50ft tower had been placed on the right of the portion, terminating in an ornamental steepled roof. At the base of the tower was the foundation stone. The whole of the exterior was faced with Kentish ragstone with Bath stone dressings, having columns and enrichments of red Mansfield stone. Over the entrance was the following inscription:

'5629-1869
This freehold land was bought and
This Synagogue was built,
endowed, and presented to the
Jewish Community by Simon

Magnus, a native of Chatham,
As a tribute to the memory of
His much-lamented and
Only son Lazarus Simon Magnus, who died 9ᵗʰ
Tebeth, 5625 — 1865, aged 39 years.'

The Minister's House was at a short distance from the synagogue, and between the two buildings, a little to the rear, a passer-by could see the burial ground with the monument to Captain Lazarus Simon Magnus.[93] The total cost of buying the ground and building the synagogue, which could accommodate up to 150 people, was £10,000.

There is no agreement about the architectural style of the Chatham Memorial Synagogue. It was variously classified as 'Moorish'[94], 'Byzantine'[95], 'Italianate', or 'Romanesque' because of its tower, spire and finials,[96] 'cathedral' and 'choral'.[97] It is probably accurate to describe it as 'eclectic', the hallmark of the 'cathedral synagogue', according to the architectural historian Sharman Kadish.[98] However, she also states that the Chatham synagogue was not built as a 'cathedral synagogue' either in scale or plan — it lacked a nave and aisles and only had one gallery at the west end facing the Ark.[99] Nevertheless, it did contain many features of the 'choral synagogue': a cloakroom, vestry, offices and a kitchen. It also incorporated a *mikveh* (ritual bath) in its basement.

The nave, divided into three parts by arches, was composed of serrated and ornamental white and red bricks with carved stone incised enrichments. The arches sprang from and were supported by clustered and coupled columns of red Mansfield stone, having floriated caps and bases, and resting on carved projecting corbels. On those arches laid the timbers of the roof, wrought and chamfered, covered with V-jointed boarding, enriched with carved fascias exposed to view. Some of the timbers were of picked yellow deal, others stained red and varnished in several tints.[100]

The white-brick walls were interspersed with carved stone enrichments and pierced with traceried stained glass windows, three on each side of the synagogue. A semi-circular enriched arch at the east end of the building was supported by polished red Mansfield stone columns, bound together with ornamental bands. The engraving on the arch, in Hebrew and English, said :

'Blessed are they that dwell in Thy house; they will be still praising Thee, Selah!' This archway acted as a frame and the entrance to the sanctuary, which was separated from the nave by a handsome carved stone screen inlaid with coloured marbles and elegantly wrought iron panelling. A convex recess in the centre of the screen was to function as a pulpit for a preacher.

The sanctuary was elevated a few feet above the level of the synagogue's floor. It could be reached by broad flights of polished marble steps with elaborate balustrading. This sacred portion of the edifice was designed as an octagonal

Elevation plan of the new synagogue, designed by Hyman Henry
Collins and (facing page), the interior. The curtain in front of the Ark was
originally absent. This was a tradition in the synagogues in Sephardi
communities and also in several orthodox 'German' synagogues on the
Continent. In 1873 Henry Jacob Nathan presented the synagogue with
a handsome cover for the reader's desk. The cloth was of rich white
silk, with gold fringe, and bore an inscription in Hebrew, beautifully
embroidered in gold, with the words (translated): '*The gift of Henry Jacob
Nathan, in memory of his wife, Jane, daughter of Simon Magnus, A.M.
5634.*' In 1875 the 'eternal light' lamp fell off the chain and was replaced
by Coleman Defries, who had donated the original lamp. In 1889 Mrs
Goodman of Frankfurt House, Chatham, presented the synagogue with
a clock in memory of her husband, Morris. The clock is still there and
fascinates children during their school visits to the synagogue[114]

apse, at each angle of which were disposed clustered pillars of variated marble. From these pillars carved ribs supported a domed ceiling, terminating in a skylight glazed with stained amber-glass, which threw a solemn and subdued light over the whole composition.

In the centre of the sanctuary was the Ark — enclosed by sliding doors, beautifully decorated with Arabesque and other ornamentation. The interior was hung with silk hangings and bullion fringe of various tints and colours. It was fitted with the dais for the reception of the Scrolls of Law.

The exhortation, 'Know before whom thou standest', was inscribed in gold letters over the Ark. Two inscriptions from the *Proverbs* 'Length of days is in her right hand' and 'And on her left riches and honours'[101] were on each side of the Ark, surrounded with naturalistic floriation.

Directly above the Ark were two stained glass windows representing the tablets of stone surmounted with 'glories' and having the Ten Commandments. Each side of those two tablets had two beautifully designed and harmoniously coloured geometrical stained-glass windows. Under those windows were the marble panels emblazoned in illuminated writing prayers for the Queen and royal family. A very elegantly jewelled, gilt cut-glass dish with the floating *Ner Tamid* ('Eternal Light', or 'The Light of Memorial') dropped from the centre of the arch. It had been presented by Coleman Defries, son-in-law of Simon Magnus, and husband of Simon's daughter, Cordelia.

An elaborate yet chaste gas candelabrum of five lights stood on each side of the apse. This sanctuary was paved with Minton's choice tessellated encaustic paving with polished marble borders. A reading desk was placed in the centre of the nave. It was approached from the floor by flights of steps, on each side, and was enclosed by iron railings, picked out in blue and gold. Burnished brass floriated pillar gas standards, designed especially for this synagogue, were elevated and positioned at each salient point.[102]

The benches were fixed pews — a fashionable fixture at the time. This was a departure from the traditional movable seating arrangement better suited for a Jewish prayer, which allowed the person to move about.[103]

The lavatories could be reached from the entrance hall by the stone stair-case. It led upstairs to the vestibule and the ladies' gallery, both at the west end of the building, facing the sanctuary. The front of the gallery was composed of decorative framing and iron balustrade of elegant design, painted in blue and picked out in gold.

The traditional synagogue is known for separation of sexes. However, in the acculturated communities, such as was Chatham, the strict separation was relaxed — women still sat away from men, but the *mechitzah*, a curtain or divider that serves as a partition between the women's and the men's sections in Orthodox Jewish synagogues, was reduced to a symbolic rail in front of the *ezrat nashim* (women's section).

Judaism forbids the portrayal of God. Over the centuries the tradition extended this prohibition to include any human form, so the ornamentation was therefore designed from natural foliage, arranged in geometrical combination. The carving had been carefully studied from the plants mentioned in the Bible. Scattered about were the lotus, vine, palm, olive, lily, pomegranate, wheatear and bulrush. Decorations were to symbolise the poetry and purity of the Jewish faith, by portraying in the design unity of conception, thus cultivating the essence of true appreciation, by appealing to both the eye and the mind.[104]

The gas fittings were by Defries of London, apart from the gas standards on the sanctuary, which were designed and executed by Brawn of Birmingham. The ironwork was by Jones and Blackstone of London, and Peart and Jackson of London. The heating, hot water and gas fitting, were installed by Spencelayh and Archer of Chatham. The stone carving was by Candy and Gibbs of London. The decorative work was produced by John Durling of Chatham. The stained-glass windows were executed by Smith and Miers, Cumberland Market, London. Upholstery was supplied by Dawson and Son of Rochester.[105]

The consecration of the new synagogue took place on Friday, 17 June 1870. It was performed by Chief Rabbi, Nathan Marcus Adler. The attendance to the ceremony was by invitation only — the demand was high, and a crowd of those unable to attend congregated outside. The weather, which in the morning seemed threatening, turned out beautifully fine. The sun shed its rays on the handsome structure, blending its powerful light with the mellow and subdued light that penetrated through the amber-coloured window at the eastern end of the synagogue. The scene was grand and imposing.[106]

The synagogue was full to the brim — about 200 people, two-thirds of whom were not Jewish were present at the event, impressed with the decorum of the building and the ceremony of the consecration.[107] Among guests of honour were Simon Magnus, Mr and Mrs Castello, Mr Defries, Mr Pyke, Mr Nathan, relatives of the founder; Messrs S. L. Miers, John Isaac Solomon, Chatham representative at the Board of Deputies, Hyman Henry Collins, architect; John Lewis Levy, Lewis Levy, Chas Levy; Henry Hart, Mayor of Canterbury; the Mayoress of Rochester; S. V. Montefiore, Professor Leopold Neumegen of Kew, Berkowitz and Barczinsky of Gravesend, a large contingent of local magistracy and town councillors, and most of the elite of Chatham and neighbouring places.[108]

The synagogue was consecrated by the chief rabbi; the officiating minister was the Rev Moss Barnett Levy, of the Western Synagogue, St Alban's Place, London, assisted by the Rev Lazarus Polack. Julius Mombach, the choirmaster and the composer of the Great Synagogue produced the musical arrangements.[109] The choir rendered his soul-stirring hymns with a grandeur and solemnity, with the especially emotive performance of the *Ode* by the quartet with the leading solo by J. Gershon, a pupil of Stepney Jewish school.[110]

The ceremony started at noon and lasted for two hours. After 'the gates of righteousness' were opened, and as the chief rabbi, bearing the Scroll of the Law, followed by the Rev Philip Magnus and the procession were

Sir Philip Magnus, nephew of Simon Magnus. For his work as an educational reformer and politician, he was created a baronet in 1917. He retained his Chatham links throughout his life

entering the synagogue, the magnificent strains of *Baruch Aba* (*Welcome*) announced that the ceremony had commenced ...[111] For the Jewish observer, familiar with the long-standing rift within the Jewish community of England, this celebration seemed the dawn of reconciliation.

The next morning, the first sermon in the new synagogue after the usual Shabbat service was preached by the Rev Phillip Magnus. Referring to the previous day, he expressed his pleasure to see that the animus once so strong between the ministers of two congregations — one professing the liberal principles, and the other adhering strictly to traditional observance, was dying out. Members of both communities at the ceremony took part in the same divine service, and each addressed in turn the bar-mitzvah youths who had that day assembled to be received into the religion of their ancestors. Other beneficial changes included a greater participation of women in attending public worship, and the adoption of pulpit instruction — a custom borrowed from the Jewish communities of Germany.[112]

However, no synagogue is complete without a school. Indeed, the school should precede the synagogue. The chief rabbi urged the congregation to establish a Jewish school at Chatham. On 24 June 1870, Philip Magnus reported that the committee room of the new memorial synagogue was to be used as a religious school. Phillip Hyman had undertaken to assist in formation of a boys' class and aid the minister in the instruction of the children.[113]

Chapter 8

After the Emancipation
1870-1914

Less than a month had passed since the opening of the new synagogue, when the death of John Alexander Kinglake, Liberal MP for Rochester since 1857, triggered a by-election.

On Tuesday evening of 12 July, the members of the Liberal Party gathered at the Corn Exchange and selected their new candidate, a 32-year-old Julian Goldsmid. Addressing the crowded auditorium, Goldsmid passionately outlined his platform: education should be compulsory and open to everyone. It was, he said, as essential as food and clothing. It was the government's duty to establish as many schools as possible, and the universities ought to be open to men of all religious creeds, including dissenters.[1] The last statement resonated well with many Roman Catholics and nonconformists, and the Chatham Jewish community, who petitioned the House of Commons in favour of the Universities Tests Abolition Bill.[2] The abolition of religious tests would have allowed them to take up degrees and professorships at the universities of Oxford, Cambridge and Durham.[3]

Passion for equality and education ran in Goldsmid's veins. His grandfather, Isaac Lyon Goldsmid, was one of the principal founders of the London University (today's University College London) in 1826. It was the first secular university institution in England open to all and admitting people irrespective of religion, in sharp contrast to the Anglican Oxford and Cambridge. In 1859, Julian graduated from the London University with first-class honours in classics and a second in animal physiology and obtained a first in his masters in classics. In 1864 he was made a fellow of the university. The same year he was called to the Bar but had to abandon his practice when in 1868 he became MP for Honiton.[4]

The Conservative Party did not propose any opposition candidate. According to the *Chatham News*, '[it] must have been a losing contest, causing expense, giving trouble all round, and creating a great deal of bitter feeling'[5]. There was some logic in this argument — Rochester had been represented by Liberals since 1857, and according to the above quotation, they were popular. However, the absence of a Conservative candidate did not mean that the election went uncontested. An independent candidate from London, Charles James Fox, put forward his candidature as an opponent of free trade and a friend to British industry. Fox was unknown to anyone in the city he wanted to represent, and newspaper reports speculated about his background and his possible connections to Rochester.

Still, the citizens of Rochester were kept waiting before they were able to meet Fox. He did not turn up for his first meeting with the prospective electorate on Friday, 15 July, but instead sent his representative, J. Roberts, chairman of the 'Association of Revivers of British Industry'.[6] In the recreation ground on New Road, Roberts addressed a big crowd for more than an hour, condemning free trade and attacking the government for the reduction of the dockyard workforce — a sore subject in the Medway Towns, and a typical consequence after each military campaign ended.[7]

Charles James Fox presented himself the next evening. He reiterated the statements of the previous meeting, pledging to promote measures for the protection of British industry against foreign competition. Much of his oration was devoted to personal attacks on his opponent. To him it seemed inconceivable that Goldsmid, a Jew, was selected to represent a cathedral city. He supported his argument with examples of the portrayal of Jews by Shakespeare and Dickens. No doubt to reinforce this point, Fox also encouraged the audience to sing the following lyrics to the popular tune *Cheer, Boys, Cheer*:

> *Rise, workmen, rise: no longer must we slumber;*
> *Why should we starve with abundance in our lands?*

Rise, women, rise: let your children swell the number,
To ask for that labour now given to Foreign hands.

It is unlikely that Fox or his audience realised that the tune with original lyrics by Charles Mackay — different from the ones above — was composed in 1850 by Henry Russell, a Jewish native of Sheerness, and formed part of his musical entertainment *The Emigrant's Progress*.[8]

Nominations took place at noon on Monday, 18 July at the Guildhall. The chamber was packed to the brim. Julian Goldsmid was nominated by S. Steele, JP, and H. Everest, JP. He was supported by nearly all aldermen and councillors, with the chief men of the Rochester Liberal Party. Charles James Fox was nominated by two electors unknown to Rochester people — William Barter and R. Hubbard, and supported by London's 'Revivers' and a number of Conservatives, many of whom were brought from Chatham, Brompton and New Brompton. The absence of the leading Rochester Conservatives was noted. They wisely distanced themselves from being directly implicated in his campaign, whose apex hinged on anti-Jewish sentiment.

The proceedings were frequently interrupted by the crowd shouting insults directed at Goldsmid.[9] In their eyes, he was a foreigner and a Jew. The fact that Goldmid was British-born, the fifth generation of Jews who had settled in the country, mattered not at all. Nor did it matter that he had the same right to represent the city in parliament since 1858, as indeed he represented Honiton in 1868. He was a Jew, and that was that.

The polling commenced the next day, Tuesday, 19 July at eight o'clock in the morning. From the start Goldsmid took the lead and kept it with increasing majority, despite the attempts of Fox's supporters to produce falsified interim results.[10] At half-past six in the evening the Guildhall was crowded when the mayor as returning officer announced the result: Goldsmid, 987; Fox, 550.

The assault on Goldsmid came from both sides, Conservative and Liberal. One of the rare pieces of evidence is a poster produced on 14 July, two days after his selection as the candidate of the Liberal Party. Written by a 'Liberal Elector', or as a handwritten note specifies, a Congregational minister, Nobbs, it spouts the all-familiar trope of 'un-Christianising' the legislature.

Another glimpse of the attacks is given by a *Chatham News* reporter immediately after Goldsmid won his seat as Rochester MP:

> '[Goldsmid is] a gentleman 'fit and proper' to represent a constituency
> by his education, his intellect, and his public spirit — a gentleman, who
> whatever his religious views, will prove to be no disgrace to 'a Cathedral
> city', for the Liberals have not chosen Mr Goldsmid because he is a Jew, but
> because he is a good representative of Liberal opinions; and the Liberals
> who have been assailing the new member of his religion may console
> themselves with recollecting, in their calmer moments, that the Jewish
> gentlemen in our House of Commons have not shown themselves rabid
> revolutionists.. They have not been eager to attack the Church … they also
> do not attempt to convert Christians; Mr Disraeli and Mr Gladstone are
> quite safe … We are not going to be overrun with Synagogues in Chatham
> and Rochester. Christianity won't be abolished yet … Half-a-dozen Jewish
> members in the Commons won't override 654 men who are Churchmen,
> Catholics, Nonconformists, or what you will — if they do, why then, Mr
> Disraeli's wild notions of the superiority of the Jewish race will be proved to
> be true.'[11]

Indeed, the period of 1868-74 saw the largest number of Jewish MPs in the House of Commons — there were eight of them.[12] After the Rochester election, the Conservatives attempted to discredit the result, citing bribery and corruption. But the allegations had no basis in truth.[13]

Julian Goldsmid went on to represent Rochester in parliament for the next 10 years. During his tenure, he was instrumental in founding the Rochester Free Library. In 1878 he offered to present 500 guineas to the city towards its foundation on condition that burgesses provide for its maintenance by adopting the Free Libraries Act, which had been in force from 1850 and which they so far had been unwilling to do.[14]

Goldsmid retained his connections with the city long after he lost his seat to Roger Leigh, a Conservative, in the 1880 election.[15] A frequent visitor to the Medway Towns, he continued his support for education and donated prizes for the Rochester Board School. In March 1894 he attended the formal opening of the rebuilt Rochester Mathematical School, of which he became a life governor until his death on 7 January 1896.[16]

A mere 10 years after its opening, Chatham Memorial Synagogue was under threat of demolition. Early in 1881 the South-Eastern Railway introduced a bill in the House of Commons to obtain permission to carry the North Kent line into Chatham. The company proposed to buy a large amount of property along Rochester and Chatham High Streets, which included the burial ground and pulling down and rebuilding part of the synagogue.[17] The Jewish community strongly opposed the bill on the grounds that it would be an act of desecration. By mid-April the House of Commons committee formed to inquire into the case, decided in favour of the community. The portion of the bill relating to the synagogue and its burial ground was struck off, and disaster averted.[18] It was also a sign of increasing equality. In 1846 the Canterbury synagogue had been demolished to make way for the railway line.

In February 1884, the Rev Lazarus Polack tended his resignation as minister, citing his advanced age.[19] On the evening of 5 May, members of the Chatham congregation and numerous friends, including two Christian ministers from the towns gathered in the synagogue's committee room to say farewell to Polack, who had served the congregation for 30 years. Phillip Hyman, the chairman presented Polack with the address, handsomely illuminated by Coleman P. Hyman, and a cheque for £328 10s, contributed by the whole community.[20]

Polack, moved to tears, reflected upon his years at Chatham, the move to the new synagogue and the changes introduced to improve services. One of such changes was introduction of decorum — quietness and reverence — not normally present in Jewish worship, which was known for its noisiness. The other feature was sermons, addressed from the pulpit, which Polack regarded

Facing page: the poster, produced by 'Liberal Elector', attacking Julian Goldsmid's selection as a Liberal candidate for Rochester in 1870

ROCHESTER ELECTION.

Is Mr. GOLDSMID the Right Man?

TO THE FREE AND INDEPENDENT ELECTORS,

As a sincere Liberal, and one earnestly concerned for the welfare of Rochester, I feel constrained to submit the following questions to the consideration of thoughtful and candid men :—

1st.—Is it not wonderful that out of Eleven Gentlemen, who had signified their readiness to become Candidates for the Representation of this Ancient Borough, the Liberal Committee should have selected the only man among them who is professedly NOT A CHRISTIAN ?

2nd.—Is it not morally certain that many Liberals will feel that their consciences and deep religious instincts make it *impossible to vote for an* UNBELIEVER ?

3rd.—Is it proper to elect a man who declines to pronounce upon the GRAVEST MORAL QUESTION of the day, and which can only be settled on Christian principles ?

4th.—Was it not, therefore, most unwise to create a division of feeling among the Liberal Constituents, a feeling all the more *intense*, because smothered for a time, which, sooner or later, must hazard the Seat to the Liberal party ? I know very well that some will exclaim, "Ah ! Religion has nothing to do with politics ! " But a great many others judge on principle that their Christianity must go into every thing ; and though they may provoke a smile, yet they shrink not from declaring that their vote as citizens is a trust for which they must "give account at the judgment seat of Christ."

However desirable it might be to decide promptly in order to prevent a division in the camp, yet intelligent and high-principled Christians will think and be prepared to act when a *General Election* comes. No great political question at present divides the strength of the Liberal Party ; but who can tell how soon a local or national one may crop up which will do so ?

Although Mr. GOLDSMID was preferred to men unquestionably more able, avowedly on the ground that he is a Young Man, yet it is a great absurdity to suppose that he will be elected when the Free and Independent Electors have fair play, and opportunity to choose freely.

A BLUNDER HAS BEEN COMMITTED, maugre the unanimity *said* to prevail ; but is it not a *coerced* unanimity, in which the voice of conscience is stifled and Christianity is insulted ?

A LIBERAL ELECTOR.

July 14th, 1870.

163

as important for the spiritual needs of the congregation.[21] To the rabbi's regret those were rare because weekly gatherings were only small. Whatever the size of the community, it seems the Chatham Jews had become pretty lax in their attendance at worship — the result of acculturation and emancipation.[22]

At the end of his speech, Polack affirmed his lifelong convictions: 'As I desire with all my heart to cultivate amicable relations with my brethren of all creeds; and you, who know my sentiments well, will acknowledge that I have never taught any doctrine more emphatically than that it is our duty to love our Christian fellow-men, and to regard them with the same sentiments as we feel for each other. I hope my non-Jewish friends will accept my assurance that I very deeply appreciate this testimony of their kind disposition towards me.'[23]

The community was now looking for a new minister, who would also be a competent *shochet* (ritual butcher) and *chazan* (cantor). The candidate would also need to be married and younger than 40. This was clearly long-term planning.[24] For about 18 months these responsibilities were undertaken by the Rev W. Barren (or Barron — there seems to be a discrepancy in the spelling), but in July 1885 the Chatham congregation elected a new rabbi, the newly married 23-year-old Bernard Joshua Salomons. Salomons was already a known face in Chatham congregation — as the reader he delivered his first sermon there in March 1884. Probably during that visit he met Elizabeth, a daughter of Kate (née Isaacs) and Abraham Goldstein, pawnbroker, whom he married at the beginning of 1885.

Born on 7 November 1862, in Radziłów, northeast Poland, then part of the Russian Empire, Bernard arrived in England with his parents, Saul and Sarah Salomons about 1879. He came from a long line of rabbinical scholars, and so it was only natural that he pursued the same path. At 19, Bernard proved such a success and was held in such high regard by the elders, that he was appointed minister to the congregation in Oxford. After two years in Oxford[25] he went to Stockton-on-Tees,[26] which he left in August 1885 to take up his appointment at Chatham in time for the High Holy Days, which that year fell in early September.[27] Very quickly the community became attached to him because of his eloquent sermons, the beautiful intoning of the services and for his efforts in teaching the young.[28]

It is hard to overestimate the significance of Salomons as leader of the

Chatham Jews and his contribution to the Medway community as a whole. Recognising the importance of preserving the history of the community, in 1887 he helped to establish a branch of Anglo-Jewish Association in Chatham and became its secretary.[29] A true follower of Jewish Law, he worked hard on alleviating the hardship of the poor, becoming an honorary secretary and almoner for the Jewish Philanthropic Society.[30] During the 1890s, the Children's Country Holidays Fund arranged holidays in the countryside for Jewish children from London's East End. Salomons led a group of the congregants, Mr and Mrs Philip Hyman, Mrs Goodman, Misses Samuels, Lou Barnard and many others to provide hospitality to the young visitors and oversaw the stay of more than 90 children each year. A day-by-day programme was devised, and the activities included sumptuous tea, a day of sports and games, a special performance at the Palace of Varieties, and so on.[31]

He worked devotedly on behalf of the Jews suffering from Tsarist persecution and helped to organise protest meetings against the atrocities during the Macedonian Struggle in the early 1890s.[32] Salomons, similar to Polack in his outlook on life, would not tolerate injustice against anyone. His efforts stemmed from conviction, though as an immigrant he would have had to overcome the distrust and prove his acceptability to the non-Jewish community. Salomons clearly won this acceptance, for in 1896 he was invited to attend and asked to propose one of the principal resolutions at a mass protest against the Armenian massacres. The meeting was held on 24 September at the Corn Exchange, and convened and presided over by Franklin G. Homan, Mayor of Rochester. Salomons proposed one of the principal resolutions. In his speech, which was described as 'spirited' and 'forcible', the rabbi was speaking on behalf of all Jews, but at the same time 'didn't confine himself to one sect or creed but rather adopted humanity as his platform.'[33]

He was vice-president of the Rochester, Chatham, and District Temperance Union; a member of the committee of the local branch of the National Society for the Prevention of Cruelty to Children;[34] a member of the local branch of the National Vigilance Committee;[35] and numerous other local charitable and cultural societies.[36] In 1892, he took part in the May Day Labour demonstration.[37] In December 1893, Salomons was the first one to address the Labour meeting at the Corn Exchange, chaired by William Lewington.[38] In January

1896, giving a talk, *Moses and the Social Problem,* to the Rochester Independent Liberal Party, he requested to be called 'comrade', aligning himself with the working class.[39]

In January 1895, the Visitation Committee of the United Synagogue and the visitors at hospitals, infirmaries, workshouses, asylums and prisons appointed Salomons a Jewish minister at Parkhurst Prison on the Isle of Wight.[40] However, after a couple of months, Salomons tendered his resignation for personal reasons.[41]

It is hard to overestimate the extent of Salomons's work in promoting and expanding on the dialogue between Jews and Christians, including the dialogue between the Jewish and Christian clerics, which was started by the previous ministers of the congregation. During his tenure, it became common for non-Jewish ministers to bring their congregation to Chatham Memorial Synagogue to hear Salomons preach.[42] One of such frequent visitors was the Presbyterian minister, S. D. Scammell, who attended Chatham synagogue for all the principal Jewish festivals.[43]

A brilliant scholar and a passionate and engaging orator, Bernard Joshua was frequently invited by the clergy as a lecturer on Jewish subjects, always to densely packed auditoria. He gave a series of lectures on Anglo-Jewish history at Eastgate House, Rochester,[44] was one of the frequent lecturers at St Andrew's Hall in Chatham,[45] at Unitarian Christian Social Institute, the Bible Christian Church[46] and Ebenezer Guild,[47] to name but a few. He continued to be invited to lecture locally long after he left Chatham. The work put such strain on the rabbi's voice that he found himself unable to lead the services and resigned from the post in 1897. The chief rabbi recommended him as an additional member of staff at Montefiore College in Ramsgate, which functioned as academy of research and study for Hebrew scholars. Salomons was the first Ashkenazi Jew accepted to the Sephardi college.[48]

It was the determination of Polack and Salomons to forge strong relationships with the local clergy, by proving their acceptability and absence of threat to Christians, that ministers of Chatham Memorial Synagogue were included as guests of honour at civic and ecclesiastical events in the Medway Towns, such as enthronement of Edward Stuart Talbot as Bishop of Rochester in 1895.[49]

Bernard Salomons with his wife Elizabeth Rachel (née Goldstein)
and their children Katie Jessie (born 1887) and Archibald Geoffrey
(born 1888). Christian ministers brought their congregants to his services

With Salomons, it was not a mere nod to the socially acceptable behavioural code at the time, it was friendship, as publicly declared by the Rev S.D. Scammell.[50] Salomons was held in such great esteem by the ecclesiastical authorities, that on 16 September 1897 they presented him with the following address:

'To the Rev Rabbi Bernard J Salomons,

'We, the undersigned, being clergymen and ministers of various Churches and Chapels of Rochester and Chatham, desire to express our sense of the loss which these towns will sustain through your departure. Your courtesy, your readiness to deliver lectures upon Biblical and Talmudical subjects, and your kindness in furthering schemes for the welfare of the people cause us to regard your transference to Ramsgate with unfeigned regret –

'T. K. Cheyne, Canon of Rochester Cathedral; T. E. Cartwright, Rector of St John's, Chatham; R. Bishop Paine, Assistant Curate of Chatham Parish Church; I. Mahon, Catholic Priest, St Michael's Chatham; R. Bullesbach, Catholic Priest, St Michael's Chatham; Edward Braddon, Assistant Priest, St Mary's Chatham; Edward J. Nash, Minor Canon and Precentor of Rochester Cathedral; J. R. Webster, Congregational Minister, Chatham; Frederic Allen, Unitarian Minister, Chatham; James Tristram, Primitive Methodist Minister, Chatham; S. D. Scammell, Presbyterian Minister and Chaplain, Royal Navy; S. Louis Warne, Bible Christian Minister, Luton Road; William Francis Ellis, Bible Christian Minister, Luton Rd; J. S. Skinner, Rector of Luton, Chatham; C. J. Ord, Vicar of St Paul's, Chatham; S. Reynolds Hole, Dean of Rochester; Ernest M. Blackie, Minor Canon and Sacrist of Rochester Cathedral; G. Anderson Miller, Baptist Minister, Rochester; Geo H. Hitchcock, Chaplain to the Medway Union —
Ellul 19th, 5657, September 16th, 1897.'[51]

The relationship between Church and Synagogue was entering a reconciliatory path. Welcoming Christian ministers to the synagogue, seeking co-operation, forging partnerships and lecturing on Jewish subjects helped to demystify and appreciate the principles of Jewish Law, recognise similarities between the religions and educate those, willing to be educated on the history of Jews and Judaism. In 1880, at the opening of a new building for out-patients at St Bartholomew's Hospital, Dean of Rochester Cathedral, Robert Scott, praised the excellency of Jewish sanitary and dietary laws[52] — the same laws for which for centuries Jews were branded sorcerers, murderers, necromancers, poisoners, and cannibals.

An invitation to Coleman Hyman of the Jewish community from the
Mayor of Chatham to the reception — a sign of acceptance and equality

In 1900, Professor T.K. Cheyne, Canon of Rochester Cathedral, while
discoursing on Christianity and the religions of the East, said that though he
did not altogether approve of Judaism, he hoped for co-operation between the
Christian and Jewish authorities as a first step to harmonial co-existence.[53]
No doubt, this was the legacy left by Lazarus Polack and Bernard Joshua
Salomons; it was also a sign of changing times.

The 1870s and 1880s were also a period when reporters frequented the
Jewish place of worship. Lengthy articles in local newspapers described the
synagogue, its liturgy, customs and festivals, even though the descriptions
were through the prism of Christianity; in one of the articles the congregation
officials are called 'church officials' and the rabbi is called a 'priest'.[54] And despite
what looked like the genuine interest on the surface, the reporter could not help

repeat the anti-Jewish diatribe about the former wealth of the community.[55]

What inspired those articles? Never before the opening of the synagogue had the community attracted so much public attention. The aim of the articles seemed to dispel the negative views about local Jews held at the grassroots, especially with increase of immigration from the Russian Empire, following its draconian laws and the subsequent pogroms. And though there were no reports of antisemitic incidents in the area, the absence of evidence is not the evidence of absence. On the official level though, the 1880s provide evidence of the Medway community's condemnation of the events in Russia.

In 1880, the Dean of Rochester, Robert Scott, publicly condemned the persecution of the Jews.[56] By February 1882 the situation for Jews in Russia worsened to such an extent that on 12 February a meeting, sponsored by Archbishop of Canterbury Archibald Tait, Archbishop of Westminster Henry Manning, the evolutionary scientist Charles Darwin, poet Matthew Arnold and social reformer Lord Shaftesbury, was held at Mansion House in London.[57] It was attended by J. Whittaker Ellis, Lord Mayor of London, members of the nobility and clergy, and representatives of corporate bodies, who had taken up the cause of the Russian Jews and established a subscription to the relief fund. The Chatham Jewish congregation was represented by senior warden Philip Hyman.[58] After the meeting, the Chatham community resolved to conduct a special service on Sunday, 19 February at three o'clock to appeal to the public.

By half-past two on Sunday afternoon, the gates of the synagogue were besieged by a large crowd anxious to obtain admission. Two policemen were keeping order. Inside, the synagogue was in full attendance, including in the ladies' gallery. Many were refused entry. High Constable Henry Jasper, Captain Cuthbertson, Dr Hutchins and most Jewish residents of the Medway Towns were present. Rabbi Lazarus Polack conducted the service and delivered the sermon:

> '… *They had come on an errand of benevolence, to protest against the fearful persecutions of the Jews in Russia, to express their horror at the slaughter and plunder, at the acts of violation and spoliation perpetrated by an ignorant and fanatic mob, to send relief to the oppressed and to raise from the depths of misery those that are ruthlessly persecuted.*

> 'Secure in the blessings of peace and living under the benign influence
> of a free government, their hearts have been suddenly and rudely pierced
> by the sharp and bitter cry of oppressions, when we thought the sword of
> persecution had become blunted and had rusted with the human blood
> which had so often died its blade'.

The first list of subscriptions to the relief fund amounted to more than £23.[59] The outrage at the persecutions of Jews in Russia and the willingness of the Gentile population to help the cause serves as proof that English Jews, at least on a local level, were now being accepted members of British society. For the Jewish community, however, acculturation and civil, political and social emancipation also brought assimilation. By the 1890s intermarriages within the community were common, and though as a result of intermarriage, the Jewish partner moved more and more away from the religion of their ancestors, they still tried to preserve their connection to Judaism. Chatham Jews even complained that *mohelim* (those trained and licensed to perform circumcision) refused to perform *brit milah* (circumcision), if a male child was born to a Jewish father and non-Jewish mother, which is contrary to *Halakhah* (Jewish Law), which stipulates that the child's religious affiliation is determined by his maternal side.[60]

Emancipation allowed English Jews to venture outside their circle and explore larger opportunities offered by the outside world. Equality also

Simon Magnus (1801-75), treasurer of the community, paid for the new synagogue in the memory of his son

freed them to vote according to their interests and opinions. From that time, Jewish political thinking as a homogenous group ceased. While the majority of the Jewish community remained Liberal, some moved to Unionism or Conservatism. The first Jewish Conservative MP was Saul Isaac from Chatham, a colliery owner, who represented Nottingham from 1874 to 1880.[61] In April 1911, Robert Sebag-Montefiore, the eldest son of Arthur Sebag-Montefiore and Mrs Sebag-Montefiore of Eastcliffe Lodge, Ramsgate, and a great-great nephew of Sir Moses Montefiore, was adopted as Unionist candidate for Rochester.[62] He held a commission as Lieutenant in the Royal East Kent Mounted Rifles, and considered himself a Tory Democrat.[63]

By the 1890s, the Chatham Jewish community was getting older. The members, who had been so prominent when Jews were fighting for their equal rights, were dying. On Tuesday, 30 November 1875, Simon Magnus, a successful coal factor and merchant, and the sole benefactor of the new synagogue, died in his home, 324 High Street in his 75th year.[64] He was the former chairman, treasurer and warden of the old synagogue.

Simon was one of the sons of Lazarus Magnus and Sarah Moses, who settled in Chatham between 1800 and 1808. In the early 1820s he married Sara, a daughter of Dr Abraham Wolff, originally from Frankfurt, and the couple had five children — the son, Lazarus Simon (born 1825) and four daughters: Jane (born 1827), Sara (born 1829), Cordelia (born 1831) and Elizabeth (born 1835). In time, the daughters married[65] and the Chatham community acquired four new members and strong supporters of the congregation.

Simon lost his wife in March 1850,[66] a couple of months after the marriage of their second daughter Sara, and remained a widower. The loss of his only son, Lazarus Simon, in January 1865 was a devastating blow. In December 1872 his eldest daughter Jane died and was buried next to her brother[67]. Simon's health deteriorated, and on the morning of 28 November 1875 he suffered a fatal stroke.[68]

In his will, after bequests to his family and numerous friends, Jewish and Christian, Simon left legacies to the Dean of Rochester and the 10 charities:

❖ The Asylum for Fatherless Children
❖ National Life-Boat Institution

Barnard's new Palace of Varieties *c.*1900. After the destruction of the
original premises, Lou Barnard, in partnership with the freeholder Watts
Charity, constructed this music hall. The plain flat-fronted red brick
structure, designed by J. W. Nash of Rochester, could accommodate
more than 1,000 patrons. Barnard's survived competition from its rivals
and was still flourishing when it burnt down in 1934. It was not rebuilt

❖ Kent County Ophthalmic Hospital, Maidstone
❖ The Merchant Seamen's Orphans Asylum
❖ The Shipwrecked Fishermen and Marines Royal Benevolent Society
❖ The Asylum for Idiots
❖ The British Home for Incurables
❖ University College Hospital
❖ West London Synagogue
❖ Metropolitan Free Hospital[69]

The number and the names of the charities tell us about Magnus's strong convictions, such as *tzedakah* and equality — equal access to health, education and welfare.

Another death took place in 1879. Dan Barnard, captain of Chatham Volunteer Fire Brigade, former High Constable of the Court Leet and a member of Chatham Board of Health, died at his home, 91 High Street, on 26 October.[70] He was 54. His funeral was attended by his many relatives, friends, the members of Board of Health, including chairman Adam Stigant, High Constable G. H. de la Cour, wearing his badge of office and Steward of the Court Leet, G. Winch.[71] To the residents of the Medway Towns Dan Barnard left two legacies — entertainment and the fire brigade.

After Dan's death, two of his sons, Lou and Charles, took over the Palace of Varieties. But fire, Dan's 'bug' since the 1860s, nearly became the family's downfall. One Monday night in May 1885 after the end of the performance, the doors of the music hall were locked and the safety checks were carried out as usual. The family and four employees, who lived above the venue retired for

Facing page: the Theatre Royal *c.*1900. The Barnards' original intention was to present 'straight plays', but they were soon forced to add musical comedies and revues to the theatre's repertoire. The theatre survived until 1955. After retail use, several unsuccessful attempts were made to raise funds for its renovation. In the late 2010s it was converted into flats, although the theatre's façade was preserved

the night. Just before dawn a watchman from the neighbouring timber wharves spotted the flames. By nine o'clock that morning, the Palace of Varieties was a heap of ash.

It was swiftly rebuilt, on a much grander scale, by the Rochester architect James William Nash. Every possible precaution was taken to avoid another fire, but the building burnt down again in May 1934, after which the Barnards decided not to rebuild.

The same fate plagued the Theatre Royal, built by the Chatham architect George Bond in 1899. The theatre, on the corner of Chatham High Street and the newly built Manor Road was almost opposite the Palace of Varieties. The venue had an ornate exterior, surmounted by a gilded figure of Victory on the roof. The inside of the theatre was richly decorated and could accommodate the audience of 3,000. But one May afternoon in 1900, after the end of the matinee production of *The Great Ruby*, it caught fire. Chatham Volunteer Fire Brigade was joined by firefighters from the Royal Marines, Royal Engineers, Lancashire Fusiliers and the Rifle Brigade, but all was in vain. The equivalent of four wagonloads of costumes and props, including a stagecoach, musical instruments and a valuable collection of sheet music destroyed. The rebuilt theatre opened on Christmas Eve 1900, but the building was damaged by fire again in 1937, after which it reopened under a different name.[72]

In 1897 and 1902 respectively, Asher Lyons and Simon Lyon, two brothers and long-standing wardens and trustees of the synagogue, died. According to Asher's obituary in the *Chatham Observer*, their forefathers settled in the area in 1747, though Simon was born in Nottingham *c.*1824 and Asher about a year later in Bedford. Both brothers, sons of Lemuel and Elizabeth Lyon, were watchmakers and jewellers, having learnt their skills from the father. Asher started work at the age of 12 and established his own business by the age of 15. During the Crimean War he acquired a reputation for making excellent watches, many of which were still in use 40 years later. He was also a splendid judge of precious stones and could have taken a high post in one of the leading London wholesale firms of jewellers and lapidaries, but he preferred to work for himself.

Both Asher and Simon took active part in politics. Old-fashioned Liberals, they lent their warm support to the local MPs — Arthur Otway, Philip

Wickham Martin, John Alexander Kingslake and Julian Goldsmid. Both had keen interest in charitable matters. Asher was one of the founders and a director of the Second Chatham Building Society and a member of Chatham Local Guardians. Simon was the oldest member of St Nicholas Board of Guardians and held the office of chairman till his death.[73]

By the end of the 19th century the community comprised only 70 people, just over a third of the community of 189 in the 1840s.[74] As the older generation died out, their children, attracted by the extensive opportunities of the wider world, moved away from the Medway Towns. The area, with the government as its main employer, offered only limited chances of earning a livelihood and progressing. However, the situation was about to change. A decade later, the Jewish population in Chatham increased dramatically to more than 170, behind only London and Birmingham.[75] The old prayer books produced in Warsaw, Kyiv and Vilna, still in possession of the synagogue, confirm the origins of the new community members.

However, the influx of new members did not mean an increase in the prosperity of the congregation, which was heavily reduced by the loss of its long-standing members. The new settlers, Jews from the *shtetls* (small towns or settlements) of the Russian Empire escaping pogroms and persecution, were mostly tailors and desperately

A volume of Deuteronomy published in Vilna, Lithuania, in 1882 chronicles the places of origin of new members of the Chatham Jewish community

poor. The number of the synagogue seat-holders decreased from 34 in 1870,[76] to 15 in 1897.[77] Within three years it shrank to 10.[78] For the first time in the history of Chatham congregation, we see in the workhouse registers Jewish names such as Barnett Barnett, who spent a short time in the Medway Union, Chatham, between 17 May and 4 June in 1884.[79]

There are only three Jewish names appearing in the Poor Law records, with Barnett Barnett being the first. The other two tragic cases relate to London residents John da Costa and Isaac Belisha.

The hawker John da Costa (born *c*.1841) and his wife Bessi (born *c*.1860), were admitted to Chatham workhouse on 2 December 1896. John died nine days later, on 11 December 1896. His place of burial was not recorded in the workhouse register, but the synagogue's records state that he was buried in the synagogue's cemetery. Two years before the couple's admission to the workhouse, John and Bessi lived at Eagle Lodge, Bow Road, London. The da Costas seemed to be doing well at the time: in July 1894, a notice in the *Jewish Chronicle* announced that a stone setting ceremony 'in fond memory of the late lamented Jane Walters, of Gravesend, dearly beloved mother of Mrs John da Costa [will take place] at the Jewish cemetery, Chatham, on Sunday next, 15 July, afternoon.'[80]

Widower Isaac Belisha, son of Samuel Belisha, was born *c*.1841 in Tangier (modern-day Morocco). He lived in Fulham in London and was admitted to Strood Union Workhouse from Northfleet on 21 October 1905. He died in the workhouse 10 days later, on 31 October 1905, and was buried in the synagogue cemetery.[81]

The appearance of Jewish names in the workhouse registers is highly unusual. Jewish communities did not rely on workhouses but provided assistance to those in need within the community. The case of Barnett Barnett, a resident of Chatham, probably points out to the impoverished state of the community itself, which was no longer in the position to help.

The cases of da Costa and Belisha, London residents, are different in this respect. The Jewish Board of Guardians, a charity established in 1859 to help Jewish poor in London, was, by the 1890s, overwhelmed by the volume of applications for help. The groups, which applied for relief included widows, children, orphans, asylum seekers and people seeking medical or financial aid.

The board tried to help those they considered to be most in need. It is not clear why da Costa and Belisha did not receive help from the board. Were they deemed not to be in that 'most in need' category? Were they then been compelled to seek help elsewhere? It is possible that having been unsuccessful in obtaining help they needed from the Jewish Board of Guardians, the da Costas and Belisha then appealed for relief to their respective parishes. The parishes then, in accordance with practice at the time, moved the applicants out of parish, to the workhouses in a different part of the country.

A trickle of immigration from Europe had been happening for decades. In 1864 the *Annual Report of the Jewish Board of Guardians* observed that most of the 'foreign poor' came from Holland.[82] However, from 1871 the numbers increased, with Jews either fleeing persecution in Romania, or after their expulsion from the Russian border regions.[83] In 1872 the *Annual Report* said: 'The poor Jews of England are now almost exclusively recruited from Poland.'[84] In 1875-76 the rate of migration increased in the run-up to the Russo-Turkish War as Jews attempted to escape conscription into the viciously antisemitic Russian Army.[85] But the peak of Jewish arrivals to the English shores came in the 1880s.

The assassination of Tsar Alexander II in 1881 was blamed on Jews,[86] and was followed by an attack on Jews in Elisavetgrad on 27 April and a subsequent wave of massacres, which spread through the Ukrainian provinces of Chernigov, Poltava, Kyiv and Kherson in the Pale of Settlement — the territories of the Russian Empire where Jews were permitted to reside.[87] The same year, Temporary Orders Concerning Jews, the so-called 'May Laws', were brought into force. The laws further restricted the mobility of the Jewish population and their rights of residence — Jews had been already been prohibited from living in St Petersburg, Moscow, and other large administrative centres unless they had a special dispensation from the authorities.[88] They were also forbidden from owning or working land or residing in the agricultural regions, and trading or engaging any other business activity on Sundays and Christian holidays, which put them in sharp disadvantage with their non-Jewish neighbours.[89]

Furthermore, Jews could be expelled from their place of residence on demand from the local Christians.[90] A sudden announcement on Passover in 1891, expelling Jews from Moscow and other centres and villages outside the Pale, displaced more than 400,000 people. Further restrictions followed, resulting in a second major wave of emigration.[91]

When a boat carrying immigrants reached Gravesend, an agent telegraphed London. Upon arrival at the Port of London, a representative of the Board of Trade, usually a member of staff of the Custom House, counted the passengers, both Jewish and non-Jewish, and took their names and other details, including particulars of whatever money they had with them. They were also medically examined. The evidence provided by the medical officers and the custom officer to the Royal Commission stated they were usually healthy, and the number of cases of infectious diseases was small.[92]

Most of them settled in London, attracted by its promise of economic opportunities. Under what conditions did they live? The historian Peter Elman, quoting Eccarius, one of the secretaries of the First International, says that they worked from six in the morning to seven or eight at night without a break in hot stuffy rooms and for extremely low wages below 16 shillings a week. Two-thirds of them died of tuberculosis.[93]

In addition to its economic prospects, London attracted the newcomers with existence of established Jewish communities with synagogues. This was coupled with the presence of family and friends, or those originating from the same *shtetl*. As a result, the East End of London, which absorbed most of the new arrivals became overcrowded. To deal with the problem, the Jewish authorities created a system of dispersal, originally to operate in London and which, in 1903, expanded to include the provinces. The suitable persons to be transferred excluded single men; the dispersion committee concentrated on married men with families. When a provincial congregation notified the dispersal committee of an opportunity for employment, the husband was sent to the place in the first instance. If the conditions were agreeable and both parties were satisfied with each other, the man was joined by his family. A small loan, including travel expenses, was advanced to be repaid in due course. Among the places qualified for transfer were Reading, Blackburn, Chester, Dover and Chatham.[94] By the end of 1906, 92 families were moved out of London.

In this light, it is interesting to see a rare piece of evidence of such a transfer from a family who were moved to Chatham between 1903 and 1906. The family, whose name is unknown, received a loan of £42, which the husband repaid, although it is not clear over what period. At the meeting of the dispersion committee in December 1906, the secretary read the husband's letter, which also contained a cheque for £5 — the last instalment. In the letter, the husband observed that the committee had done him 'a great favour which I will never forget'.[95] Clearly, Chatham trumped London economically and socially.

The influx of poor Jewish immigrants threatened the status quo of the English Jewry, who now viewed themselves fully English. Being confined to specific areas in the Pale of Settlement, Russian, Lithuanian and Polish Jews had little chance of venturing outside their immediate social circle, and as a result, the process of acculturation did not take place. Having arrived in England, they stood in sharp contrast with their emancipated English counterparts, who were distancing themselves from the newcomers and viewed them with disdain.

The conviction was that Jews had earned civic equality by the high level of their contribution to English society and in compliance with English norms, and any deviation from these accepted ways could jeopardise their civil status.[96] It is possible to gauge the sentiments, of many prominent Jews by reading the opinion of a distinguished Jewish journalist and historian Lucien Wolf:

> *'With every sympathy for the immigrants it was impossible to deny that they were of an undesirable type. Centuries of oppression had left their mark on the Russian Jew, and though they had not degraded him below the level of average provincial life in Russia they had certainly not helped him to raise himself very much above it. He belonged to a stratum of culture distinctly inferior to that which prevailed in Western Europe.'[97]*

Nathan Joseph, the chief rabbi's brother-in-law and an important figure in Jewish immigration to England, was a staunch opponent of an open-door policy:

> *'This class constitutes a grave danger to the [Jewish] community. Its members were always paupers and useless parasites ... Many of these were*

never persecuted but came with the persecuted.'[98]

English Jewry feared that the immigrants threatened to transform the 'high English character' of the community, the character that had developed as a result of acculturation, emancipation and assimilation. A big anti-immigration campaign ensued, with many eminent Jews travelling to Eastern Europe to try to discourage emigration.

In addition, the un-English characteristics of the new arrivals were feared would jeopardise the amicable relations of the English Jewry with the Gentiles and ignite a new wave of antisemitism. Indeed, a less-than-subtle hostility towards Jews became discernible. Samuel Henry Jeyes, an influential writer, expressed his view in no uncertain terms:

> *'English Jews ... have their faults but they're English to the core ... But [the immigrants] from Russia and Poland have all the vices which are generated by many centuries of systematic oppression. This immigrant class would never be popular in Britain 'since they succeed, if not taking the bread out of English mouths, at least in reducing the margin of wages which might be spent on beer and gin [and] they are naturally and not quite fairly detested.'*[99]

Joseph Banister, a rabidly antisemitic writer, in his work *England Under the Jews* referred to all foreign Jews as thieves, sweaters, usurers, burglars, forgers, traitors, swindlers, blackmailers, and perjurers.[100]

Arnold White, a journalist and a virulent antisemitic campaigner against immigration, spouted the diatribe about 'the rich and powerful Hebrews who really the rulers of the civilised world'.[101] In 1886 he and Lord Dunraven formed and financed a Society for the Suppression of the Immigration of Destitute Aliens, with White wanting to stop 'the leaks which take in the riff-raff from other countries'.[102]

White's views were challenged by the historian Stephen Fox, who used statistical data as evidence against hostility towards pauper immigration. The data showed that immigrants were no burden on the communities and the local rates; to the contrary, they were a source of profit, having introduced two additional branches of trade — shoe manufacturing and tailoring.[103]

However, anti-Jewish attacks were not restricted to Conservatives; the Liberal Party had its own antisemites. Hilaire Belloc was concerned with 'Jewish peril', while Professor Goldwin Smith was convinced that it was beyond the power of any legislation to make Jews patriots — his vicious attack prompted the chief rabbi to pen an article entitled *Can Jews Be Patriots?* in terms commended by William Gladstone.[104]

In the Medway Towns the antisemitic insults, no doubt numerous, did not make it into the papers unless accompanied by physical violence. One of the common insults related to trustworthiness and honesty — Jews were seen as inherently dishonest and untrustworthy, such as in the case of an assault on an inmate of the Medway Union Workhouse. During the trial, the perpetrator though admitting the charge, nevertheless called the victim 'a Jew, who would swear anything'. Neither of the inmates was Jewish.[105] However, the hostilities were not merely verbal. There are several cases in the local newspapers that provide us with insights of the local atmosphere at the time. Two of them concern a Jewish photographer, Abraham Zisblon Cohen, originally from Poland. In May 1899 Cohen brought charges against a bargeman, Thomas Allen, for wilfully damaging his photographic camera and chemicals to the value of £2 18s on Sunday, 23 April. The attack happened in Upnor at three o'clock in the afternoon. Cohen was about to take a photograph of a young man, when the drunken Allen knocked over his apparatus. The complainant represented himself in court, while the defendant was represented by a solicitor, G. Robinson. During the hearing, Cohen's cheap equipment was mocked by the lawyer as 'a sunlight box on perambulator wheels' — a remark that elicited laughter from the public attending the hearing; Cohen's case was trivialised, and his memory and ability to describe the assailant questioned and dismissed. It also transpired that on that day a number of children, or men, depending on the statement of the solicitor or the defendant, jeered at Cohen for being a Jew and sang at him a ditty *Only a Jew*, which again prompted laughter from the audience. Despite the obvious discrepancies in the testimonies of Allen and his solicitor, the case was dismissed.[106]

Jeering, insults and derision look like the everyday reality, in which Jews lived. There are no newspaper reports about insults — defamation law hardly existed, and the Race Relations Act did not come into force till 1965.

A year later, on Sunday 2 July 1900, Cohen, while taking photographs opposite the pier in Upnor, his preferred spot, was attacked again. This time the dark slide of his apparatus was broken and his bottles of chemicals upset, spilling over his coat. The total damage was 45 shillings. The assault started at 2.30 in the afternoon when five defendants, four stokers from Northumberland, and a private in the 5th Battalion Rifle Brigade, came up to Cohen, taunting and insulting him with what were probably antisemitic remarks, but which the newspaper called 'disgraceful names'. It escalated when Private John McGrath suggested drowning Cohen. The attempted murder was averted only by a woman from a nearby house, who helped Cohen to get away from the assailants. During the hearing it transpired that McGrath had had an encounter with Cohen the previous Sunday, when he had also damaged Cohen's apparatus, but that attack was dismissed by the court as irrelevant to the case. The defendants denied all charges. This time the court awarded damages, though the total sum was insulting — 12s 6d. However, the most insightful glimpse into the attitudes towards Jews at the time is the trivialisation of the case by the chairman, who declared that 'he didn't think on this occasion the defendants intended any particular harm'.[107]

Another example of antisemitism that permeated society, and which made into the newspapers, was the July 1904 case of Gershen Grodberg, a cabinetmaker, originally from Russia. Grodberg was in debt and filed for an administration order. During the hearing the judge found it appropriate to ask Grodberg if he did not think he had better go back to Russia, though it is hard to see how this question related to the case at hand. Grodberg stated that his children were born in England. The judge then proceeded to ask the applicant whether he wanted to go back to Russia and fight, in a reference to the Russo-Japanese War, which was being waged at the time. Grodberg, who was no doubt well-acquainted with the virulent antisemitic realities of the Russian Army and terrified at the thought of having anything to do with it, replied in the negative. His reply elicited a contemptuous 'I don't wonder' from the judge.[108]

The congregation experienced hostility even when on the synagogue's premises. Many outpatients of St Bartholomew's Hospital regularly sat on the wall dividing the hospital and the synagogue's cemetery, observing the burials and stone consecrating, and often throwing medicine bottles onto the burial ground. When asked to withdraw, they jumped over the wall and used the cemetery as a passageway to the High Street. By 1902 the situation had become so bad that the wall between the hospital and the cemetery had to be raised.[109]

The attacks prompted Jews to apply for naturalisation, if they could afford the fee, in an attempt to secure their legal position in the country. Salomons's naturalisation in 1889 as well as the naturalisation of many other members of the Chatham Jewish congregation, is evidence of the precarious situation in which Jews found themselves.

The intensification of the anti-Jewish campaign, and pressure on the government by the anti-immigrant lobby, resulted in the introduction of an Alien Bill in March 1904. One of the requirements was that applicants should be able to speak, write and read English, which excluded Yiddish-speaking Jews. The bill was rejected, but the agitation remained.

The next year the government introduced a new bill. Despite statistics proving the contrary, most anti-bill politicians, wary of being branded 'the aliens' friends', changed their mind. The change was even more dramatic on the Liberal front benches. The bill hastily passed through the House of Lords and received the Royal Assent on 10 August 1905.[110] It enabled immigration officers to refuse entry to anyone they considered 'undesirable'.

If in the 1880s the ecclesiastical authorities in the Medway Towns were eager to show solidarity with the rabbis in their plight against the atrocities against Jews perpetrated in the Russian Empire, by 1891 the situation had changed. In his statement relating to persecution, Randall Davidson, the Bishop of Rochester, now questioned the extent, or indeed evidence itself of such persecution:

'... *The difficulty of course ... is to ascertain with accuracy what are the actual facts, and what are the circumstances which have led to the cruelty and outrage ... It is evident that those who have impartially studied the whole subject are not entirely of one mind about it ...*'[111]

When the Russian authorities revived the medieval 'blood ritual' accusation against Jews in 1913, a protest meeting was held in London. This time, though notes of sympathy were sent, no bishop joined the protesters. Moreover, some of them, including the Bishop of Rochester, questioned the truthfulness of the accusation.[112]

The local newspapers, which in the 1880s were writing glowing articles about the synagogue, the customs and the practices of Judaism, now found it appropriate to publicise a lecture delivered to the large audience in the Vines Institute by a Wesleyan minister from London, the Rev W. Kingscote Greenland, *The Jew — Monotheist, Martyr, Moneylender*. Among other ideas he propagated the diatribe about all powerful Jewish conspiracy, controlling the money markets of the world.[113]

Chapter 9

The Great War
1914-1918

On 4 August 1914 the sound of bugles called for military and naval personnel to report immediately to their respective barracks. The previous day the German Empire had invaded Belgium, violating the Treaty of London of 1839 that recognised and guaranteed the country's independence and neutrality. Following its treaty obligations, Britain declared war on Germany. Reservists were called to their units, and the Medway Towns were flooded with servicemen. The barracks were full, and every available hall appropriated.[1]

To justify the country's involvement from a religious and moral perspectives, politicians, clergy and journalists employed highly emotive rhetoric of 'a final battle against 'good' and 'evil'', a 'holy war' and a 'just war' against the now-'pagan' Germany. In autumn 1914 prime minister Herbert Asquith argued that Germany had become ruthlessly expansionist and was no longer guided by Christian principles. 'We do not covet any people's territory', Asquith declared in October 1914, oblivious to the irony of his statement: 'We have no desire to impose our rule upon alien populations. The British Empire is enough for us.'[2]

Some clergymen, alarmed by the prospect of war between Christian nations, advocated diplomacy. In his sermon at Westminster Abbey in August 1914, Randall Thomas Davidson, the Archbishop of Canterbury and former Bishop of Rochester, advised the congregation that the 'resolute and unshakeable disbelief' in the necessity of war was gaining ground. However, by 1915 his pacifism had transformed itself into nationalistic jingoism; in his sermon at St Paul's Cathedral he declared that the British were fighting for 'a cause which we can, with clear conscience, commend to God', that of 'resistance to the ruthless dominance of force, and force alone'.[3]

Anti-alienism was already present before the war — the 1905 Aliens Act conferred the power to immigration officers to refuse entry to anyone considered 'undesirable'. Under war conditions, the anti-alien legislation was strengthened further — on 5 August 1914 the Aliens Restriction Act was presented to parliament and rapidly became law. Under its provision, foreign nationals were required to register with the police, and enemy aliens were forbidden to live in the designated prohibited areas, which included the Medway Towns. However, the speed with which the act was adopted created much confusion, and the Jewish population of the area became the target for suspicion, as in case of Morris Weinstein, a peddler from Vilna, Lithuania, whose nephews were serving in the Russian and British Armies,[4] or a 'Russian Pole', Jacob Green, who was registered in London, but had lived in the Medway area for more than a year and worked for the outfitters Featherstone & Co;[5] or Annie Brabonder, 52, who had been living in Britain since she was three, and was convinced that she was English by virtue of long residence.[6]

The proximity of the area to the Continent, and its dockyard and the barracks meant that the Medway Towns were very important from a military perspective. This in turn caused many local spy scares, both real and perceived. Ronald Baldwin, a local historian, in his *Gillingham Chronicle*, mentions a network of German spies and agents established in all British naval towns by Gustav Steinhauer, head of the British section of the German Admiralty's intelligence service, as early as 1902. On the other hand, on 4 August 1914, returning home with a sailing party, aldermen John Featherby and George Swain, both former Mayors of Gillingham, were arrested, interrogated and released only after their identities were verified.[7]

The image of the Christian 'knight' on crusade against the 'pagan' forces of Germany, evoked by politicians, journalists and ecclesiastics, exacerbated the collective hostility and xenophobia of the earlier years. Britain's residents, either aliens, or naturalised British subjects, but identified by their German-sounding names, became an easy target.[8] To distract attention from their

German connections, some anglicised their names, as was the case with the Fehrenbachs, local jewellers and naturalised British subjects, who became Fairbank.[9] Even King George felt compelled to change from Saxe-Coburg-Gotha to Windsor in 1917.

However, on 14 October 1914 Superintendent A. E. Rhodes of Chatham Police issued the Article to the Alien Restriction (Consolidation) Order 1914, which stipulated the prohibition on changing foreign-sounding names,[10] increasing anti-German animosity among the local population. Jews were on the receiving end of it, as the overwhelming majority of them had German-sounding names. One of numerous examples was the case of Morris Weinstein, when the magistrate was convinced that he was German because of his name.[11] Yiddish, which many Jews used when conversing between themselves, was interpreted as German, adding to the fear that Jews were acting as spies on behalf of Germany. The Geigels[12] were one of many similar cases.

To dispel malicious rumours some felt compelled to give interviews to reporters or write to editors requesting to publish their statements. One of them was Coley Goodman, a cinema pioneer, who in partnership with his brother Sidney, opened the Gem Cinema in Gillingham in January 1910 — the first cinema in the Medway Towns. On 22 August 1914, the *Chatham News* published a small announcement denouncing the gossip and explaining that he was of Russian extraction, naturalised in the 1880s. 'I am satisfied that one would have to take a very long journey to find a more patriotic Britisher than Mr Goodman,' the reporter concluded.[13] Solomon Halpern, another member of the Chatham Jewish congregation, declared in the *Chatham News* in October 1914:

'A warning to disseminators of a false report — I Soley Halpern, Confectioner, of High St and Canterbury St, Gillingham, Kent, hereby give notice that I shall take immediate legal proceedings against any person or persons who attempt to damage me in business by stating that I am a German or an Austrian. By birth I am a Pole, and I am now a naturalised Englishman. I have the official papers in my possession which can be seen by anyone interested. They have been shown to the Business Manager of this paper.'[14]

The sinking of the *Lusitania* on 7 May 1915, followed by the story of a crucified Canadian soldier — a kind of a military version of the blood libel — published in *The Times* two days later, and subsequent graphic stories, escalated anti-German feeling. Germany was now being portrayed not only as anti-Christian, but as actively hostile to Christianity — a place historically allocated to Jews. The propagandists in support of the war, channelling the aspects of religious antisemitism by conflating 'German' and 'Judas', aroused and fuelled a spirit of revenge.[15]

One can only imagine the toxic atmosphere, with the Jewish community being on the receiving end of it: malicious rumours, menacing encounters, and not everything was reported in newspapers. Jewish businesses affixed notices on their windows denouncing any connections with Germany;[16] Halpern again sent his public declaration to the newspapers, to be published on 15 May.[17] To so many Jews the atmosphere reminded them of their homeland, Russia or Poland, — from which they believed they had escaped. They tried to keep their heads down, hoping it would all 'blow over'. But worse was to come.

On Saturday, 22 May 1915, *Chatham Observer* reported rioting in Gravesend with Jewish shops wrecked, including one of Mr Schiltz, a member of the town council, who had been a printer in the town for more than 50 years.[18]

On Thursday, 27 May a large crowd gathered outside the business premises of L. Levy and H. Goldberg & Co, outfitters,[19] based on the corner of Fair Row and Chatham High Street. The flags of the Allies decorated the names of the proprietors at the front and notices in the windows stated: 'This firm is in no way connected with Germans. We

The declaration issued by John Lyon of the Chatham congregation on 1 June 1915

No German Jews in the Chatham District.

To the Editor of the " Observer."

Sir,—I must apologise for asking you to insert a few lines in your widely circulated newspaper. As many of my co-religionists have been subject to much annoyance lately, will you kindly give publicity to the fact that there are no German Jews in thhis neighbourhood. Those of the Jewish persuasion who are not English are Russians.—Faithfully yours,

JOHN LYON, President,
Chatham Jewish Congregation.
Memorial Synagogue. Rochester, June 1st, 1915.

Solomon Halpern's confectionary in Canterbury Street, Gillingham, was established at the turn of the century. Solomon (right) threatened to sue anybody who said that he was German

are English-born'. However, a rumour had started that the business harboured German subjects, and the crowd turned aggressive, only to be restrained by a police presence.

On Saturday, 29 May after 9pm a drunken sailor was arrested outside Levy's premises. The arrest of a drunken sailor was nothing out of the ordinary for Chatham, but this time it became a trigger. A mob of 200 quickly assembled, some shouting threats, and the situation escalated rapidly. Stones and bottles were thrown through the windows, damaging the mannequins.

Petrified staff managed to leave the building by the side door, escorted by the police. When at 11pm the shop manageress, Mrs Barnett, returned, the crowd was still there. It was dispersed only when a contingent of the Middlesex Regiment — a second lieutenant, five serjeants and 40 men — arrived from Chatham Barracks to help the police.[20]

The only arrest made during what *Chatham News* described as 'a lively and exciting incident', was that of a tinker, who was fined 13 shillings for using bad language.[21]

For refugees from Russia the incident reminded of pogroms — still a fresh memory for many. For English-born Jews, who believed that they had earned an equal place in British society by having developed a high-quality Jewish character, it shattered their world view — there was no distinction between them. Fear became the main feeling permeating the whole of the community. And it was that fear that compelled John Lyon, president of the congregation, to write a humble request to both local newspapers:

> 'Sir, I must apologise for asking you to insert a few lines in your widely circulated newspaper. As many of my coreligionists have been subject to much annoyance lately, will you kindly give publicity to the fact that there are no German Jews in this neighbourhood. Those of the Jewish persuasion who are not English are Russians.
> — Faithfully yours, John Lyon, President, Chatham Jewish Congregation, Memorial Synagogue, Rochester, June 1 1915.'[22]

Rumours and suspicions about Jews, including those who joined the army, led sometimes to tragic results, as was the case of Albert Isaacs, Lieutenant of the 5th Battalion, Middlesex Regiment, stationed in Brompton during summer 1917. Born in 1880, a son of Pauline, a German national, and Samuel Isaacs, who was Jewish, Isaacs grew up in Vryborg, South Africa. Pauline died when Albert was one year old. His father soon remarried, and the boy was brought up in the Jewish tradition by his father and stepmother. As a young man he took part in the Second Boer War. In 1915 Albert Isaacs joined the Cullinan Horse Brigade of the Eastern Force under the command of Colonel C.A.L. Berange, and participated in the invasion of the German South-West African Colony.

During the action Isaacs established himself as a translator, having co-operated with the intelligence staff, and rendered most valuable assistance, using his first language to translate captured German papers into English. In

1917, he applied to the War Office for a position of an interpreter and was commissioned to join the army with the rank of lieutenant.

According to the *Supplement to the London Gazette* for the 27 August 1917 and the *Army List for September* 1917, Lieutenant Albert Isaacs, with a group of six officers from the South African Defence Force, joined the 12th Battalion of the Middlesex Regiment on 24 June 1917.[23] He arrived in England on 27 July and was drafted to the regiment on 23 August 1917. On a temporary basis he was attached to the 5th reserve battalion of the same regiment, stationed in Gillingham.

During those last days of August, Isaacs took drills, which he found awful. He attended two or three interviews in London, but despite his impeccable military record, was turned down each time. Isaacs brooded over his rejections. He tried to resolve the situation by speaking to one of the training instructors of the officer class and explaining himself. He said he felt he was in a false position, although he was an interpreter and knew German better than English, he was repeatedly being turned down, because his mother was German. He knew nothing about infantry work and felt that he was more inefficient in it than even the rawest recruit.

He was offered a job as a miner, listening out for German miners and tunnellers in the trenches, but that position did not attract him. It was a waste of his language skills. The instructor suggested persevering, which did not ease the situation. Every day Isaacs became more and more agitated and complained about not being able to get away from infantry life. The army clearly was not interested in utilising his best skills. On 1 September he wrote several letters, which he stamped but did not post. In a letter to his father Albert wrote that things 'turned out so differently to my expectations'.

On Sunday 2 September Isaacs arrived at the Queen's Head Hotel, Brompton, at 1.45pm for his lunch. It was his third visit to the hotel — their cooking was definitely better than in many other places. He quickly had his meal and left the place before 2.30. At 6.30pm he returned for his dinner. In the bar he had half a bitter and dry ginger and then proceeded to a private room where he ate his meal in solitude while reading. At five minutes to nine Isaacs asked the manageress of the hotel whether he could have a wash and was shown to the bathroom on the first floor. To everyone who saw him that evening he looked normal, though rather quiet.

With hindsight, it is obvious that under this pretended quietness and calmness, Isaacs was suffering from immense stress and a combination of emotions — being rejected and wasted in the army, hurt, feeling under suspicion on account of his excellent knowledge of German, his detestation of infantry work and a sense of total helplessness. At 9.30pm, Isaacs fired three shots into his chest through an opening in the front of his tunic. He was found still conscious by an officer from a neighbouring regiment. As the latter rushed out to call for a doctor, Isaacs fired two more shots through the same wound. The inquest verdict was 'suicide during temporary insanity.'[24]

Discrimination and prejudice against Jews wishing to enlist was reported widely by the *Jewish Chronicle*. At the same time, the war fuelled accusations that Jews were not 'doing their bit'[25] despite the evidence to the contrary.

Archibald G. Salomons, the only son of Rabbi Salomons, was drafted to the Royal Engineers upon joining the army.[26] Lieutenant Gerald George Samuel, the youngest son of Sir Marcus Samuel, Bt, of The Mote, Maidstone, fought with the Royal West Kent Regiment and was killed on 8 June 1917.[27]

At the end of September 1915 Captain Robert Sebag-Montefiore, the former Unionist candidate for Rochester, went with his regiment, the Royal East Kent Yeomanry, to Gallipoli. He was wounded in the thigh, left shoulder and right knee when a bomb accidentally exploded in a trench on 23 October. He died he next month at the 17th General Hospital in Alexandria.[28]

Gunner Maurice Samuel, nephew of the clothier Mark Samuel, of 184 Chatham High Street, joined Kitchener's Army at the beginning of the war. In 1916 he went to France with his regiment. On 19 December, while he and others were in a farmhouse at Ypres, a German shell killed 10 of his comrades and wounded another. Samuel succeeded in getting his wounded comrade to a place of safety while under heavy fire. He then twice returned to the farmhouse to ascertain if any other occupants were alive, and to free any surviving horses. Samuel was wounded by shrapnel in 10 places, and on coming out the last time he was caught by a gas shell. After undergoing about six months of treatment he was invalided from the army and was awarded the new Military Medal for gallantry on the field.[29]

The Rev Michael Adler described incidents when Jewish soldiers attempted

A group of Jewish servicemen with the military chaplain the Rev Herman
Shandel, Chatham, 1917. The image appeared for the first time in the
British Jewry Book of Honour edited by the Rev Michael Adler

to undermine enemy morale by shouting insults in Yiddish, which the Germans
could understand.[30] But although British Jews and Gentiles fought and died
alongside each other, Jewish civilians faced ostracism and attack, and Jewish
soldiers encountered hostility from their fellow-combatants,[31] occasionally
resulting in tragedy, as was the case of Lazarus Jacobs, a fishmonger from
Hackney, east London.

Jacobs enlisted on 1 May 1917 and was attached to the 5th Battalion of the
King's Royal Rifles, stationed at Sheerness. He struggled with military drills
and was probably picked upon. According to Lazarus's roommate, Rifleman
Henry James Freeman, Jacobs was depressed at intervals because of the drills.
On evening 9 May when several men were in the room joking together about
them, Jacobs said: 'I think I shall cut my head off tomorrow.' The following
morning, having got out of bed he remarked: 'It's my birthday. Wonder what
will happen today.' He paraded in the ordinary way, and at 1.30pm Freeman

left Jacobs in the room. Several minutes later Rifleman Frank Dean discovered Jacobs sitting in the latrine against the wall with a razor in his hand.. Dean rushed to call for the serjeant-major and the captain. When all three of them found Jacobs, he was lying on the ground with his neck cut from ear to ear. Lazarus was taken to Fort Pitt Hospital in Chatham but died on the way there. The coroner recorded the verdict 'suicide during temporary insanity' — a decision commonly used to avoid the verdict of a military offence contrary to the Army Act 1881 sec 38(2).[32]

In Jewish Law the prohibition on suicide is based on the verse from *Genesis*, in the Noah Ark's story: 'And surely your blood of your lives will I require.'[33] The Talmud interprets this verse 'And surely the blood of your lives I will demand,'[34] as one should not wound their body. Even more so, they may not take their own life. There is also a deep spiritual consequence to suicide: the soul has nowhere to go — it cannot return to the body, which is destroyed, nor it is let into any of the soul worlds, because its time has not come. The soul remains in a permanent painful state of limbo. In this world, problems can be solved; after death there are no solutions, only consequences.

Halakhah also provides a definition of suicide. It is the state that 'one who [explicitly] states that he is ascending to the roof [to jump], and then is seen immediately ascending to the roof in anger and falling to his death, is assumed to have committed suicide.'[35] This essentially means that suicide can be committed only by a person in the state of clear and sound mind, free from internal or external coercion. Fear, pain, mental distress are considered among those internal factors that 'coerced' the person into suicide; the person was not of clear and sound mind.[36]

Both Lieutenant Albert Isaacs and Rifleman Lazarus Jacobs were interred in the Chatham synagogue burial ground.

Conscription was introduced by the passing of the Military Service Act in January 1916. Recognising the status of Russian Jews as refugees from Tsarist Russia and acknowledging their unsurprising reluctance to fight on the same side as the regime that had oppressed them, the home secretary exempted them from conscription, but they could continue to join on a voluntary principle. This exemption created resentment and suspicion and intensified already present hostility towards Jews.[37]

Furthermore, after the Russian Revolution of 1917,[38] and the subsequent abdication of Tsar Nicholas II, the separate terms 'Russian', 'Bolshevik' and 'Jew' speedily became interchangeable. The politicians and the press again quickly divided British Jewry into good and bad groups. When trying to escape the bombing raids, many fled from the East End to the home counties and south coast. This triggered many adverse comments.[39] A 'conscription or deportation' campaign, launched by politicians and newspapers in the East End, swiftly spread to the national press, and in July 1917 the Military Service Act was extended to include Russian Jews.[40]

Those who felt they should be exempt from the draft on medical grounds, potential damage to their business, being in work seen as essential to the war effort, family hardship, or conscientious objection, applied to a local Military Service Tribunal. Both local newspapers, the *Chatham News* and the *Chatham Observer*, widely reported tribunal hearings where the cases involving Jews were particularly aggressive.

The following are the cases of four tailors, originally from Russia: Adam Baltushka from Chatham; Maurice (or Morris) Woolf (or Wolff) from Chatham; Jacob (Jack) Koski from Chatham; and Lewis Vishinsky from Old Brompton. All four applied for exemption on medical grounds.

Adam Baltushka, who had been rejected as unfit by the Russian Army, was classified as suitable for sedentary work at home only (C3). This prompted the mayor to remark that bespoke tailoring — Baltushka was a master tailor — was in the latest schedule of trades, and his application was refused.[41]

In 1916 Maurice Woolf, a 23-year-old tailor, received an exemption due to his family circumstances. He was the only breadwinner for two families — his own and his brother's, who was suffering from tuberculosis.[42] Within a year, Maurice contracted pulmonary tuberculosis and was referred to the Central Medical Board, who after what appeared to be a cursory examination lasting for 'only half a minute', declared him to be category A, fully fit for active service.[43] Fortunately, for Woolf, for the first time a tribunal disagreed with the medical board.[44]

Lewis Vishinsky, who had seven children, was originally rejected in 1915 when he volunteered to join the army. Vishinsky suffered from bronchitis and tuberculosis. Despite this, in 1917 he was classified B1, fit for the service abroad. After months of going through appeals and medical examinations, the Central Medical Board confirmed him as being totally unfit for military service. This elicited a rather telling remark from the chairman of the tribunal, Alderman George Swain: 'You are very lucky.'[45]

The case of Jacob Koski, or Strikowski, was particularly hostile, as if the military were hellbent on catching him out. Strikowski was born in 1888 in a small settlement near Warsaw. Escaping the antisemitic Russian Empire, the young tailor arrived in England in 1910 via Hamburg,[46] settled in Chatham and was naturalised in 1912, adopting the name of Jack Koski.[47]

During the war his father and four brothers were serving in the Russian Army, while he was rejected because of his poor eyesight. The British medical board certified him as C1, fit for garrison duty at home only.[48] In early 1917 wishing to contribute to the war effort, Jack partially closed his business and found a position at the engine and steamroller factory of Aveling & Porter, which had switched to munition production during the war. The army, though, was determined to conscript him. Two appeals against Koski's exemption were lodged; both were dismissed.[49] At the review in August 1917 the army representative, Colonel Atkinson, directly accused Koski: 'The idea I have from my instructions is that the local comment is that you have gone into munitions to avoid the Army.'[50] The panel decided in Koski's favour.

The army appealed again; at the same time the recruiting officer put pressure on Aveling & Porter to dismiss Koski. He was sacked, though received good recommendations for his work. Koski then obtained work as a fitter at Short Brothers' aeroplane works, and here again his work was satisfactory. In October 1917 the tribunal adhered to their original decision.[51]

The army appealed again. The hearing this time took place at the West Kent Appeal Tribunal in Maidstone, where the reason for such determination from the army to draft Koski in was finally made clear — he was considered a foreigner despite his legitimacy as a British subject, and as such, under grave suspicion in the eyes of Colonel Atkinson. However, reason prevailed, and the tribunal gave Koski another six months' exemption on condition that he worked full-time as a fitter in an aeroplane factory.[52]

Comparing the above cases with cases of non-Jews, it is obvious that the treatment they received was different in language, attitude and decision. The military often had fewer objections to exemption for Gentiles. Based on the newspaper reports, the encounters during the hearings were usually amicable, with sometimes humorous conversations between the members of the panel and the applicants, as in case of the Epps brothers, fat boilers and sausage skin makers, who joked with the mayor, presiding at the hearing that they had ousted the Germans from Chatham in this particular business.[53]

In September 1917, a single man, Wilfrid Miles, applied for an exemption because of his family circumstances. The greengrocer said his mother was a widow and could not carry on the business by herself. He was classified as C3, suitable for sedentary work at home — the same grade as Adam Baltushka. The military representative offered no opposition, and the tribunal granted the customary exemption for six months.[54]

The newspapers especially honed onto the stories about Jews seeking exemption as conscientious objectors. Coupled with existing suspicions, the sensationalist, bigoted and mocking language of the article titles — "Conscientious Jews",[55] "Attitude of Russian Jews",[56] "Men with Elastic Consciousness", "Munition Workers Do Not Want to Fight",[57] — worked as an additional trigger for escalating anti-Jewish feeling.

There are only four people, four tailors, who applied for exemption on the grounds of being a conscientious objector — Jacob (Jack) Wolfe and the Posner brothers — David, John and Joseph. There is only one small report about Jacob Wolfe, whose tribunal hearing took place in March 1916, and whose fate is unknown, but there is more information about the brothers.

The Posners, with their elderly father, Henry, worked as a family tailoring business, supplying the outfitters firm F&H Newcomb with field jackets for military and naval uniforms at a rate of 14-20 coats per week. The initial hearing took place in the early days of March 1916; the eldest, Joseph was granted a temporary exemption of four months, while David and John's applications were refused. The brothers appealed.[58]

The appeal took place the next month. The atmosphere was intimidating; the appellants' awkward demeanour and their answers, provided the source of sadistic entertainment for the panel — Colonel Atkinson's derision in response to the appellants' statements elicited frequent laughter from the members of the tribunal.[59] The brothers' appeals were rejected. David was drafted into the

King's Royal Rifle Corps, only to be discharged two months later as totally unfit for service.[60]

In July 1916, Joseph was attested and certified for garrison duty at home. However, his appeal was dismissed,[61] and he was called up for 13 December 1916, but he failed to appear. On 14 December 1916 he was arrested, fined 40 shillings and handed over to the military authorities.[62]

During those years of enormous stress, the synagogue nevertheless had to function and find a way to be able to feel part of a wider community. The community arranged concerts for the armed forces, be it to collect funds for the widows and orphans of the men who lost their lives on the *Princess Irene* in 1915,[63] or to raise morale and the spirits of the disabled soldiers and sailors.[64] Jewish servicemen stationed in the vicinity could attend special services and parades conducted by the Rev Herman Shandel, the military chaplain stationed at Chatham, which attracted audiences of 150 men.[65] He was assisted by the Rev Marks Fenton, who had been rabbi of the Chatham congregation since the summer of 1903.[66]

Providing solace and spiritual guidance was particularly tricky. Fenton, as a minister of religion, was exempt from military service; but he was a refugee from Warsaw who arrived in England *c.*1895, and undoubtedly was under suspicion. He also had to administer the last rites more frequently during those years.

On 11 June 1915 the congregants gathered in the synagogue's cemetery for the burial of Sarah Haffkin. She and her husband, the Rev Lazarus Haffkin, refugees from Russia, lived in the Egyptian port of Alexandria.

The Rev Marks Fenton (born *c.*1864), was rabbi of the Chatham congregation during the Great War and died just after the armistice

Lazarus died in March 1915, and that May his widow joined the *SS Sadieh* as stewardess — the only female in the crew of 54. The unarmed vessel was on its way to Hull carrying 8,000 tons of onion and cotton seeds, onions and bones. On 1 June at about 2pm, when the boat was in the Thames Estuary, about six miles northeast of the Elbow Buoy, it was torpedoed without warning by a UB-6 submarine under the command of Kapitänleutnant Erich Haeker. Seven crew in the engine room died instantly. The rest climbed into the boats. Sarah's boat swung and dropped forward, sending people overboard. Within three minutes they were rescued by the captain's boat. Sarah was was already dead when she was brought on board.[67]

In 1917 the community buried two servicemen, Lazarus Jacobs and Albert Isaacs. However, the saddest time for the community was the burial that took place on 28 January 1919, two months after the war — the rabbi himself. Marks Fenton had originally settled in the Birmingham area upon arrival to England *c.*1895, married Clara Weber, daughter of Simon Weber, from Birmingham. The couple established their home in Dudley, but despite Fenton's best efforts, he struggled to revive a Jewish community there[68], and in 1902 they moved to Rochester, joining the Chatham congregation. After the armistice in November 1918, he was taken ill, slowly sank and died early on Sunday 26 January 1919. The Rev M. Rosenbaum, of Borough Synagogue, Walworth officiated.[69]

Chapter 10

The Turbulent Peaceful Years 1919-39

After the 'war to end all wars' ended, the battered and much diminished Chatham Jewish community turned to rebuilding their lives. It was not an easy task — for years the congregation had felt under attack, and the death in 1919 of their spiritual leader, Rabbi Marks Fenton, left the community disorientated and in need of a new rabbi. The Rev Joseph L. Babitz, Fenton's successor, was appointed by the end of the year, but did not stay long. In November 1921 he conducted a short service at the funeral of John Lyon and left Chatham soon after.[2] For a while the community had to rely on rabbis from London — in October 1922, the Rev L. Ticktin consecrated Lyon's memorial stone.[3]

The synagogue needed repairing — it had sustained significant damage during the war. On 18 July 1923 the Chief Rabbi, Dr Joseph Hertz arrived to reconsecrate both the restored and renovated synagogue and the burial ground. The service was conducted by the newly appointed rabbi, the Rev Abraham Samet.

In the evening Dr Hertz gave a lecture, *The Bible as a Book*. The room in Chatham Town Hall was packed to the brim with people of all denominations. According to the newspaper reports, 'the gathering was a record — not merely in size — but in enthusiasm and intense appreciation'. The mayor, E. A. Billingshurst, speaking on behalf of Chatham generally, said that the whole of the borough appreciated the chief rabbi's visit. During his stay Dr Joseph Hertz also visited Rochester Cathedral and the deanery, where he was welcomed by the dean, Dr John Storrs.[4]

The horrors of the war were over, and the suspicions, malicious rumours circulating during the war had all been forgotten; the relationship between both communities was restored. When on Saturday, 26 April 1924, the Prince of Wales unveiled the Royal Naval War Memorial on the Great Lines,[5] Jewish residents were represented by the Rev Abraham Samet; Solomon Halpern, president; Samuel Heiser, warden; Gershon Posner, treasurer; M. Noble, secretary, and ex-servicemen belonging to the Jewish community. A wreath was placed at the base of the memorial on behalf of the congregation.[6]

If one is to rely on newspaper reports, it is easy to assume that civilian life was restored with no aftermath from those four ravaging years. The reality was, however, different. The war left all participating countries in disarray, facing economic problems and high level of unemployment. In 1921, more than 16 per cent of British population was jobless, and dissatisfaction was widespread.[7]

Although the Medway Towns escaped the worst of the devastating effects of the war, the Admiralty laid off much of the dockyard force and there were rumours of the dockyard being closed.[8] The rising level of discontent in the country culminated in the General Strike in May 1926, called by the Trades Union Congress on behalf of the miners. Printers, railwaymen, tram workers, stevedores, barge workers and Medway engineering workers of both Short Brothers aircraft works and Aveling & Porter all joined the action. There was no strike at the dockyard, however — trade unionism was discouraged, and the workers were prevented from joining the action.

The backdrop of the post-war crisis and class conflict, intensified by the Russian Revolution, provided fertile ground for the establishment of the first British fascist organisation in 1923. For those hankering for the 'good old days', the allure of Mussolini's fascist movement with its promises of 'discipline' and 'order', destruction of democracy, outlawing the trade unions and parties to the left, and opposition to egalitarianism, was irresistible.[9] By November 1924, the British fascist movement was well established and going strong in Gillingham.[10]

In 1926 an advertisement on the front page of the *Chatham News* publicised a British fascist meeting at Gardiner Street, Gillingham. The local HQ was at

Mazaler House, Beresford Road — the residence of the area commander and recruiting officer Albert J. Bullock.[11]

Meanwhile, in Germany, Adolf Hitler, the new leader of the National Socialist German Workers' Party, attempted to seize power, while pursuing a similar agenda to Mussolini. British Jews first encountered Hitler in the spring of 1923. The *Jewish Chronicle*, one of the few English newspapers to scrutinise events in Germany, closely observed his trial in April 1924, following the 'Beer Hall Putsch', his botched attempt at a coup in Bavaria. The *Chronicle* pleaded for Hitler to be taken seriously and quoted widely from the *Völkischer Beobachter*, the principal Nazi newspaper. Editorials in 1930-31 emphasised that the Nazi leadership meant exactly what it said. Alas, to no avail.[12]

In October 1929 the American stock market crashed, sending a tidal wave across the world. Within three years, unemployment in Britain rocketed to almost three million. Medway townspeople, who had already been suffering from large-scale layoffs at the dockyard during the 1920s, faced further cuts. Between October 1929 and October 1931, Chatham's Employment Exchange registered an increase in jobless from 3,634 to 6,531.[13]

The Labour government under the leadership of Ramsay MacDonald stuck to traditional economic policies, making cuts to balance the budget, keeping the pound overvalued, and upholding free trade, despite the changed economic reality and growing criticism. One of his critics, Winston Churchill, discussed in his Oxford lecture of 1930 the 'failure' of democracy and appealed for alternative methods of governing. In consequence, some aristocrats, fearing the loss of their estates through taxation, advocated for more authoritarian rule and the temporary disbandment of parliament. In such an event, they proposed Churchill as leader.[14]

The other critic was a Tory defector, Sir Oswald Mosley. When a memorandum, in which he proposed an expansion of credit, protectionism to revive the economy and increased public spending, was rejected, Mosley resigned from the cabinet and turned the Mosley Memorandum into the Mosley Manifesto. In December 1930, 17 Labour MPs, including Frank Markham, MP for Chatham, signed the manifesto.

On Saturday, 31 January 1931, under the auspices of the Chatham Labour Party, Markham and Mosley addressed a meeting at Rochester Corn

Exchange. Markham defended the Labour government's achievement on job creation and declared that the Tory policy on running down the dockyard was being reversed. Regarding Mosley's proposals, he remarked that they were also supported by the previous MP for Chatham, John Moore-Brabazon, a Tory.

Mosley, however, regarded the 200,000 posts created by the government to be inadequate, taking into account more than a million job losses since 1929. Instead of socialism he favoured a comprehensive system of import controls as an immediate means to save jobs. A month after his speech at Rochester, on 28 February 1931, Mosley declared the establishment of the 'New Party' (Nupa).[15]

Over the next months the government crisis deepened resulting in the prime minister calling a general election for 27 October 1931. In a high-profile campaign, the New Party contested 24 constituencies, including Chatham. Its candidate for the dockyard town was Martin Francis Woodroffe, 20, a radio engineer from Wimbledon. He was also the head of the Nupa Youth Movement, the party's youth wing, nicknamed Mosley's 'Biff Boys' — a reference to Mosley's earlier remark that followers would rely 'on the good old English fist'. On Saturday, 3 October 1931, Woodroffe's election campaign was launched at an open-air meeting in Batchelor Street, Chatham. One of the speakers was the East End Jewish boxer Ted 'Kid' Lewis, born Gershom Mendeloff. A week later, at Chatham Town Hall, Mosley spoke in support of the Chatham candidate.

Despite its extensive push, the New Party won no seats in the country. However, the campaign led to the establishment of the Rochester and Chatham branch of the party and on 1 December 1931 it held an annual meeting at the City Café by Rochester Bridge. The reported membership stood at 40 (including 11 women). On 6 January 1932 the branch held a 'carnival ball' at the Rochester Casino attended by Rochester's mayor and mayoress, and the town clerk. Mosley was awarded a dancing trophy, and half of the evening's proceeds were reportedly donated to St Bartholomew's Hospital.

By March 1932 the direction of the party was clear — Mosley talked about the need for a disciplined body of young men to resist the threat of communism. Party representatives were dispatched to study Nazi Party methods, and Mosley visited Italy to meet Mussolini. In May 1932, the New Party's open-air meeting at Batchelor Street, Chatham, which had become an equivalent of London's Hyde Park Speakers' Corner, featured the loudspeakers broadcasting the *Fascist Hymn* as party members gave the fascist salute.[16]

During that year, however, the New Party rapidly lost members as they realised its close association to fascism. To pursue his ideas of a protectionist economy and strong government, Mosley needed to find a solution, and to find it quickly. On 1 October 1932, amalgamating the diehard members of the New Party and other far-right groups, Mosley founded the British Union of Fascists (BUF). Believing that he was the only saviour against the communists, Mosley managed to convince Mussolini and Lord Rothermere, owner of the *Daily Mail*, to provide financial backing. Parroting Mussolini's movement, BUF members wore blackshirt uniforms and operated as a paramilitary organisation.

Meanwhile, the economic crisis in the country was deepening, and the number of unemployed surged further. By November 1932 Chatham's Employment Exchange registered 7,687 — an increase of 1,156 from October 1931, and more than twice as many than in 1929.[17]

At the start, the BUF denied institutional antisemitism, though it had a fair share of antisemites and racists. When challenged by the *Jewish Chronicle* to disown them, Mosley's response was rather ambiguous. The BUF 'would never attack Jews because they are Jews', he said, but if Jews attacked the BUF or were 'international capitalists' or subversives, then the BUF reserved a right to counter-attack.[18] However, Mosley's thin veneer of political respectability slipped in October 1934, when he launched into a demagogic assault on an 'international Jewish conspiracy',[19] drawing his attack from the *Protocols of the Elders of Zion*. This fabrication, which originated in Russia about 1905, from the annals of the Tsarist police, was created to stoke the anti-Jewish feeling and inspire pogroms. It claimed that the ultimate aim of the Jews was world domination, using any means necessary, through political and financial gain. The document reached Britain in 1920 and was exposed as fake news in 1921.[20] However, that did not stop it being widely used by both the far right and the Establishment, exploiting the image of the Jew as both capitalist, motivated by financial greed, and communist, hungry for political influence among dissatisfied working classes plotting a revolution.[21]

Mosley visited the Medway Towns several times. His first visit was on

30 October 1934 when he addressed an audience of more than 1,000 at the Pavilion dance hall in Canterbury Street, Gillingham. A crowd of between 300 and 500, which congregated outside to protest, was restrained by 30 policemen to allow him into the venue.

Twenty uniformed blackshirts stood guard around the hall. During his speech he denounced democracy and presented his plan for a 'corporate state', and also targeted Jews. Mosley told the audience that the BUF fought Jews 'because they have opposed the interests of fascism and the interests of Britain'. The Jews 'have to choose whether to put Britain first or Jewry first'.

Outside, the blackshirt 'guards' were pelted with eggs as the crowd chanted and sang the *Red Flag*. In nearby Skinner Street anti-fascist speakers addressed impromptu meetings.[22]

On his emergence after the meeting Mosley was spat upon and his entourage was attacked with missiles, including bottles. One Blackshirt was hit on his head; a policeman's hand was cut by flying glass. The crowd also attempted to overturn Mosley's car. A *Chatham Observer* reporter at the scene commented: 'There was in this crowd an element of sheer blackguardism which had given itself over to the ugly influence of mob fury'. Contrasting the crowd with Mosley's BUF boys he noted that 'not the slightest evidence of any act of violence on the part of any of the large contingent of Blackshirt present, despite the fact that several of them had been pelted with eggs by someone in the crowd whose aim was remarkably accurate.'[23] But the reporter's observations were not the full story — a young female member of the Labour League of Youth was beaten up outside the Pavilion, away from the eyes of press and the crowd.[24]

On 16 March 1935 Hitler announced Germany's rearmament in violation of the Treaty of Versailles; in October the same year Mussolini invaded Abyssinia. Britain started its own rearmament. The Medway Towns' population, most of whom always relied on the government's military campaigns for their employment, began expanding the numbers of the dockyard's workforce. In June 1935, Chatham's Employment Exchange registered fewer than 4,000 unemployed for the first time since 1930.[25]

Mosley visited the Medway Towns again on Monday 23 June 1936. This time the venue was Rochester Casino on the corner of the Blue Boar Lane and

Corporation Street. A large crowd gathered to see him enter the building, and many police were drafted in.

The spacious auditorium was lined with blackshirts. A detachment of them formed an arch down the central gangway and gave the fascist salute as Mosley approached the platform to the fascists' marching song.

Addressing the audience, Mosley claimed that the fascist regime would carry out the 'will of the people' unlike the current parties, which existed only to slow progress. To win the peace, he said, Britain had to ally with Germany, Italy and Japan. Mosley argued that fascism was the only antidote to socialism and the saviour against the Soviets. 'The British government had been passive dupes of the Jew, [Maxim] Litvinoff [the Soviet foreign secretary], who sought to set them at rest while the communist jackals feasted on the ruins of western civilisation,'[26] — a common conflation between Jews and Bolshevism, caused by Karl Marx's Jewish heritage and the perceived prominence of Jews in the ranks of the Bolsheviks.[27]

The speech was received with almost no interruptions, perhaps because of the line of blackshirts around the hall. However, a quite a few in the audience opposed Mosley's views. The audience applauded vigorously when a young Jew rose and asked why Jews who were prepared to die for England should be penalised because of their race. There was no direct answer from Mosley; he repeated his ambiguous statement about the choice Jews had to make in order not to be attacked by him and the BUF: England or Jewry.

Meanwhile, a group of communists, bearing a red flag, held a meeting outside. They were singing the *Internationale* and *We Must Get Rid of the Rats* as they waited outside the main entrance. Mosley slipped out through the side door and a detachment of his men formed a square around his car as he climbed into it. The crowd rushed towards the square, breaking the police lines and stopping the traffic along Corporation Street. There was a sudden movement to surround the car, but the rush was held up by the barrier of blackshirts.[28]

About a week after Mosley's Casino speech, the Rev B. Williamson, Vicar of St Paul's Church, Chatham, hosted a meeting when the guest speaker was the Rev I. Livingstone from the Golders Green Synagogue, who talked about Jews in Germany. Quoting the opinions of the Archbishop of Canterbury, the Bishop of Dover and many other clerics and distinguished people who had condemned the persecution of the Jews, Livingstone contended that the German public itself was not antagonistic towards Jewry, but the hatred emanated from the Hitler regime. The people of Germany regarded the Jews in much the same light as the people of England did; it was only the violence of their present rulers that had stirred the bitterness that had not previously existed.[29]

The presence of fascists was visible across Kent. Blackshirts perceived themselves as unique saviours from the evil of communism. Bessie Pullen, from Tankerton, attended fascist meetings in Rochester proudly wearing her full fascist uniform. In her letter to the *Whitstable Times* in December 1936, she complained about the presence of communists, who turned up and were distributing their leaflets. She appealed to conservative readers of the newspaper:

> *'... To the Communists our common crime will be that we believe in God, in law and order and decency. Of course, they reserve their deepest hatred for fascists because as yet the fascists are the only party that is out to fight them and their evil. I only hope that the rest of the country will not wake up too late.'[30]*

The common conflation of Communist and Jew gives this letter a more sinister undertone.

The perception and the attitude of the Medway Towns' councils towards Mosley and his party were inconsistent, to say the least. The fascists held their meetings at the Old Corn Exchange and the Casino at Rochester,[31] at the Pavilion and Paget Hall in Gillingham,[32] but were repeatedly refused the use of Chatham Town Hall.[33] Instead, in Chatham they held their meetings outdoors, in Batchelor Street, a traditional meeting-place.[34] The BUF was permitted to promote its free publications at Chatham Library,[35] but Gillingham Library refused to allow this,[36] and there are no records regarding the distribution of their publications at Rochester Library.

In January 1937, there were concerns about the existence and distribution of the fascist documents and propaganda at Chatham Dockyard, including a meeting, where a prospective BUF candidate, Noel Kennedy, addressed a crowd of 1,000.[37] The same month, Sir Stafford Cripps, Labour MP for Bristol East, said Chatham Dockyard was a hot spot for the open distribution and sale of fascist literature. Cripps claimed that he provided Sir Samuel Hoare, First Lord of the Admiralty, with the name of the man responsible, but despite the man being known for his political activities and displaying a large fascist sign on his locker, he was not apprehended and his locker not searched.[38]

The next month, Ernest Thurtle, Labour MP for Shoreditch, asked Hoare if he had had an opportunity of making further inquiries into the distribution of fascist literature at the dockyard and that it had been permitted by responsible authorities. Hoare said no evidence had been forthcoming to substantiate the allegations.[39]

Whether it was a cover-up, as Cripps hinted,[40] or indeed there were no fascists in the dockyard, it is obvious that they had support and were active in the Medway Towns. The party's local HQ was at 22b Chatham Hill in 1937,[41] moving to 20 Arden Street, Gillingham, the next year.[42] In the next election the BUF was preparing to contest Chatham, where it believed it had sympathisers.[43] The candidate was 32-year-old Noel Kennedy,[44] in whose support Mosley spoke at the Paget Hall in Gillingham in April 1938.[45]

Mosley and his party were a great source of concern for the Chatham Jewish community, which by that time comprised only a dozen extended families. This time there were no riots or attacks on business premises, but who could predict what would happen later? In 1928 the Rev Abraham Samet resigned after his wife and his son died within two years of each other.[46] The new rabbi, Samuel (Sam) Wolfe appointed in 1930,[47] devised a strategy — education and engagement with the wider community. With two London rabbis, the Rev M. Rosenbaum, of Borough Synagogue, and the Rev I. Livingstone, of Golders Green Synagogue, and Harry Samuels, a barrister and a member of the Fabian Society, he delivered lectures across Medway.

The first took place in March 1933 at a meeting of the St Andrew's Literary Society and was entitled *Jew and Gentile*.[48] The following year, the Rev M. Rosenbaum gave a talk, *What the Jews Have Contributed to Civilisation*, at the inaugural meeting of Medway and District Social and Literary Club. Rosenbaum spoke of the role of Jews in early times and the Middle Ages as the carriers of learning from the East to the West in philosophy, medicine

The Rev Abraham Samet, *c.*1925, was the Chatham rabbi only briefly

and mathematics. The meeting, which took place at the Methodist school in Rochester, was presided over by the Rev Sam Wolfe and supported by Mayor of Rochester Joseph W. Leech; Mayor of Chatham Cllr Mark Packer; Alderman H. F. Whyman and E. D. Clark, headmaster of Sir Joseph Williamson's Mathematical School.[49]

The topics that started from historical and religious perspectives became more and more political, as Hitler's antisemitic propaganda and policies escalated, and Mosley and his party were gaining support from the public and press in the UK. They ranged from *The Mosaic Religion and its Relation to Everyday Life*'[50] to *Jewish Ideals of Citizenship* delivered to the Medway Towns branch of the Workers' Educational Association in 1935[51]; from *Jew in the World Today*,[52] to *The Jews in Germany* in 1936,[53] to *The Jew and his Neighbour with Special Reference to Antisemitism and to the Plight of German Jewry* in 1939.[54] Some lectures, such as *Jew and Gentile*[55] and *Jew in the World Today*[56] were repeated, their content updated as the political situation in Germany and the UK worsened.

In March 1937 a reporter from the Chatham Jewish community sent a note to the *Jewish Chronicle*: 'During this blackshirt business we in Chatham have not heard any nasty remark passed against Jews. We mix with our Christian friends in clubs and keep on the best of terms with all residents.'[57] It is not clear what precise 'blackshirt business' the reporter referred to, but the mere necessity of sending the note to the national Jewish newspaper points to an attempt to reassure everyone, including members of the Chatham community. The reality was, perhaps, more dangerous than the correspondent wanted us to believe.

However, the most telling statement, giving an insight into grave concerns about the more and more precarious position of Jews in the society, was made by Rabbi Rosenbaum. 'He had found that the Jews were as good as any other people,' said he during his repeat *Jew and Gentile* talk on 31 October 1938.[58]

The venues for the talks were offered by clergymen, nonconformist and Anglican. In Gillingham it was the Methodist Church,[59] Chatham — St Paul's[60] —and Rochester offered two venues — Bethel Methodist Church[61] and The Vines Congregational Church.[62]

The lectures attracted large audiences, attended by clergy and the mayors of Chatham and Rochester. It is not clear whether representatives from Rochester Cathedral ever participated.

On 13 March 1938, German troops marched into Austria. The same year Chamberlain's government abandoned its ally, Czechoslovakia, allowing Hitler to annex its Sudetenland. In July 1938, the Evian Conference of 32 countries, convened to manage the increasing numbers of refugees from Nazi Germany, produced no result. Hardly any country loosened its immigration restrictions. The inability or unwillingness of the countries to take decisive steps in resolving the issue, emboldened Hitler, who saw it as endorsement to escalate his antisemitic attacks.

On the night of 9 November 1938, which became known as 'Kristallnacht', or 'Pogrom Night', Jews and their property were attacked across Germany, Austria and Sudetenland. The pogroms continued the next day and in some areas violence carried on longer. Over 48 hours more than 1,000 synagogues were burnt or otherwise damaged; about 7,500 Jewish businesses were looted and ransacked; at least 91 Jews were killed; Jewish hospitals, schools, cemeteries and homes were vandalised, often by neighbours. About 30,000 Jewish males aged 16 to 60 were arrested; and the concentration camps of Dachau, Buchenwald and Sachsenhausen were expanded to accommodate new prisoners. On 15 November Jewish children were barred from attending schools and local authorities were ordered to impose curfews. By December

1938, Jews were banned from most public places in Germany.[63]

The November events were reported in the press, including the local newspapers. Letters to the editor followed. Two weeks after the pogroms, in the *Chatham Observer* R.G. Baker from The Quest, Yorkletts, Whitstable, complained about 'sob-stuff on the persecution of the Jews in Germany and elsewhere (with the object perhaps of getting more of them here)'. Baker blamed Jews for their own persecution, the source of which he saw in the Talmud, which, according to him, confirmed all those Jewish conspiracy theories.[64]

A week later the only public response to the letter was that of Rabbi Sam Wolfe. In restrained language the rabbi explained that despite the Jews suffering losses the same way as the Germans, the devastating economic situation in post-war Germany was blamed on Jews. When Hitler, the master of populist propaganda, was sworn chancellor in January 1933, he promised the unhappy Germans prosperity, 'a new heaven and earth, coupled with the persecution of the Jews. Unfortunately, new heaven and earth could not be manufactured to order, but the persecution of the Jews could'. It began with the 'Cold Pogrom' on 11 March 1933, when 'brownshirt' stormtroopers attacked Jewish-owned shops.

As for the Talmud — the commentary to the Torah, comprising 26 volumes, and written in the fifth century CE, Wolfe pointed to the Golden Rule: 'Thou shalt love thy neighbour as thyself' (Leviticus 19:18); the Talmud explains this verse as: 'Whatever is hateful unto thee, do it not unto thy fellow.'[65]

On Sunday 8 January 1939, the rabbi spoke at The Vines Congregational Church in Rochester, where he denounced in scathing terms the treatment meted out by the Nazis to Jews during recent months. He recounted the account of two Baptist ministers who had motored through Germany. They saw Jewish synagogues burnt and the houses and business premises of Jews wrecked by the mobs while the police looked on. They found groups of Jews, old and young, wandering about the streets, afraid to go back to their ruined homes. They said even war and revolution could not be worse than the ghastly sights they saw.

Wolfe thanked the English Christian friends for their warm-hearted response to the appeal by 1st Earl Baldwin of Bewdley (the former Conservative prime minister Stanley Baldwin) to save the children out of Germany, and also

'Yours forever, loving Sam': the Rev Sam Wolfe, in the 1930s

the people of Kent for their sympathy and hospitality to German child refugees, referring to the children who had arrived by Kindertransport.

But it is rather telling that as if to remind the audience that Jews really 'did their bit' during the Great War, he also mentioned that 50,000 served in His Majesty's Forces; more than 2,000 were killed and 7,000 were wounded. To justify the worthiness of Jews, to prove that they deserved to be treated as equal and be accepted, Wolfe mentioned the names of Benjamin Disraeli, who served twice as prime minister, and Sir Isaac Isaacs, recently governor-general of Australia. Jews, he said, had become British statesmen, administrators and servants of the Empire. British Jews would be found among the men of eminence in art, science, medicine, law and literature. The history of the Jews showed that many of those who came to Britain from abroad as refugees from lands of persecution brought new ideas and established industries that increased the wealth of the nation and created employment for hundreds of thousands.[66]

On 15 March 1939 Hitler tore up the 'peace in our time' Munich Agreement and invaded Czechoslovakia. Several days later Mosley visited the Medway Towns again, giving an hour-and-a-quarter speech at the Paget Hall. He concentrated on the developments in Europe, defended Hitler's actions and ranted against Jews and refugees, accusing them of taking jobs from the two million British still unemployed.[67]

British re-armament was well under way, and the new war in Europe started to look imminent.

Postscript

Afeter the end of the Second World War, the few surviving members of the community returned. They were determined to revive the Jewish community life in the Medway Towns. The war severely damaged the synagogue and the Minister's House. The ironworks and railings were requisitioned during the war, and both buildings looked abandoned, desolate and dejected. There were no funds to restore the damage; the slowly dilapidating rabbi's house was becoming uninhabitable.

For the next two decades the congregation numbers were growing again, boosted by young families with children. By the mid-1960s the congregation urgently needed a community space. In 1965, the centenary year of the foundation of the Chatham Memorial Synagogue, a newly formed centenary committee launched an appeal scheme. It had two aims: to restore the synagogue to its previous glory and to build a much-needed community centre. The next seven years were devoted to raising funds. With the help from the Ministry of Public Building and Works, Rochester Council (predecessor of the current Medway Council) and a member of the Jewish community, the original décor of the synagogue was restored. The derelict minister's house was demolished; in its stead, in June 1972 the congregation inaugurated the Mid-Kent Youth and Community Centre. The synagogue restoration work, the design and the building of the centre were conducted by Halpern and Partners of London, international architects and town planners — Hilary Halpern, a grandson of Soley Halpern, was keeping the promise he had made to his grandfather many years ago.

On Sunday 26 January 2003, the eve of the liberation day of Auschwitz and the Holocaust Memorial Day in the UK, a new stained-glass window was unveiled in the synagogue. Designed by Hilary Halpern, it was crafted by Sharif Amin, a Muslim artist. The 24ft-long window in the roof of the synagogue features the names of 22 of the Nazi death camps. The design includes symbols of barbed wire, watchtowers, chimneys, and the Star of David. A circle of clear glass in the middle is surrounded by rays of coloured glass, which fade from yellow to orange and red into purple and black. The dark, menacing colours suggest the horrors of the Holocaust, but the luminous explosion of light in the centre is a glimmer of hope.

Since the congregations of Gravesend, Canterbury and Sheerness ceased to exist, the Chatham Memorial Synagogue has become the only one in mid-Kent. Its congregation had its peaks and troughs, expanding and contracting depending on the state of economy and opportunities offered. But no matter how big or small the community is, its members carry on playing an active role in local civic life. They host educational visits for schools across Kent and deliver teacher-training workshops; take part in the work of the Standing Advisory Council for Religious Education and are school governors, committee members of Medway Inter-Faith Action and lead and take part in numerous events and fundraisers — advocating for education, equality and co-operation. The Magnus legacy continues.

Appendix 1

Jewish entries in the parish records 1660-1780

The following four tables relate to the Jewish entries in the 17th and the 18th centuries.

This data was extracted from the indices kept at Medway Archives Centre and verified from Ancestry database. Information relates to the 18th century records from the following churches: St Nicholas Church, in the city of Rochester, St Margaret's Church, outside Rochester city walls, and St Mary's Church in Chatham. The cut-off point in extracting data is 1780 — the year of the first explicit record relating to the synagogue, which provides us with the name of one the synagogue founders.

The data is arranged alphabetically according to the surname, as it appears in the index, chronologically and according to the type of record — baptism, marriage, burial.

In deciding whether to include the person, according to the surname, caution was exercised. Some surnames, such as Abraham/Abrahams are typically Jewish. However, certain variations and anglicised versions of surnames, such as Brams, Braham, Barham (corrupted versions of Abraham) were included, especially if the person or at least one of the parents had Jewish sounding first names. However, if the surname was ambiguous, and the first name, neither of the person nor of his/her parents sounded Jewish, the surname was not included. Some strange-sounding names were also included.

Jewish entries in the parish records 17th century

Name	Parents	Record	Date	Church
Abraham, John	John & Mary	baptism	21 Oct 1693	St Margaret, Roch
Cassell		baptism	Apr 1696	St Mary, Chatham
Lyon		baptism	Mar 1687	St Mary, Chatham
Moise		baptism	Apr 1678	St Mary, Chatham
Moise		baptism	May 1680	St Mary, Chatham
Moise		baptism	Dec 1684	St Mary, Chatham
Moise		baptism	Feb 1688	St Mary, Chatham
Moses		baptism	Sep 1677	St Mary, Chatham
Moses		baptism	Apr 1683	St Mary, Chatham
Moses		baptism	Jun 1687	St Mary, Chatham
Gelfs		baptism	Aug 1694	St Mary, Chatham
Levy, William		marriage	1694	St Mary, Chatham
Raphuen (Raphael?), Isaac		marriage	1695	St Mary, Chatham

Jewish records in the parish entries, 1701-80

Name	Parents	Record	Date	Church
Aaron, Benjamin	Jonathan & Mary	baptism	11 Jun 1749	St Mary, Chatham
Abraham	—	baptism	Oct 1718	St Mary, Chatham
Abraham, Elizabeth	John & Mary	baptism	3 Feb 1739	St Margaret, Roch
Abraham, Richard	John & Elizabeth	baptism	16 May 1742	St Mary, Chatham
Abrahams	—	baptism	Oct 1721	St Mary, Chatham
Abrahams	—	baptism	Aug 1725	St Mary, Chatham
Abrahams	—	baptism	Jan 1728	St Mary, Chatham
Abrahams, Nathaniel	Thomas & Mary	baptism	13 Jul 1740	St Mary, Chatham
Abrahams	—	baptism	May 1744	St Mary, Chatham
Abrahams, Michael	John & Elizabeth	baptism	19 Oct 1746	St Mary, Chatham
Abrahams	—	baptism	Aug 1752	St Mary, Chatham
Abrahams, Allen	Robert & Elizabeth	baptism	15 Dec 1754	St Mary, Chatham
Abrahams	—	baptism	Feb 1755	St Mary, Chatham
Abrahams, Robert	Robert & Elizabeth	baptism	6 Feb 1756	St Mary, Chatham
Abrahams, Richard	Robert & Elizabeth	baptism	28 Jan 1758	St Mary, Chatham
Abrahams, Nathaniel & Hallaway, Grace	—	marriage	12 Oct 1762	St Mary, Chatham
Abrahams	—	baptism	Mar 1763	St Mary, Chatham
Abrahams, Nathaniel	NathanieL & Grace	baptism	6 Mar 1765	St Mary, Chatham
Abrahams, Sarah	Michael & Elizabeth	baptism	12 Aug 1770	St Mary, Chatham
Abrams	—	baptism	Jun 1733	St Mary, Chatham
Abrams, Michael & Gattrell (Gettrell?), Elizabeth	—	marriage	17 Oct 1769	St Mary, Chatham
Alexander, Harry & Samuel, Elizabeth	—	marriage	5 May 1760	St Mary, Chatham
Alexander, James & Barrett, Sarah	—	marriage	31 Oct 1760	St Mary, Chatham
Barham, Mary	Gabriel & Ann	baptism	26 Feb 1758	St Margaret, Roch
Barram	—	baptism	Apr 1724	St Mary, Chatham

Caster	—	baptism	Aug 1713	St Mary, Chatham
Dazada	—	baptism	May 1714	St Mary, Chatham
Donleevy, Mary	Hugh & Mary	baptism	2 Feb 1752	St Mary, Chatham
Goold, Edward	Edward & Suzannah	baptism	6 Jul 1746	St Margaret, Roch
Hambro, Mary	Roger & Mary	baptism	19 Oct 1759	St Mary, Chatham
Hambro, John Morris	Richard & Susanna	baptism	4 May 1768	St Margaret, Roch
Hebron, Elizabeth	Arthur & Susanna	baptism	17 May 1754	St Mary, Chatham
Honniker, Sarah (wife of Moses)	—	burial	30 Nov 1751	St Mary, Chatham
Isaac, Edward John	Abraham & Mary	burial	3 Feb 1779	St Mary, Chatham
Jacques, Jacob	—	burial	17 May 1739	St Mary, Chatham
Kagin, John	John & Mary	baptism	2 Dec 1750	St Mary, Chatham
Kedshebe	—	baptism	Apr 1727	St Mary, Chatham
Keser, Henry Franklyng	John & Martha	baptism	25 Sep 1763	St Margaret, Roch
Keser, Sarah	John & Martha	baptism	30 Jul 1769	St Margaret, Roch
Kirsha	—	baptism	Oct 1717	St Mary, Chatham
Kuwn, Joannah	John & Joannah	baptism	15 Mar 1746	St Mary, Chatham
Leven	—	baptism	Sep 1738	St Mary, Chatham
Levens, George	John & Earte	baptism	5 Nov 1741	St Mary, Chatham
Levi, Samson & Dadd, Sarah	—	marriage	10 Sep 1764	St Margaret, Roch
Levi, Maryann	Samson & Sarah	baptism	27 Dec 1767	St Mary, Chatham
Levi, Thomas William	Samson & Sarah	baptism	27 Sep 1765	St Margaret, Roch
Levi, Sarah	Samson & Sarah	baptism	24 Oct 1771	St Margaret, Roch
Levins	—	baptism	Apr 1745	St Mary, Chatham
Levinton	—	baptism	Feb 1770	St Mary, Chatham
Lewens, Robert	John & Mary	baptism	15 Feb 1749	St Mary' Chatham
Lewins	—	baptism	Mar 1740	St Mary, Chatham
Lewins	—	baptism	Jul 1742	St Mary, Chatham
Lewins	—	baptism	May 1744	St Mary, Chatham
Lewins	—	baptism	Jul 1746	St Mary, Chatham
Levy, William	—	burial	28 May 1712	St Mary, Chatham
Lion, James	Daniel & Mary	baptism	3 Sep 1759	St Mary, Chatham
Lucy/Lewey/Lewsy	—	baptism	1713	St Margaret, Roch

Lucy/Lewey/Lewsy	—	baptism	1715	St Margaret, Roch
Lucy/Lewey/Lewsy	—	baptism	1717	St Margaret, Roch
Lucy/Lewey/Lewsy	—	baptism	1722	St Margaret, Roch
Lewey, William	Joseph &Judith	baptism	10 May 1724	St Margaret, Roch
Lyon, Elizabeth	Joel & Ann	baptism	1 Mar 1761	St Mary, Chatham
Maires	—	baptism	Mar 1715	St Mary, Chatham
Mases	—	baptism	Jul 1756	St Mary, Chatham
Mattas, Thomas	Charles & Ann	baptism	25 Oct 1761	St Mary, Chatham
Mauze	—	baptism	Feb 1733	St Mary, Chatham
Mauze	—	baptism	Mar 1736	St Mary, Chatham
Mayes	—	baptism	Jan 1721	St Mary, Chatham
Mayrs	—	baptism	Aug 1706	St Mary, Chatham
Meires	—	baptism	Jul 1718	St Mary, Chatham
Meirs	—	baptism	Nov 1716	St Mary, Chatham
Melior	—	baptism	1779	St Margaret, Roch
Menzies, Mihel	—	baptism	1711	St Margaret, Roch
Meuris, George Lewis	George & Catherine	baptism	5 Dec 1766	St Mary, Chatham
Meyer, Matthew & Goold, Sarah	—	marriage	9 Feb 1773	St Mary, Chatham
Mizen, Isaac	Richard & Sarah	baptism	28 Jun 1741	St Nicholas, Roch
Morris & King	—	marriage	Feb 1711/12	St Mary, Chatham
Moses & Wreake	—	marriage	Mar 1711/12	St Mary, Chatham
Moses, Sarah	Abraham & Mary	baptism	9 Aug 1750 (b. 16 Jul 1750)	St Mary, Chatham
Moses, Abraham	Abraham & Jane	baptism	25 Aug 1751	St Mary, Chatham
Moses, Abraham (husband of Jane, will proved on 1 Jul 1776)	—	burial	21 Jun 1776	St Mary, Chatham
Moses, George	Abraham & Jane	baptism	15 Jan 1764	St Mary, Chatham
Moses, William	Abraham & Jane	baptism	10 Jan 1768	St Mary, Chatham
Moses, William	Abraham & Jane	burial	21 Mar 1770	St Mary, Chatham
Phenuke (?)/Phenke, Anne	—	baptism	11 June 1721	St Margaret, Roch

Raphael, Sarah	Nicolas & Mary	baptism	19 Oct 1746	St Mary, Chatham
Raphael, Ann	William & Catherine	baptism	9 Mar 1760	St Mary, Chatham
Raphael, John	William & Catherine	baptism	25 Oct 1761	St Mary, Chatham
Sach	—	baptism	1766	St Margaret, Roch
Sach	—	baptism	1770	St Margaret, Roch
Sach	—	baptism	1775	St Margaret, Roch
Sampson	—	baptism	May 1762	St Mary, Chatham
Sampson	—	baptism	May 1763	St Mary, Chatham
Sampson	—	baptism	Nov 1765	St Mary, Chatham
Sampson	—	baptism	Jun 1768	St Mary, Chatham
Sampson	—	baptism	May 1771	St Mary, Chatham
Samson	—	baptism	Sep 1760	St Mary, Chatham
Samuel, Susan (aged about 19 years)	—	baptism	16 Mar 1746	St Nicholas, Roch
Samuel, Sannel	—	baptism	Aug 1763	St Mary, Chatham
Samuel	—	baptism	Jan 1741	St Mary, Chatham
Saul	—	baptism	Jul 1744	St Mary, Chatham
Saul	—	baptism	Aug 1745	St Mary, Chatham
Saul, Elizabeth	George & Sarah	baptism	15 Jul 1748	St Mary, Chatham
Sigal, John	John & Ann	baptism	10 Sep 1760	St Mary, Chatham
Sison	—	baptism	Jun 1708	St Mary, Chatham
Sison	—	baptism	Apr 1710	St Mary, Chatham
Sison, Mary	Edward & Mirabella	baptism	4 Apr 1742	St Mary, Chatham
Sison, Sarah	Edward & Mirabella	baptism	21 Aug 1743	St Mary, Chatham
Sison	—	baptism	Apr 1745	St Mary, Chatham
Sison, Elizabeth	Edward & Mirabella	baptism	19 Jul 1747	St Mary, Chatham
Sison, Martha	Edward & Mirabella	baptism	26 Dec 1749	St Mary, Chatham
Sisson	—	baptism	Nov 1703	St Mary, Chatham
Sisson	—	baptism	Nov 1706	St Mary, Chatham
Solomon, Thomas	Thomas & Elizabeth	baptism	5 Jul 1747	St Mary, Chatham
Solomon, Henry	John & Elizabeth	baptism	23 Apr 1749	St Mary, Chatham
Solomon, John	John & Elizabeth	baptism	14 Jul 1751	St Mary, Chatham
Symons, Isaac	Daniel & Sarah	burial	19 Aug 1756	St Mary, Chatham
Turzer, Daniel	—	burial	13 Dec 1751	St Mary, Chatham

The number of baptisms, marriages and burials when at least one partner is Jewish; parish records 1701-1780

Decade	St Margaret, Rochester	St Nicholas, Rochester	St Mary, Chatham	Total
1701-10				
Baptism	—	—	5	5
Marriage	—	—	—	—
Burial	—	—	—	—
Total	—	—	5	5
1711-20	—	—		—
Baptism	4	—	7	11
Marriage	—	—	2	2
Burial	—	—	1	1
Total	4	—	10	14
1721-30				
Baptism	3	—	6	9
Marriage	—	—	—	
Burial	—	—	—	
Total	3	—	6	9
1731-1740				
Baptism	1	—	6	7
Marriage	—	—	—	
Burial	—	—	1	1
Total	1	—	7	8
1741-50				
Baptism	—	2	25	27
Marriage	—	—	—	—
Burial	—	—		—

Total	—	2	25	27

1751-60

Baptism	1	—	15	16
Marriage	—	—	2	2
Burial	—	—	3	3
Total	1	—	20	21

1761-70

Baptism	7	—	16	23
Marriage	1	—	2	3
Burial	—	—	1	—
Total	8	—	19	27

1771-80

Maptism	3	—	1	4
Barriage	—	—	1	1
Burial	—	—	2	2
Total	3	—	4	7

Overall number of the Jewish records for 1701-80

Record	St Margaret, Rochester	St Nicholas, Rochester	St Mary, Chatham
Baptisms	19	2	81
Marriages	1	—	7
Burials	—	—	8
Total	20	2	96

Appendix 2

Excerpts from Rochester Cathedral records relating to the alms given to Jews in the early 18th century (DRc/FTb)

D ean & Chapter accounts of Rochester Cathedral for the 18th century show that people receiving alms came from every corner of the world: Turks, Armenians, Poles, Germans, Italians, French, Flemish, Greek… not to mention Scots, Welsh, Irish and those who arrived from other parts of England. Some of them were passing through and needed some help to proceed on their way; others settled in the area. The excerpts below relate to Jews, appearing in the accounts. The record either states explicitly that the alms relate to a Jew, or the person, receiving the alms has a Jewish sounding name and/or his toponymic relates to a place known to have a large Jewish community.

Date	Record, including the alms given
8 Feb 1715	[alms given] to one David Blank a poor Hamburgher cast away Isle of Wight (2s)
16 Aug 1715	Simon Fisher etc with a pass from Leghorn (6d)
26 Sep 1715	Tho' Levet & his wife with a pass (6d)
6 Nov 1717	John Boacham, Levite Thomas & others that had been cast away coming from Indies (5d)
8 March 1724	Daniel Moses, a Dutchman (6d)
25 July 1724	to one John Meyer, a poor Hollander

15 Jan 1727	to Solomon Gillingham being very poor (1s 6d)
23 May 1729	to a converted Jew (1s)
17 Jan 1730	to a converted Jew (1s)
9 Feb 1730	to a converted Jew (5s)
23 May 1731	to a converted Jew (1s)

Appendix 3

Early synagogue leases (CH2/15)

1 September 1808:
Lease to Solomon Mordecai and others, 2 tenements in St Margaret's for 40 years from Midsummer 1808 between:
Trustees of St Bart's of the first part

and

SOLOMON MORDECAI, silversmith, City of Rochester
HUMPHREY SOLOMON, of Rochester, salesman
ISAAC ABRAHAM, late of St Margaret's next the said City, but now of Sheerness, tobacconist
HART COHAN of Chatham, salesman
MICHAEL ABRAHAM of Chatham, salesman
ABRAHAM MOSES of Chatham, salesman
Of the second part

and

Said Solomon Mordecai
Humphrey Solomon
Isaac Abraham
Hart Cohan
Michael Abraham

Abraham Moses
SIMON DAVIS, shopkeeper
LAZARUS MAGNUS, Chatham, shopkeeper
JOSHUA ALEXANDER, Chatham, shopkeeper
SAMUEL SIMONS, Frindsbury, shopkeeper
LION BENJAMIN, Chatham, shopkeeper
AARON MOSS, Sheerness, shopkeeper
Of the third part

Witnesseth that the said Brethren as well for and in consideration that the said Solomon Mordecai, Humphrey Solomon, Isaac Abraham, Hart Cohan, Michael Abraham and Abraham Moses have surrendered and do hereby surrender unto them one lease by Indenture bearing the date the 15th day of July 1794 granted to them and to Levi Israel and Israel Levi both since deceased, of the messuages or tenements and premises hereafter … all those two small messuages, tenements or dwelling houses (now used as a Jews' Synagogue), alleyway and with the ground backside and gardens thereunto belonging or therewith now or heretofore demised, used and occupied or enjoyed (in St Margaret's) formerly in the tenure or occupation of Wiiliam Scolcop and Widow Wilson since of John Tilghman and Widow Harris…"

23 April 1823
Trustees of St Bart's of the first part

and

ISAAC ABRAHAM, of Sheerness, tobacconist
HART COHAN, late of Chatham, now of Liverpool, salesman
MICHAEL ABRAHAM, of Chatham, salesman
JOSHUA ALEXANDER, of Chatham, shopkeeper
SAMUEL SYMONS, of Frindsbury, shopkeeper
LION BENJAMIN, of Chatham, gentleman
AARON MOSS, of Sheerness, shopkeeper
Of the second part

and

Joshua Alexander, Lion Benjamin, Moses Aaron, Moses Aaron
MARCUS HYMAN of Chatham, apothecary
SOLOMON LUCAS of Chatham, slopseller
SAMUEL SIMON LAZARUS of Chatham, slopseller
LEVY SIMONS of Chatham, slopseller
LEWIS COHAN of Chatham, slopseller
BERMAN ISACHER BARNARD, hardwareman
ABRAHAM MOSS, slopseller
LEWIS ALEXANDER of Chatham, butcher
JONATHAN ZACHARIA of Chatham, salesman
Of the third part
(Solomon Mordecai, Humphrey Solomon, Abraham Moses, Simon Davis
and Lazarus Magnus all since deceased)
New 40-year lease

Appendix 4

Early Jewish entries in the Freemasons' records

Kentish Lodge of Antiquity. From Moderns Grand Lodge 1768-1813, Register of Admissions: Country and Foreign, vol II, fols 1-649 (online)

Initiation	Name	Age	Occupation	Residence
January 1764	Meuris, George		Gunner	—
January 1764	Taylor, William		Tailor	—
6 January 1794	Moises, Hugh	30	W.Middlesex surgeon	Rochester
4 January 1808	Solomon, Joseph	23	Attorney	Rochester
15 February 1808	Moss, Edward	25	Jeweller	Strood
17 September 1810	Morris, Griffith	30	Capt	Chatham

Lodge No 243 (Globe Inn, Chatham). From Antients Grand Lodge 1771-1813; Membership Registers: Country, Foreign and Military, vol I, #7-271 (online)

Initiation	Name	Occupation	Residence
8 October 1798	Aarons, Moses	Hatter	Chatham
8 October 1798	Lucas, Brm(?)	Sergeant 71	Chatham
8 October 1798	Sherenbeck, Henry	Jeweller	Chatham
17 January 1800	Magher, Jas	Tailor	
January 1810	Taylor, Samuel	Merchant	Brompton
August 1810	Morris, Thomas	King's Force	
December 1812	Myers, John	Sergeant Royal Marines	Chatham

Globe Lodge, Chatham. From United Grand Lodge of England 1813-1836; Register of Admissions Country and Foreign 'C', #291-418 (online). The lodge merged with Lodge No 306 in 1825

Initiation	Name	Age	Occupation	Residence
5 January 1810	Taylor, Samuel		Coal trade	Chatham
4 September 1823	Casper, Lewis	38	Watchmaker	Chatham
4 September 1823	Cohen, Lewis	35	Navy agent	Chatham
4 September 1823	Cohen, Mark	32	Gentleman	Liverpool
4 September 1823	Isaacs, John	35	Silversmith	Chatham
4 September 1823	Levi, Thomas	34	Musician	Chatham
4 September 1823	Lucas, Solomon	34	Slopseller	Chatham
4 September 1823	Marks, Montague	33	Slopseller	Chatham
4 September 1823	Moss, Abraham	30	Slopseller	Rochester
6 January 1825	Morris, J. [?] K.	37	Lieutenant, Royal Marines	—

Royal Marine Lodge, Chatham. From United Grand Lodge of England;
Freemason Membership Registers 1751-1921. United Grand Lodge of
England 1813-1836. Register of Admissions: Country and Foreign 'C',
#291-418 (online)

Initiation	Name	Age	Occupation	Residence
13 January 1814	Myers, John	—	Serjeant	Chatham
14 July 1814	Aaron, Lyon	—	Draper	Chatham
22 September 1814	Levy, Thomas	—	Drummer	Chatham
8 December 1814	Levy, George	—	Private	Chatham
1814	Aaron, Isaac	—	Navy agent	Globe Lane (from Lo 259 Sheerness)
1814	Isaacs, John	—	Jeweller	Globe Lane
1814	Magnus, Lazarus	—	Slopseller	High St
25 January 1815	Cohen, Lewis	—	Watchmaker	Globe Lane
25 January 1815	Lucas, Solomon	—	Army agent	High St
25 January 1815	Solomon, Morris	—	Slopseller	Military Rd
25 September 1817	Cohen, Asher	—	Pawnbroker	Chatham, Liverpool
25 September 1817	Lyon, Aaron	—	Navy agent	
22 January 1818	Moss, Abraham	31	Slop merchant	Rochester
27 May 1819	Marks, Montague	28	Slop merchant	Chatham
23 March 1820	Cohan, Mark	28	Gentleman	(from Lo 20)
23 March 1820	Sherenback, Henry	58	Optician	
25 January 1821	Schnebbelie, Jacob Christ	44	Pastry cook	Rochester (from Lo 20)

Royal Kent Lodge of Antiquity No 20, Chatham. The lodge was named in 1819; its earlier name was Kentish Lodge of Antiquity. From United Grand Lodge of England 1813-1836; Register of Admissions: Country and Foreign 'A', #17-140, fols 1-277 (online)

Initiation	Name	Age	Occupation	Residence
20 October 1801	Sherenbeck, Henry	55	Jeweller	Chatham
3 February 1817	Magnus, Lazarus	—	Slop merchant	Chatham
1 December 1817	Sloman, Joseph	36	Gentleman	Chatham
1 December 1817	Solomon, Samuel	32	Gentleman	Chatham
25 November 1818	Sloman, John	23	Gentleman	Rochester
19 April 1819	Franklin, James	31	Coal merchant	Rochester
1 December 1819	Schenebelie, Jacob, Ch.	45	Confectioner	Rochester
26 December 1819	Mellingen, John Gideon	40	Hospital surgeon	Fort Pitt
18 July 1820	Cohan, Mark	—	Gentleman	Rochester
2 August 1820	Schnebelie, John	39	Professor of music	Brompton
1827	Solomon, Joseph	—	Pawnbroker	Chatham
27 July 1831	Solomon, John	—	Comedian	—

Brompton Lodge. From United Grand Lodge of England 1813-1836; Register of Admissions Country and Foreign 'C', #291-418 (online)

Initiation	Name	Age	Occupation	Residence
11 August 1814	Morris, Richard	-	Surgeon	Brompton
11 January 1816	Casper, Lewis	-	Silversmith	Chatham
12 August 1818	Tailor, Leonard	53	Royal Navy	-

Appendix 5

Jewish residents of St Margaret Parish, Rochester, in Militia Ballot, 1821

From *A Transcript with Index of the 1821 Militia Ballot List for the Parish of St Margaret, Rochester, Kent.* Cuxton: Allen, 1995)

Name	Age	Occupation	Children	Notes
Levy, Henry	58	Jew Rabbi	no small children	
Levy, Lewis	29	shopkeeper	no children	exempt licence hawker
Moss, Abraham	39	broker		rheumatism

Appendix 6

Jewish navy agents of Chatham

The following three tables relate to the Chatham Jewish navy agents. The data below is extracted as it appears in the following work: Green, Geoffrey L (1989) *The Royal Navy and Anglo-Jewry 1740-1820: Traders and Those Who Served. London*: G. L. Green

Register of Jewish navy agents in Chatham.

Name	Address	Date	Trade	Notes
Aaron, Abraham	203 High St	Dec 1815-Sep 1820		from Deal
Aaron, Isaac	Globe Lane	Dec 1815-Dec 1818	umbrella maker	
				licence revoked 14/12/1818 for not
				accounting to John Briggs late of
				HMS Caledonia for prize money;
				licence restored 14 Jan 1819 at an address in Maidstone
Aaron, Joseph	Chatham	July 1803-Dec 1806		moved to Sheerness
Aaron, Lyon	High St	Nov 1814-Jul 1819		
	Grove Lane	Jul 1819-Sep 1820		moved to London
Abrahams, Abraham	321 High St	Sep 1822-Sep 1827	Slopseller & tobacconist	
	Military Rd	Sep 1827-Sep 1828		from Poole, moved to London
Barnett, Joel	Chatham	Dec 1809-?	—	—
Cohen, Asher	73 High St	Nov 1814-Sep 1820	Pawnbroker	moved to Liverpool

Cohen, Lewis	Globe Lane	Dec 1815-Sep 1838	Slopseller, furniture broker	
Cohen, Mark	Chatham	Dec 1809-?	—	—
Davis, David &				
Lazarus	68 High St	Nov 1842 - Oct 1847	Pawnbrokers	
			moved to Northfleet	
Davis, Samuel	68 High St	Dec 1816-Sep 1832	Slopseller	
Samuels & Martha		Sep 1832-Oct 1847	Silversmith	
		widow carried on the business at the same address		
Isaacs, Isaac	11 Hamond Place	Aug 1828-Sep 1831	Slopseller	—
Isaacs, John	92 High St	Apr 1838-Sep 1844	Watchmaker, clockmaker	
	68 High St	Sep 1844-Sept 1854	and silversmith	—
Lucas, Solomon	309 High St	Dec 1815-Jul 1819	Slopseller	—
Magnus, Lazarus	302 High St	Dec 1809-Sep 1828	—	—
Magnus, Simon	302 High St	Nov 1842-Sep 1852	Silversmith & pawnbroker	—
Moss, Elias	Chatham	Dec 1809-Dec 1815	—	moved to Plymouth
Sloman, Joseph	91 High St	Dec 1817-Sep 1821	Pawnbroker	—
Solomon, Lewis	89 High St	Oct 1833 - Sep 1842	Slopseller	—
	3 Hamond Place	Sep 1842 - Oct 1861	Slopseller	—
Solomon, Samuel	40 High St	Jul 1819 - Sep 1838	Slopseller	—

Comparative table of licensed navy agents in Chatham and Sheerness between 1809 and 1820.

	Chatham	Sheerness
Total, 1809	7	11
Jewish Navy Agents, 1809	5	5
Percentage, 1809	71.5	45.5
Total, 1816	10	17
Jewish Navy Agents, 1816	6	9
Percentage, 1816	60.0	53.0
Total, 1820	9	6
Jewish Navy Agents, 1820	7	5
Percentage, 1820	77.7	83.3

Battle of Trafalgar prize money received by Chatham navy agents

Name	Number of seamen acted for	Amount collected	Commission received
Barnett, Joel	2	£3 15s 5d	1s 10½d
Cohen, Asher	3	£5 13s 1½d	2s 9¾d
Magnus, Lazarus	16	£48 6s 4d	£1 4s 1½d
Moses, Abraham	1	£1 17s 8½d	11¼d
Moss, Elias	63	£103 15s 7d	£2 11s 10½d

Appendix 7

Comparison table for the attendance to the places of worship in two cathedral cities — Rochester and Canterbury, and in the dockyard places of Chatham and Sheerness, 1851

The data below is extracted from the following work: Yates, Nigel (1984) 'The Major Kentish Towns in the Religious census of 1851', *Archaeologia Cantiana* v100, pp400-401.

Yates identifies four major groups of worshippers, divided as follows:

1 Church of England;

2 Old Dissent, which sprang directly from the Reformation, and comprised:
  – Independents, or Congregationalists,
  – Various groups of Baptists,
  – Presbyterians,
  – Society of Friends,
  – Calvinists,
  – Unitarians;

3 New Dissent, groups ceded from the Church of England, as a result of the 18th-century evangelical revival, and which consisted of
  – Methodists,
  – Countess of Huntingdon's Connexion;

4 The rest — groups that comprised:
  – Roman Catholics,
  – The Latter-Day Saints,
  – Jews, the only non-Christian group.

Place	C of E	Old Dissent	New Dissent	Roman Catholics, Latter-Day Saints, Jews
Canterbury	60.5	19.1	18.8	1.6
Rochester	69.2	14.0	15.8	1.0
Chatham	46.5	25.7	23.1	4.7
Sheerness	37.6	22.2	26.8	13.4

Appendix 8

Summary of Jewish congregations in Kent, 1847 (from JC 23/7/1847).

Congregation	Ba'ale batim	Seat-holders	Individuals
Canterbury	8	4	106
Chatham	16	40	189
Dover	4	0	31
Sheerness	2	10	13

Attendance at Sabbath services on 28-29 March 1851, and average attendances on Sabbath for the previous six months. Jewish congregations in Kent.

The data below is extracted from the following works: Lipman, V. D. (1951) "A Survey of Anglo-Jewry in 1851", *Transactions JHSE* v17, pp171-188; *1851 Census of Worship*, PRO, H.O.122

It is interesting to note that Sheerness Jewish community is not included in the census. The Sheerness Jewish community was established originally in 1810. It still appears in the *Summary of Jewish congregations of the British Empire*, published by the Jewish Chronicle in July 1847 (see table above). However, it seems that the organised Jewish community did not exist by the beginning of 1851. The Sheerness Jewish community was re-established in 1853 with the help of Lazarus Simon Magnus, who was elected as their deputy for the Board of Deputies of British Jews. The Sheerness new synagogue officially opened on 9 November 1853 with 15 seat-holders. (JC 5/8/1853; JC 18/11/1853).

28-29 March, 1851			Average			
Congregation	Fri eve	Sat morn	Sat aft	Fri eve	Sat morn	Sat aft
Canterbury	26	30	20	28	35	20
Chatham	30	24	—	—	20	—
Dover	60	60	—	not stated	not stated	—
Ramsgate	30	45	20	30	30	20

Table of births, marriages and interments, and number of seat-holders of the Jewish congregations in Kent and the port places of Plymouth, Portsea and Southampton, January 1853-January 1854. (from JC 26/5/1854)

Forty-two organised Jewish communities in the country were recorded that year.

Place	Births	Marriages	Deaths	No of seat-holders
Canterbury	2 (male)	—	—	13
Chatham	5 (2 male; 3 female)	2	4 (1 male; 3 female)	32
Dover	—	2	—	12
Plymouth	7 (3 male; 4 female)	4	5 (2 male; 3 female)	42
Portsea	2 (1 male; 1 female)	2	3 (1 male; 2 female)	55
Ramsgate	1 (male)	1	—	Private synagogue
Sheerness	—	—	—	15
Southampton	—	—	—	16

Table of births, marriages and interments, and number of seat-holders of the Chatham Jewish congregation, 1852-1900

Data below is extracted from the following source: Board of Deputies, *www.jewishgen.org* — accessed 18/3/2007

Year	Birth	Marriage	Burial	No of Seat-holders
1852	2 births (female)	2 marriages	1	30
1860	-	-	6	31
1870	-	-	2	34
1880	-	-	1	30
1890	-	2	-	15
1900	1	-	4	10

Appendix 9

Jewish community of the Medway Towns from the directories, 1790s-1860s

The next seven tables provide a glimpse into the number and the nature of the Jewish businesses in the decades between the 1790s and the 1860s, before the opening of the new synagogue. Most of the businesses concentrated on the High Streets of Chatham and Rochester and nearby streets. The Medway Towns of Chatham and Rochester and their respective High Streets were and are a contiguous area, which makes it hard to determine where one place finishes and the other begins; the boundary problem was noted by many visitors over the centuries. The municipal boundaries were moved too. It is also useful to bear in mind the renumbering of Chatham High Street, which took place in the 1880s.

Additional complication was to determine whether the person was part of the local Jewish community, especially if they do not appear in any other Jewish records. To provide consistency, if a person had an unusual, i.e. not typical Christian surname, his/her name was included in the list.

It is also useful to remember that an entry into any directory required a certain amount of wealth. As a result, there is a high possibility that other Jews did not appear in the directories, as they were too poor to merit an entry. On the other hand, some names merited more than one entry, or were operating from more than one premises. In such cases, their name is listed only once, but separate businesses and/or premises are listed as they appear in the directory.

Universal British Directory for 1792 lists the following Jewish names for Chatham and Rochester and Brompton. The Brompton area, next to the dockyard was then recorded as part of Chatham.

	Name	Occupation	Place
1	Hayler, Benjamin	Pawnbroker	Chatham
2	Iserel [sic, Israel], Levi	Silversmith	Chatham
3	Levi, Israel	Salesman	Rochester
4	Levi, Simon	Salesman	Chatham
5	Mordecai, Solomon	Salesman	Rochester
6	Moss, Abraham	Silversmith	Chatham
7	Morris, Benjamin	China-man	Chatham

In addition, Michael Pearson in his book *Kent Clocks & Clockmakers* lists the following clock- and watchmakers, operating in 1792-1800:

	Name	Occupation	Place
1	Barrett, Daniel	Watchmaker	Chatham
2	Asher, Mordecai	Clockmaker	Rochester
3	*Phillip, Myer	Clockmaker	Rochester

(source: Pearson, Michael (1997) Kent Clocks & Clockmakers. Ashbourne: Mayfield Books)
*Phillip, Myer seems to have operated in Rochester in 1767, according to Pearson.

The Holden Directories, 1811-1815 and *Underhill's Directory* for 1816-17.
CHS = Chatham High Street; RHS = Rochester High Street.

Name	Occupation	Place	Years
Abrahams, Michael	Slopseller	Chatham	1811-15
Benjamin, Benjamin	China & glass warehouse	Chatham	1811-15
Benjamin, Lyon	Slopseller	Chatham	1811-15
Cohan*	Slopseller & pawnbroker	Chatham	1811-15
Cohen *	Pawnbroker, etc	Chatham	1816-17
Davies	Silversmith	Chatham	1816-17
Hayler	Watchmaker/silversmith	Chatham	1811-15
Jonas, S	Silversmith	Rochester	1816-17
Mordecai, Solomon	Silversmith	Rochester	1811-15 1816-17
Moses, Abraham	Slopseller	Chatham	1811-15
Moss	Slopseller	Chatham	1811-15
Schubbelie, J & Co	Confectioners	RHS	1811-15
Sheeringback, John **	Jeweller	CHS	1811-15
Sheringbeck, John **	Jeweller	CHS	1811-15
Solomon, H	Clothes salesman	Eastgate, Rochester	1811-15

* Cohen and Cohan are possibly the same person.

** Sheeringback, John and Sheringbeck, John are possibly the same person. He's probably a relative of Henry Sherenbeck, jeweller and actor.

Pigot Directory for 1826. All streets are in Chatham unless stated. CHS = Chatham High Street; RHS = Rochester High Street.

Name	Occupation	Address
Abrahams, Abraham	Slopseller & salesman	
	Tobacconist	331 CHS
Abrahams, Coleman	Slopseller & salesman	44 CHS
Abrahams, Michael	Slopseller & salesman	47 CHS
Alexander, Jacob	Tailor	337 CHS
Alexander, Joshua	Furniture broker	147 CHS
Barnard, Berman J	Hardwareman	70 RHS
Barnard, Samuel	Slopseller & salesman	34 CHS
Cohan, Henry	Slopseller & salesman	7 CHS
Cohan, Lewis	Furniture broker	Hamond Place
	Slopseller & salesman	1 Hamond Place
	Dealer in marine stores	CHS
Hart, Jacob	Silversmith	St Margaret's Banks, Roch
Isaacs, John	Slopseller & salesman	CHS
Isaacs, Lewis	Furniture broker	307 CHS
Levy, Aaron	Tobacconist	37 CHS
	Watchmaker, jeweller & silversmith	343 CHS
Levy, John	Stationer & salesman	119 Eastgate, Roch
Levy, Lewis	Slopseller & salesman	Military Rd
Lucas, Solomon	Slopseller & salesman	309 CHS
Lyons, Isaac	Slopseller & salesman	CHS
Magnus, Simon	Pawnbroker	302 CHS
Moss, Abraham	Furniture broker	St Margaret's Banks, Roch
Sherenbeck, Henry	Optician, etc	347 CHS
Simons, Levy	Slopseller & salesman	CHS
Sloman Jos & Chas	Pawnbroker	46 CHS
Soloman, John	Slopseller & salesman	154 CHS
Soloman, Lewis	Slopseller & salesmann	Military Rd
Soloman, Samuel	Slopseller & salesman	126 CHS

| Woolf, Aron | Slopseller & salesman | St Margaret's Banks, Roch |

The names below were extracted from the *Pigot Directory* for 1832-34 and *Wright's Topography* for 1838. All streets are in Chatham unless stated. CHS = Chatham High Street; RHS = Rochester High Street.

Name	Occupation	Address	Year
Abraham, Coleman	Slopseller & salesman	44 CHS	1834
	Salesman, tailor & renovator	10 Watt's Place	1838
Abrahams, Abraham	Slopseller & salesman	112 CHS	1834
	Clothes salesman	As above	1838
Alexander, Jacob	Furniture broker	St Margaret's Banks,	1834, 1838
Barnard, Asher	Tailor	341 CHS	1834
Barnard, Berman J	Hardware dealer	Eastgate, Roch	1834
Barnard, Samuel	Slopseller & salesman	33 CHS	1834
Benjamin, Mrs	Gentry	CHS	1838
Casper, Leius	Watchmaker, jeweller, etc	3 Watt's Place	1838
Cohan, Lewis	Furniture broker	45 CHS	1834
Cowan, James	Lieutenant, Royal Navy	26 Cazeneuve St,	
		Troy Town, Roch	1838
Davis, E	Furnishing ironmonger	311 CHS	1838
		10 Hamond Place	1838
Davis, M. & D.L.	Pawnbrokers	CHS	1838
Davis, Samuel	Slopseller & salesman	68 CHS	1834
	Silversmith	As above	
Harris, Solomon	Slopseller & salesman	337 CHS	1834
Isaacs, Henry	Furniture broker	11 Military Rd	1834
Isaacs, Isaac	Slopseller & salesman	11 Hamond Place	1834
	Army clothier &		
	fancy repository	310 CHS	1838
Isaacs, John	Slopseller & salesman	87 CHS	1834
	Silversmith, jeweller	92 CHS	1838
Isaacs, Lewis	Furniture broker		

(Possibly the same as	Slopseller & salesman	86 CHS	1834
Isaac, L.)	Army outfitter & general	As above	As above
	furniture warehouse	Garden St, Brompton	1838
Isaacs, Samuel	Army & navy clothier	79 CHS	1838
Jacob, James	Leather-cutter, etc	114 Eastgate Roch	1838
Jacobs, W.P.	Surgeon	154 RHS	1838
Levy, John	Furniture broker &		
	general dealer	St Margaret's Banks	1834, 1838
	Gentry, clergy, etc	St Margaret's St, Roch	1838
	Ship-store dealer	Nicholson's Wharf	1838
Levy, Lewis	Furniture broker	3 Military Road	1834
Lyons, George	Bricklayer's Arms	High St, Brompton	1838
Lucas, Samuel	Slopseller & salesman		
	Army & navy clothier	12 Hamond Place	1834
		309 CHS	1838
Magnus, Simon	Pawnbroker, silversmith, etc.	302 CHS	1834; 1838
Marks, Montagu	Furniture broker	342 CHS	1834
Simons, Levy	Slopseller & salesman	128 CHS	1834
Simons, Samuel	Slopseller & salesman	48 CHS	1834
Sloman, John	Wheelwright & timber dealer	St Margaret's Banks	1834, 1838
Sloman (Slowman in W.T.),			
Joseph and Chas	Pawnbrokers	46 CHS	1834, 1838
Soloman, L & S	Watchmakers & toymen	2 Military Rd	1838
Solomon, Samuel & Lewis	Slopsellers & salesmen	89 CHS	1834; 1838
Zachariah, Jonathan	Slopseller & salesman	331 CHS	1834

The names below were extracted from the *Pigot Directory* for 1840; Bagshaw, Samuel (1847) *History, Gazetteer and Directory of the County of Kent*, volume 1; *Williams Directory* for 1849. All streets are in Chatham unless stated. CHS = Chatham High Street; RHS = Rochester High Street.

Name	Occupation	Address	Year
Aaron, Ann	Umbrella maker	Clover St	1840
Abrahams, Abraham	Slopseller & salesman	112 CHS	1840
Abrahams, Coleman	Slopseller & salesman	Globe Lane	1840
		Tobacconist & clothier	1849
Alexander, Joshua	Tailor	Road St	1840
Alexander, Reuben	Clothes broker	(old) Globe Lane	1847
Barnard, Daniel	Hardware dealer	292 CHS	1847
	Newsagent	333 CHS	As above
	Tobacconist	As above	As above
	Clothier	9 Hamond Place	1849
	General dealer	292 CHS	As above
Barnard, Hannah & Son	Hardware dealers	Eastgate, Rochr	1847
Barnard, L	Clothes dealer	Globe Lane	1849
Barnett, Barnett	Clothes broker	241 CHS	1847
	Clothes dealer	CHS	1849
Barnett, Barney	Clothes dealer	Globe Lane	1849
Braham, James	Grocer & tea dealer	4 Hamond Place	1847
Casper, Lewis	Watch & clockmaker & silversmith	2 Watts Place, CHS	1840, 1847
Cohn, Simon	Cap maker	351 High St	1847
Cohen, Mrs	Gentry	3 Clarence Place, Roch	1849
Coleman, Abraham	Clothes broker	7 Globe Lane	1847
Davis, Joseph	Tobacconist	154 Eastgate, Roch	1847
Davis, Martha & David Lazarus	Pawnbrokers	68 CHS	1840
Defrates, William	Tailor	Almon Place, Roch	1847

Goldsmith	General dealer	343 CHS	1849
Goldsmith, Michael	Toy dealer	343 CHS	1847
Goldsmith, Morris	Clothes broker	251 CHS	1847
	Clothier	As above	1849
Harris, Barnet	Clothes broker	341 CHS	1847
		Wood St, Brompton	1847
Harris, Solomon	Slopseller & salesman	337 CHS	1840
	Clothes broker	382 CHS	1847
Hayler, William	Silversmith & jeweller	59 CHS	1847
	Watch & clock maker	As above	As above
Heitzman, Anthony	Watch & clock maker	168 CHS	1847; 1849
Isaacs & Son	Outfitting warehouse	94½ CHS	1849
Isaacs, Henry	Furniture broker	11 Military Rd	1840
Isaacs, Charles & Isaac	Outfitters (Army & Navy)	94 CHS	1847
Isaacs, Isaac	Army clothier	14 Hamond Place	1840
	Bookseller & stationer	As above	As above
	Slopseller & salesman	11 Hamond Place	As above
Isaacs, John	Watch & clockmaker & silversmith	92 CHS	1840
	Outfitters (Army & Navy)	68 CHS	As above
	Silversmith & jeweller	As above	1847
	Watch & clockmaker	As above	As above
	Jeweller	As above	1849
Isaacs, Lewis	Furniture broker	Garden St, Brompton	1840
	Cabinet maker & furniture warehouse	As above	1847
Isaacs, Samuel	Bookseller & stationer	79 CHS	1840
	Outfitter	As above	As above
	Tailor & drape	As above	As above
	Tobacconist	As above	As above
	Outfitters (Army & Navy)	71 CHS	1847
	Military outfitter	CHS	1849
Isaacs, Saul	Furniture dealer	308 CHS	1849
Jacob, Myers	Tailor & draper	223 CHS	1847

Jacobs, James	Boot & shoemaker	Eastgate, Roch	1840
	Beer house proprietor	Eastgate, Roch	1847
Jacobs, John	Greengrocer	331 CHS	1847
Legis, Casper	Clock & watchmaker	2 Watts Place	1849
Levy, Mrs Sarah	Gentry	St Margaret's Banks, Roch	1847, 1849
Levy, Chas	Merchant & marine store	St Margaret's Banks, Roch	1847
Levy, Isaac	Clothes broker	355 CHS	1847
	Clothes dealer	High St, Brompton	As above
Levy J & J	Furniture broker	351 CHS	1840
J Levy & Sons	General dealers	St Margaret's Banks, Roch	1840
Levy, Jacob	Clothes broker	(old) Globe Lane	1847
Levy, John Lewis	Marine stores, ship & barge owner	St Margaret's Banks, Roch	1847
Levy, Joel	Salesman	350 CHS	1849
Levy, Nathan Chas	Dealer in marine stores	83 RHS	1847
		High St, Strood	1849
	Coal merchant	CHS	1847
Levy, Noah	Clothes dealer	184 CHS	1840
Lucas, Samuel	Outfitter	309 CHS	1840
	Slopseller & salesman	As above	As above
	Outfitters (Army & Navy)	As above	1847
Lyons, Asher	General dealer	157 RHS	1849
Lyon, Symon	Tobacconist	Eastgate, Roch	1847
	Tobacconist	112 RHS	1849
Magnus, Simon	Pawnbroker	302 CHS	1840
Magnus Simon & Son	Outfitters (Army & Navy)	302 CHS	1847
	Silversmith & jeweller	As above	As above
Marks, Hannah	China, glass & earthenware dealer	86 CHS	1847
	Furniture broker	As above	As above
Marks, John Montagu	China, glass & dealer	CHS	1840
	Outfitters (Army & Navy)	18 Watts Place	1847
	General dealer	86 CHS	1849
	Outfitters	16-17 Watts Place	As above

Marcus, John	Tailor	Whittaker's Place	1849
Morris, Caroline & Anne	Academy or school	Rome Lane	1840
Nathan, John	Clothes broker	210 CHS	1847
	Tailor & draper	As above	As above
Phillips, Jehiel	Jewish Rabbi	St Margaret's Banks, Roch	1847
Pyke, Joseph	Watchmaker, etc	302 CHS	1849
Salmon, Adolphus S	Wine & spirit merchant	St Margaret's Banks, Roch	1847
	General dealer	Levy's Place Roch	1849
Schage, Henry	Hatter	12 Military Road	1849
Schnebblie, John	Professor of music	Wood St, Brompton	1849
Silvester, Samuel	China, glass & earthenware dealer	84 CHS	1847
Simons, Levy	Slopseller & salesman	128 CHS	1840
	Clothes broker	St Margaret's Banks, Roch	1847
	Clothier	RHS	1849
Simons, Samuel	Slopseller & salesman	47 CHS	1840
	Clothes broker	As above	1847
Sloman, Joseph & Charles	Pawnbroker	46 CHS	1840
	Pawnbrokers	As above	1847
Solomon, John	Furniture broker	Military Rd	1840
Solomon, John & Charles	Furniture brokers	14 Military Rd	1847
	Furniture brokers	13-14 Military Rd	1849
Solomon, Samuel & Lewis	Navy agents, slopsellers & salesmen	89 CHS	1840
	Outfitters (Army & Navy)	3 Hamond Place	1847
	Clothiers	3 Hamond Place	1849
Solomon, Samuel & Lazarus	Watch & clock maker	357½ RHS	1840
Symons, Jane	Milliner & dressmaker	St Margaret's Banks, Roch	1847
Woolf, Samuel	Marine stores dealer	211 CHS	1840
	Umbrella maker	Chatham Hill	1847
	Umbrella maker	Chatham Hil	1849

The names below were extracted from the *Phippen Directory*, 1858. All streets are in Chatham unless stated. CHS = Chatham High Street; RHS = Rochester High Street.

Name	Occupation	Address
Abrahams, Elizabeth	Tobacconist	Globe Lane
Alexander, Reuben	Clothier	301 CHS
Barnard, D	Hardware man	292 CHS
Barnard Daniel	Railway Tavern	CHS
Barnett, Abraham	Clothes dealer	RHS
Barnett, Anna	Old clothes dealer	241 CHS
Barnett Benjamin	Clothes dealer	Globe Lane
Cowan, Mark	Gentry	11 Maidstone Rd, Roch
Davis, Joseph	Tobacconist	154 RHS
Defrates, John	Licensed beer seller	RHS
Defrates, William J	Tailor	RHS
Goldsmith, Morris	Clothier	251 CHS
Goodman, Morris	Clothier	167 CHS
Harris, Barnet	Clothes dealer	87 CHS
Isaacs, Charles	Gentry	1 Milton Terrace
Isaacs, Charles, Samuel & Saul	Outfitters	12 (64) Hamond Place
		71 CHS
		Joselyn's Wharf
Isaacs, C.S & S	Clothiers	71 CHS
		Jocelyn's Wharf
Jacobs, Abraham	Town carter	Brook
Jacobs, John	Corn factor/fruiterer	331 CHS
Jacobs, John	Agent for the sale of Packham's trusses & surgical bandages	331 CHS
Lazarus, Hermann	Photographist & picture dealer	Military Rd
Layzul, Abraham	Publican Maidstone Arms	Crow Lane, Roch
Levy, Charles	General dealer	High St, Strood
Levy, John Lewis	Coal merchant & general dealer	Chatham Intra

Levy, Nathan	Marine store dealer	North St, Strood
Lyons, Asher	Silversmith	332 CHS
Lyons, Ellis	Clothes dealer	Brook
Lyons, Simon	Silversmith	Eastgate, Roch
Magnus & Son	Coal merchant	324 CHS
Marks, John Montague & Isaac	Outfitters	86 CHS
		307 CHS
Pyke, Joseph	Silversmith	302 CHS
Samuel, Joseph	Clothes dealer	CHS
Samuels & Co	Curriers	Globe Lane
Schatzle, Xaver	Watchmaker	RHS
Sloman, Charles	Pawnbroker	46 CHS
Sloman, Joseph	Gentry	CHS
Solomon Samuel & Lewis	Navy agents	Hamond Place
Solomon, John & Charles	Upholsterers	260 CHS
		147 CHS
Solomon Louisa	Shopkeeper	Fair Row
Woolf, Myer	General dealer	CHS
Woolf, Samuel	Umbrella maker	CHS

The names below were extracted from the *Simpson Directory*, 1865. All streets are in Chatham unless stated. CHS = Chatham High Street; RHS = Rochester High Street.

Name	Occupation	Address
Abrahams, C	Clothier	Globe Lane
Barnard, D	China shop	79 CHS
	Upholsterer	309 CHS
Barnett & Co	Dyers & French cleaners	11 Military Rd
Barnett, B	General dealer	148 CHS
Barnett G	Publican, Marlborough Head	Frindsbury, Strood
Baurle, L	Watch & clock maker	391 RHS
Crowheim, J	Print seller & frame maker	7 Watts Place
De Frates, J	Beer retailer	Cazeneuve St, Roch
Frankenstein, L	Hairdresser & picture frame maker	20 Cazeneuve St, Roch
Goodman, Morris	Clothier	236 CHS
Haisman, Mrs	Gentry	7 Orange Terrace, Roch
Heizman, A	Watch & clockmaker	167 RHS
Hyman, Philip	Clock, watch maker, jeweller & silversmith	4 Military Rd
Jacob, R	Baker	Park Place, New Brompton
Layzul, Abraham	Publican, Maidstone Arms	Crow Lane Roch
Levy, C	Furniture broker & general dealer	49 High St, Strood
Levy, J L	Coal merchant	Chatham Intra
Lewin, G	Coal dealer	Brook
Lyon, S	Watch maker & jeweller	123 Eastgate, Roch
Lyons, A	Silversmith, etc	332 CHS
Lyons, Simon	Silversmith, watchmaker & jeweller	123 Eastgate, Roch
Maas, J W	Draper	306 CHS
Pyke, Joseph	Jeweller etc	Beacon Lodge, Chatham Hill (residence) 302 CHS
Riedel, L	Watchmaker	Medway St
Solomon, A	Beer retailer	King St, Roch

Samuel, Joseph	Clothier	198 CHS
Schultheiss, J T	Watchmaker	283a CHS
Solomon, A	Beer retailer	King St, Roch
Solomon, Isaac	Hardware man	CHS
Solomon, J[acob]	Surgeon	Fair Row
Solomon, J & C	Furniture brokers	260 CHS
Woolf, Samuel	Umbrella maker	350 CHS
Woolf M	Furniture broker	223 & 224 CHS

Appendix 10

List of residential rabbis of Chatham synagogue

t is difficult to draw up a definitive list of the rabbis. This is especially true in regard to the early years of the community. It is known that there was no residential rabbi in 1777. The records show that a marriage, which took place that year, was solemnised by a travelling Rabbi Ash of Dover, who was operating in London and Kent between 1768 and 1818.

Name	Years
The Rev Barlin	c.1802-c.1807
The Rev Abraham Lyon Benjamin	c.1808-1821?
The Rev Henry Levy	1821
The Rev Jeniel Phillips	1831-54
The Rev Lazarus Polack	1854-84
The Rev W. Barron (or Barren)	1884-85
The Rev Bernard Joshua Salomons	1885-97
The Rev Moses David Isaacs	1897-1903
The Rev Marks Fenton	1903-19
The Rev Joseph Babitz	1920-21
The Rev Abraham Samet	1923-29
The Rev Samuel Wolfe	1930-42

Appendix 11

Poems

The poems below refer to Jews and the Medway Towns. The first three poems, written by local poets, were published in the 18th century. The second set of three short poems, also written in the 18th century, gives us a glimpse of what people thought about the area and its residents. The last poem relates to the Jewish struggle for emancipation in the 19th century.

The following poem was written in 1756 by the Rev Thomas Austen, MA, Vicar of Allhallows, who became a minor canon at Rochester Cathedral. The poem was republished in the second volume of *The Kentish Garland* in 1882.

Some Verses on Stroud Fair, by the Rev Thomas Austen, 1756

A FAIR there us just centr'd in a Town,
More fam'd for ruder Fisherman than Clown,
Next to an open Marsh the Stalls are plac'd,
And with one double Row of trifles grac'd.
Here come, from Roffa's further Street, a throng
Of various Maidens, Beauties old and young,
Who, having laid aside for one small space,
Their darning, knitting, needlework, and Lace,
Like snow that gathers o'er ye ground,
In smaller parcels other heaps surround.
Each new Acquaintance from ev'ry quarter meet,

In gabbling prate much a dish of Chat complete;
These are in walking so cemented close,
That face to face they rush, and chin to nose:
Then laugh aloud, and frown, and bless the Fool
For awkward blindness just deriv'd from School,
Whose dangling sword blades dignify their skull
With much such grace as ribbons do a Trull.
Here titt'ring Miss advances in the rear,
And proudly urges you the way to clear:
That hence her Hoop may meet no flouting squeeze,
But safe convey her passing on with ease.
Here one remarks the garb, the gait, the view
Of all the male, or airy female crew.
Some with too many tawdries deck their head,
And scarce in form, if better taught than fed.
This ogling sly, This bridling up her chin,
Would fain be deem'd a mortal Seraphin.
With eyes aslant some mark what others buy,
Unnotic'd, wou'd your gen'rous temper try.
This thoughtful Sage steps slow, with glove and cane,
And moralizes on each Object vain;
Another wishes for the Evening's close,
For nappy ale and pipe to toast his nose:
With oysters fresh, and Company beside,
Voluptuously to make his minutes glide.
Here nuts and almonds in the whole heaps are spread;
Here Children gaping squall for Gingerbread.
Here some with copper halfpence try their luck,
And others urge th' advent'rous chance of Chuck.
Here ribbons, ear-rings, grace a Lady's stall;
There other fancies do the Eyes enthrall.
Here Jews, with pencils, seals, and gaudy rings,
Convert your money into needless things.
But would you have the Quintessence of all,

Then step you to the Oyster-wenches' Stall;
There crabs and shrimps (both stinking) new you'l buy,
Your palate teasing till you come to try.
The Noise thus made alarms each gaping Fool,
With much Proverbial Cry, but little Wool.

The poem below appeared in the *Kentish Gazette* on 19 November 1771 and was republished in 1882 the second volume of *The Kentish Garland*.

The Chathamites, A Song (Tune — Nancy Dawson)
Of all the spots on Britain's shore,
Examine ev'ry country o'er,
Sure ne'er was seen the like before,
The well-known town of Chatham.

Fair truth directs my honest muse,
Here drunken soldiers and ship crews,
Whores, Baptists, Methodists, and Jews,
Swarm ev'ry part of Chatham.

Possess'd of ev'ry female grace,
Of shape, and air, and blooming face,
By Nature made for Love's embrace,
Are fam'd the Girls of Chatham.

Whene'er inclin'd to am'rous play
The wanton God points out the way,
The who so kind, and fond as they?
Ask all the Bucks of Chatham.

Great shade of Hoyle, assist my quill,
To tell how much thy dear Quadrille,
Is eager sought Old Time to kill,
In every house of Chatham.

Such ruptures rushing through each breast,
When e'er a Pool the Gamester's blest;
"What pity Sunday's made for rest!"
Exclaim the Belles of Chatham.

Proud Rochester and Strood may talk
Of pavements smooth, and roads of chalk,
For those who chuse to ride or walk:
Not so the folks of Chatham.

Contented in their dirty hole,
They hobble on with meaner soul,
Contriving how to save the cole;
Who would not live at Chatham?

The poem below originally appeared in the fourth volume of the
Canterbury Journal **on 8 October 1771 and was republished in 1881 in**
the first volume of ***The Kentish Garland.***

A *Tour through Kent. By West-country party. An irregular Ode.*

The tenth of May, At break of day, Our Joe and I, and sister Dolly,
And uncle George, and couzen Polly,
Down we went, Helter, skelter, Into Kent:
Hurry, Scurry, Down we went.

The road was dousty; hedges white; And such a cloud Along the road,
You could not zee us out of zight.
My couzen Poll And zister Doll Rode gallop, heigh, ge, ho!
And uncle George, and I and Joe, Vull of laughter, Rode vast after:
So we went Hoity, toity, Into Kent, Into Kent:
Whisky, Vrisky, Down we went.

At Zhooter's-hill we made an halt, For Polly's Zaddle was in vault;

And Joe was dry, And so was I, But George was wonderous testy;
Then Dolly zaid, "As I'm a maid, I'ze travel not zo hasty"-
We call'd a pot Of piping hot, But Couzen wodna tas'te it;
Zo George and she Had gin and tea, And zister call'd for rattifee,
But I warrant they didna wast it:
Zo we went, Cherry, merry, Into Kent, Into Kent,
Winking, blinking, Down we went.

At Dartford we heard how a Gauger was skeer'd,
Who to zearch in a hearse had a vancy;
Thof the driver did zwear he had only a Bear,
That could handle a musquet and dance-y.
Then poor master Gage flew outright in a rage,
And zowre like a zailor at Whapping,
If the Mabob was there, with old Scratch and a Bear,
He'd zeize every zoul of 'um napping;
Zo Whipcord alighted and open'd the door,
While the Gauger, cock-zure of a hundred,
Pop'd into the hearse — Whipcord zhut it zecure,
And away with his carriage he thunder'd.
A Greenland Bear with zaucer eyes Was in the hearse zecreated;
Gage view'd the moster with zurprize, And dropt a zent most vetid.
He hallo'd aloud, Protezted and vow'd
If Whipcord would open the door
And once set him clear From the paws of the Bear,
He'd ne'er zearch his vehicle more.
But deaf as a stone Old Whipcord was grown
To the cries of the woeful Exzise-man;
Nor did he release Poor Gage from disgrace
Till he promis'd at act like a wize-man.
Dolly laugh'd at the joke Till her lacing was broke;
Joe laugh'd till he waundry near split was,
Uncle zhook his vat zide, Couzen laugh'd till she cry'd,
But I conna zee where the wit was.

Thus we went, Touzy, blousy, Into Kent, Into Kent,
Tattle, prattle, Down we went.

At Rochester a bridge we past, Zo high no rain can vlood ye,
And underneath a river vlows With rapid stream and muddy.
A narrow turn, and winding, Leads hence into the Zitty,
Where we zaw naught worth minding To grace a tale or ditty.
But when we came to Chatham, Zure ! how we wonder'd at 'um!
There was zuch a racket With trouser and jacket,
With zhipwrights, and blackzmiths, and ropers,
We thought we were got in A place vull of zotting,
'Mongst mariners, mermaids, and topers.
Zo we went, Hurly burley, Through Kent, Through Kent,
Vlaring, staring, Thus we went.

Joe sed he never saw a dock, Zave Varmer Ploughshear's villy,
And that the Varrier (being drunk) Cut off amazing zilly.
Zo we agreed, without dispute, That Joe shud see the dock-head,
And when he view'd the wond'rous zight, He gap'd like any block-head.
A zhip there was a hugey zize, Upon the stocks a building,
As bigger than a country barn As elephant than gelding.
They zhow'd us cannons zmall and great, With grape-zhot, bombs, and mortars,
And zed that these were made to kill The heathen Jews and Tartars.
Joe thought it was a burning shame, With those destructive things,
To murder Martyrs, Turks, and Jews, And all to pleasure Kings.
Here was hemp in zuch stores (They zed, beaten by……)
As would vurnish out plenty of halters,
To hang in terrorem Great villains, and Quorum, Are — and public Defaulters.
Zo we went, Prying, spying, Through Kent, Through Kent,
Wond'ring, blund'ring, Thus we went.

Richard Ranger

The following set of three short poems by G.M. Woodward originally appeared as 'written by a Tourist in 1790' in *Eccentric Excursions of Literary and Pictorial Sketches of Conntenance, Characters and Country in Different Parts of England and South Wales interspersed with curious Anecdotes....* The volume was published in London in 1796 by Allen & Co. It gives us an insight into three of the Medway Towns — the cathedral city of Rochester, Chatham with its masculine and rowdy atmosphere of sailors and soldiers, and Strood, which is on the other side of the River Medway. And though Jews are not explicitly mentioned, their presence is implied in the occupations of tailors and slopmen.

'Rob'em, Starve'em and Cheat'em' stated a contemporary proverb; or as an 'intelligent foreigner' M. Aubry de La Motraye affirmed in 1725, quoted in *The Kentish Garland*: '[the towns] make up a kind of Triopolis or Triple City'.

The poems are extracted from the book by Smetham, Henry (1899) *History of Strood*. Strood: Parrett and Neves.

The People of Stroud

'The people of Stroud,
Talk long and talk loud,
And herd in a croud,
Traducing their innocent neighbours;
While envy by fits
Mid the congress sits,
Gives a whet to their wits,
And smiles on their scandalous labours.

This place, like an eel,
Where the publicans steal,
Is dirty, base, long, foul, and slippery;
And the belles flirt about,
With their persons deck'd out,
With run muslin, and second-hand frippery.

'Rochester's a town
Of specious renown,
Full of tinkers and taylors,
And slopmen and sailors,
And magistrates who often blunder'd;
Coquettes without beauty,
Old maids past their duty,
And Venus' gay nymphs by the hundred.

Vile inns without beds,
And men without heads,
By which poor Britannia's undone;
Extortionate bills,
Anti-venery pills,
And port manufactur'd in London.

Honest DICK WATTS of yore,
Their good name to restore,
Decreed (such enormities scorning)
Each travelling wight,
A warm couch for the night,
And fourpence in cash in the morning.

'Old Chatham's a place,
That's the nation's disgrace,
Where the club and the fist prove the law, sir;
And presumption is seen
To direct the marine,
Who know not a spike from a hawser.

Here the dolts show with pride
How the men-of-war ride,
Who Gallia's proud first-rates can shiver,
And a fortified hill
All the Frenchmen to kill
That land on the banks of the river!

Such towns and such men,
We shall ne'er see again,
Where smuggling's a laudable function;
In some high windy day,
May the de'el fly away
With the whole of the dirty conjunction.'

The poem below comes of the Kent History Centre's collection of political posters (U1210/Z3). It was written and widely circulated in the 1850s, while a debate about allowing Jews to take seat in parliament took place. Sir Walter Buchanan Riddell unsuccessfully contested West Kent seat in 1857 parliamentary election as a Tory candidate.

RIDDDEL'S Proud Boast!
Sing hey, diddle, diddle,
Says candidate Riddle,
I don't care a rap for the Blues;
They may chuckle and laugh,
They may spurn me as chaff,
But something I'll pledge, win or lose.

For the Church, Queen and State,
I'll uphold every rate,
To keep the Dissenters in awe:
And as for relaxing,
The system of taxing,
I'll never consent to such law.

But the Grant to Maynooth,
I'll oppose nail and tooth!
Because it will vex poor old Pam!
Yet the truth I'll declare,
I believe in Grant fair!!
And ought to be paid without sham.

Now the Ballot comes next,
'Tis a Chartist pretext
Which purple and orange can't stand:
'T will damage conversion,
Destroy our coercion!!
And knock up the great feudal band:

No! No! my brave Tories,
We'll stick to our glories;
Nor yield up a tittle of right:
Let the renegade Blues
Fraternise with the Jews;
But the Ballot, we'll choke the first night.

The Jews are all fretting,
The Commons to get in;
The Whigs give them courage and hope;
But I'll take jolly care
They shall never get there:
I'll die first — or hang in a rope!

Then tune up the fiddle,
With hey diddle, diddle;
The purple and orange for me:
I'll prop up the Tories,
(Tho' rotten their core is!)
Triumphant my flag you shall see.

Notes

Abbreviations used for the following periodicals:
CN: the *Chatham News*
CO: the *Chatham Observer*
ILN: the *Illustrated London News*
JC: the *Jewish Chronicle*
RG: the *Rochester Gazette*
SE Gazette: the *South East Gazette*

Chapter 1. The First Community: from William the Conqueror to Edward I, 1066-1290

1 Appelbaum, Shimon (1951) 'Were there Jews in Roman Britain?', *Transactions JHSE* v17, p189-205.

2 Mundill, Robin R. (2010) *The King's Jews: Money, Massacre and Exodus in Medieval England*. London: Continuum, pp1-20.

3 Romain, Jonathan (2011) 'River Jews: Medieval Jews along the Thames as a Microcosm of Anglo-Jewry', *Transactions JHSE* v43, p21.

4 Hurscroft, Richard (2006) *Expulsion: England's Jewish Solution*. Stroud: Tempus.

5 Romain, Jonathan (2011) 'River Jews: Medieval Jews along the Thames as a Microcosm of Anglo-Jewry', *Transactions JHSE* v43, p22.

6 Hertz, J.H., ed. (1937) Pentateuch & Haftorahs. 2nd ed. London: Soncino Press.

7 Mundill, Robin R. (2010) *The King's Jews:*

Money, Massacre and Exodus in Medieval England. London: Continuum, p5; Golb, N. (2012) *The Jews in Medieval Normandy — a Social and Intellectual History*. Cambridge: Cambridge UP, p114.

8 Romain, Jonathan (2011) 'River Jews: Medieval Jews along the Thames as a Microcosm of Anglo-Jewry', *Transactions JHSE* v43, p23.

9 Lipman, Vivian D. (1965) 'The Anatomy of Medieval Anglo-Jewry', *Transactions JHSE* v21, p72.

10 Romain, Jonathan (2011) 'River Jews: Medieval Jews along the Thames as a Microcosm of Anglo-Jewry', *Transactions JHSE* v43, p21-42; Lipman, V.D. (1981) 'Jews and Castles in Medieval England', *Transactions JHSE* v28, pp1-18.

11 Hillaby, Joe (1990) 'London: the 13th-Century Jewry revisited', *Transactions JHSE* v32, p100.

12 Smith, Frederick F. (1928) *A History of Rochester*. London: The Daniel Company, p6.

13 RCA/L2/32/66.

14 *www.opendomesday.org*, accessed 14/12/16.

15 Oakley, Anne M. (1975) 'The Cathedral Priory of St. Andrew, Rochester', *Archaeologia Cantiana* v91, p48-50.

16 Hope, W.H. St John (1898) 'The Architectural History of the Cathedral Church and Monastery of St. Andrew at Rochester', *Archaeologia Cantiana* v23, p.227; Gervais of Canterbury, *Opera Historica* (Rolls Series 73), i. 100 Cott. MS *Vespasian* A. 22 (f.28b); Cott. MS, *Vespasian* A. 22, f. 30; Gervais of Canterbury, *Opera Historica* (Rolls Series 73), i. 292.

17 Jacobs, Joseph (1893) *The Jews of Angevin England: Documents and Records from Latin and Hebrew Sources, Printed and Manuscript, for the First Time Collected and Translated*. London; p73; 27 Hen, II, Sudhantesc.
Indeed, Rochester at that time possessed a mint. The city had acquired its own mint by 810 and continued till the reign of King John. (Pyrefoy, Peter B (2008) 'The Coinage of William I in Kent', *Archaeologia Cantiana* v128, p60; Smith, Frederick F (1928) *A History of Rochester*. London: The Daniel Company, p231).

18 Jacobs, Joseph (1893) *The Jews of Angevin England: Documents and Records from Latin and Hebrew Sources, Printed and Manuscript, for the First Time Collected and Translated*. London; p90; Pipe Rolls 32 Henry II, p192; Pipe Rolls 32 Hen II, Chent.

19 Brown, Reva B. & Sean McCartney (2004) 'David of Oxford and Licoricia of Winchester: Glimpses into a Jewish Family in Thirteenth-Century England', *Transactions JHSE* v39, pp1-34.

20 Hope, W.H. St John (1900) 'The Architectural History of the Cathedral

Church and Monastery of St Andrew at Rochester', *Archaeologia Cantiana* v24, p60.

21 Roth, Cecil (1949) *A History of the Jews in England*. 2nd ed. Oxford: Clarendon Press, pp10-11; *medium.com/the-christ-church-heritage-a-to-z/j-is-for-jewry-682baec8da11*, accessed 24/05/2020.

22 Hurscroft, Richard (2006) *Expulsion: England's Jewish Solution*. Stroud: Tempus, p51.

23 Hillaby, Joe (2013) 'Prelude and Postscript to the York Massacre: Attacks in east Anglia and Lincolnshire', in Jones, Sarah Rees and Sethina Watson, eds. *Christians and Jews in Angevin England: The York Massacre of 1190, Narratives and Contexts*. York: Boydell & Brewer, York Medieval Press, p52.

24 Adler, Michael (1911) 'The Jews of Canterbury', *Transactions JHSE* v7, p24.

25 Hillaby, Joe (1992) 'The London Jewry: William I to John' *Transactions JHSE* v33, p37; Rymer, T., Foedera (1816) Record Commission Ii, 51.

26 Hurscroft, Richard (2006) *Expulsion: England's Jewish Solution*. Stroud: Tempus, p56.

27 Adler, Michael (1911) 'The Jews of Canterbury', *Transactions JHSE* v7, p26.

28 Adler, Michael (1911) 'The Jews of Canterbury', *Transactions JHSE* v7, pp19-96; PRO Exchequer KR, accounts No 249.2.

29 DRc/T572/14.

30 Anon (1772) *The History and Antiquities of Rochester and its Environs. Rochester*: Fisher, pp129-130.

31 Newark hospital marks the foundation of Strood as a separate independent parish. (Smetham, Henry (1899) *History of Strood*. Strood: Parrett & Neves, p1).

32 Bishop Glanville died in 1214 and was buried in the cathedral, on the north side.

The chronicler in recording his death, gleefully adds 'that he was buried like Jews and heretics, without the Divine offices, because he died during the Interdict, and that as soon as he was buried, the Interdict was removed'. (Hope, W.H. St John (1898) 'The Architectural History of the Cathedral Church and Monastery of St. Andrew at Rochester', *Archaeologia Cantiana* v23, p313).

33 Oakley, Anne M. (1975) 'The Cathedral Priory of St. Andrew, Rochester', *Archaeologia Cantiana* v91, pp50-52.

34 Epstein, I (1935) 'Pre-Expulsion England in the Responsa', *Transactions JHSE* v14, pp187-205; Lipman, Vivian D (1965) 'The Anatomy of Medieval Anglo-Jewry', *Transactions JHSE* v21, pp64-77.

35 Jenkinson, Hilary (1915) 'Records of Exchequer Receipts from the English Jewry', *Transactions JHSE* v8, p43.

36 Elman, Peter (1945) 'Jewish Finance in Thirteenth-century England' *Transactions JHSE* v16, p93.

37 Mundill, Robin R. (2010) *The King's Jews: Money, Massacre and Exodus in Medieval England*. London: Continuum, p62.

38 Epstein, I (1935) 'Pre-Expulsion England in the Responsa', *Transactions JHSE* v14, pp203-204.

39 Cott MS Nero D. 2, f. 123.

40 William was officially canonised in 1256.

41 Hurscroft, Richard (2006) *Expulsion: England's Jewish Solution*. Stroud: Tempus, pp59-60.

42 Mundill, Robin R. (2010) *The King's Jews: Money, Massacre and Exodus in Medieval England*. London: Continuum, p150.

43 Rigg, J.M., ed. (1905) *Calendar of Plea Rolls of the Exchequer of the Jews*. v1 London: Macmillan, p15, membrane 4d.

44 Fine Roll C 60/29, 14 Henry III (1229-30), membrane 7.

45 Martin, C. Trice (1896) 'Documents Relating to the History of the Jews in the Thirteenth Century', *Transactions JHSE* v3, p198; Close Rolls 15 Henry III.

46 Fine Roll C 60/52, membrane 14; Fine Roll C 60/52, membrane 13.

47 Mundill, Robin R (2010) *The King's Jews: Money, Massacre and Exodus in Medieval England*. London: Continuum, pp104-5.

48 Mundill, Robin R. (2010) *The King's Jews: Money, Massacre and Exodus in Medieval England*. London: Continuum, pp108-109.

49 Anon (1894) 'Jewish Tallies of the Thirteenth Century' *Transactions JHSE* v2 miscellanies, p20; Stacey, Robert C (1985) 'Royal Taxation and the Social Structure of Medieval Anglo-Jewry: The Tallages of 1239-1242' *Hebrew Union College Annual*, p215; (online); accessed 24/05/2020 Available from *www. academia.edu/37074665/Robert_C._ Stacey_Royal_Taxation_and_the_Social_ Structure_of_Medieval_Anglo-Jewry_The_ Tallages_of_1239-1242_Hebrew_Union_ College_Annual_56_1985_175-249.*

50 Smetham, Henry (1899) *History of Strood*. Strood: Parrett & Neves; pp149-150.

51 Lord, Evelyn (2004) *The Knights Templar in Britain*. Harlow: Pearson.

52 Churchill, Irene J., Griffin, Ralph and F. W. Hardman, eds. (1956) *Calendar of Kent Feet of Fines to the End of Henry III's Reign*. Ashford: KAS, p71.

53 Churchill, Irene J., Griffin, Ralph and F. W. Hardman, eds. (1956) *Calendar of Kent Feet of Fines to the End of Henry III's Reign*. Ashford: KAS, p75.

54 Churchill, Irene J., Griffin, Ralph and F. W. Hardman, eds. (1956) *Calendar of Kent Feet of Fines to the End of Henry III's Reign*. Ashford: KAS, p81.

55 Smetham, Henry (1899) *History of Strood*. Strood: Parrett & Neves, p252.

56 Barber, Malcolm (1994) *The New Knighthood: a History of the Order of the Temple*. Cambridge: Cambridge UP.

57 Tout, T.F. (1967) *Chapters in Medieval Administrative History of Medieval England; the Wardrobe, the Chamber, and the Small Seals*. Manchester: Manchester University Press; New York, Barnes & Noble, i. 250, 181; M.P., i. 175; p127.

58 Mundill, Robin R (2010) *The King's Jews: Money, Massacre and Exodus in Medieval England. London*: Continuum, pp88-89; Rigg, J.M., ed. (1905) *Calendar of Plea Rolls of the Exchequer of the Jews*. v1; London: Macmillan, pp132-133.

59 Smith, Frederick F. (1928) *A History of Rochester*. London: Daniel Company; pp19-21; Cotton MS, Nero D ii, Brit Mus.

60 PRO E/101/249/10.

61 Adler, Michael (1911) 'The Jews of Canterbury', *Transactions JHSE* v7, p43. However, only two years after the horrors of the Baronial War we find that Isaac, son of Benedict of Bedford, and Sampson, son of Josce, pay 1 bezant each to leave Canterbury and reside in Sittingbourne. Also, Leo, son of Solomon pays 1 bezant to leave Canterbury to live in Ospringe. (Rigg, J.M., ed. (1905) *Calendar of Plea Rolls of the Exchequer of the Jews*. v1; London: Macmillan, p134).

62 Romain, Jonathan (2011) 'River Jews: Medieval Jews along the Thames as a Microcosm of Anglo-Jewry', *Transactions JHSE* v43, p22.

63 Rigg, J.M. (1901) *Select Pleas, Starrs, and Other Records from the Rolls of the Exchequer of the Jews, AD 1220-64* vXV. Selden Society; ppli-lv.

64 Mundill, Robin R. (2002) *England's Jewish Solution: Experiment and Expulsion, 1262-90* Cambridge: Cambridge UP, p119; B Cotton MS Nero D ii, folio 179.

65 Adler, Michael (1911) 'The Jews of Canterbury', *Transactions JHSE* v7, p53.

66 Elman, Peter (1945) 'Jewish Finance in Thirteenth-Century England', *Transactions JHSE* v16, p96.

67 Mundill, Robin R. (1988) 'Anglo-Jewry under Edward I: Credit Agents and Their Clients', *Transactions JHSE* v31, p4.

68 Close Rolls 1272-79 Edward I P 362; Membrane 13.

69 Rigg, J.M. (1901) *Select Pleas, Starrs, and Other Records from the Rolls of the Exchequer of the Jews, A.D. 1220-1264* vXV. Selden Society, p78.

70 Rigg, J.M., ed. (1905) *Calendar of Plea Rolls of the Exchequer of the Jews*. v2; London: Macmillan, p242.

71 Hillaby, Joe (1990) 'London: the 13th-Century Jewry revisited', *Transactions JHSE* v32, p152; Close Rolls 1290, 96; Mundill, R.R. (1990) 'Jewish Entries in the Patent Rolls, 1272-1290' *Transactions JHSE* v32, p83; Patent Rolls 205 27 July 1290 378.

72 Roth, Cecil (1949) *A History of the Jews in England*. 2nd ed. Oxford: Clarendon Press, p85. Both destructions of the Jewish First and the Second Temple occurred on the 9th of Av, though 655 years apart. Jews were expelled from England and Spain on the 9 Av, 18 July 1290 and 31 July 1492 respectively.

Av is the 11th month of the civil year and the fifth month of the ecclesiastical year in the Hebrew calendar. It usually falls on July or August.

73 Mundill, Robin R. (2010) *The King's Jews: Money, Massacre and Exodus in Medieval England. London*: Continuum, p158.

74 Elman, Peter (1945) 'Jewish Finance in Thirteenth-century England' *Transactions JHSE* v16, pp89-96.

75 Mundill, Robin R. (2010) *The King's Jews:*

Money, Massacre and Exodus in Medieval England. London: Continuum, p157.

76 Mundill, Robin R. (2010) *The King's Jews: Money, Massacre and Exodus in Medieval England*. London: Continuum, p159.

Chapter 2. Out/with the Jews, 1290-1656

1 Adler, Michael (1899) 'History of the 'Domus Conversorum' from 1290 to 1891', *Transactions JHSE* v4, pp53-54.

2 Adler, Michael (1899) 'History of the 'Domus Conversorum' from 1290 to 1891', *Transactions JHSE* v4, pp27-28.

Domus Conversorum continued to receive baptised Jews, almost without a break to the days of James I. Adler states that there were no admissions of Jews to the Domus after 1609. However, in 1717 an application was made was made for the payment of the royal pension to a converted Jew in London. (Adler, Michael (1899) 'History of the 'Domus Conversorum' from 1290 to 1891', *Transactions JHSE* v4, p21, 49).

3 Edwards, Lewis (1953) 'Some Examples of the Mediaeval Representation of Church and Synagogue', *Transactions JHSE* v18, p63, 66-67.

The figure of the church was 'restored' by the architect Lewis Nockalls Cottingham, who carried out the restoration of Rochester Cathedral in 1825-30. Either ignoring or being ignorant of the iconographical significance of the figure, he decorated it with the mitred bearded bishop's head. The mistake was corrected only in the 1890s by the efforts of Miss Louisa Twining, writer on ecclesiastical iconography and a major social reformer. (Hope, W.H. St John (1898) 'The Architectural History of the Cathedral Church and Monastery of St. Andrew at Rochester', *Archaeologia*

Cantiana v23, p76).

4 Smith, Frederick F. (1928) *A History of Rochester*. London: The Daniel Company, p285.

5 Hope, W.H. St John (1898) 'The Architectural History of the Cathedral Church and Monastery of St. Andrew at Rochester', *Archaeologia Cantiana* v23, pp1-85.

6 Livett, Grenvile M (1895) 'Mediaeval Rochester', *Archaeologia Cantiana* v21, pp56-58.

7 Anon (1772) *The History and Antiquities of Rochester and its Environs*. Rochester: Fisher, p203.

8 *The Guardian* 4/5/2012.

9 Julius, Anthony (2010) *Trials of the Diaspora: a History of Anti-Semitism in England*. Oxford UP, pp167-170.

10 Wolf, Lucien (1919) *Notes on the Diplomatic History of the Jewish Question* (online). London: Spottiswoode, p126; accessed 22/06/2018 Available from *archive.org/details/ notesondiplomati00wolfuoft/page/126/ mode/2up*.

11 Conversos (old term Marranos) were crypto-Jews, or 'New Christians', the Jews of Spain and Portugal, who were forced to convert to Christianity. Outwardly, they behaved as Catholics by attending church and participating in all services. However, in privacy of their homes they secretly continued to practise Judaism, despite the permanent threat from the Inquisition.

12 Roth, Cecil (1949) *A History of the Jews in England*. 2nd ed. Oxford: Clarendon Press, p136-7.

13 Fines, John (1962) 'Judaising' in the Period of the English Reformation — The Case of Richard Bruern', *Transactions JHSE* v21, p145.

14 Councer, C.R. (1935) 'The Dissolution

of the Kentish Monasteries', *Archaeologia Cantiana* v47, p131.

15 Bishop John Fisher (*c.* 9 October 1469-22 June 1535), Master of Queen's College, Cambridge, and chancellor of the university, was appointed to the See of Rochester in 1504. During his 31 years of tenure he mostly resided in Rochester. He was imprisoned in the Tower of London on 21 April 1534 for upholding the Roman Catholic Church's doctrine of papal supremacy, and for refusing to accept the king as supreme head of the Church of England. He was executed on Tower Hill on 22 June 1535 and subsequently declared a martyr and saint by the Catholic church. (Anon (1772) *The History and Antiquities of Rochester and its Environs. Rochester*: Fisher, pp153-154).

16 Flaherty, W.E. (1859) 'A Help Toward a Kentish Monasticon', *Archaeologia Cantiana* v2, pp50-51.

17 At the time of dissolution, the priory's value was £486 11s 5d.

18 Anon (1772) *The History and Antiquities of Rochester and its Environs. Rochester*: Fisher, pp79-80.

19 Flaherty, W.E. (1859) 'A Help Toward a Kentish Monasticon', *Archaeologia Cantiana* v2, p58.

20 Anon (1772) *The History and Antiquities of Rochester and its Environs. Rochester*: Fisher, p82.

21 Anon (1772) *The History and Antiquities of Rochester and its Environs. Rochester*: Fisher, p85.

22 Prior, Roger (1988) 'A Second Jewish Community in Tudor London', *Transactions JHSE* v31, p149.

23 Roth, Cecil (1949) *A History of the Jews in England*. 2nd ed. Oxford: Clarendon Press, p146.

24 Fines, John (1962) ''Judaising' in the Period

of the English Reformation — The Case of Richard Bruern', *Transactions JHSE* v21, p323; 325.

25 Roth, Cecil (1949) *A History of the Jews in England*. 2nd ed. Oxford: Clarendon Press, p132.

26 Wolf, Lucien (1924) 'Jews in Elizabethan England', *Transactions JHSE* v11, p3 note 4.

27 Wolf, Lucien (1924) 'Jews in Elizabethan England', *Transactions JHSE* v11, p4.

28 Prior, Roger (1988) 'A Second Jewish Community in Tudor London', *Transactions JHSE* v31, p149.

29 Roth, Cecil (1949) *A History of the Jews in England*. 2nd ed. Oxford: Clarendon Press, p139.

30 Roth, Cecil (1949) *A History of the Jews in England*. 2nd ed. Oxford: Clarendon Press, pp139-140.

31 Roth, Cecil (1949) *A History of the Jews in England*. 2nd ed. Oxford: Clarendon Press, pp143-144.

32 Julius, Anthony (2010) *Trials of the Diaspora: a History of Anti-Semitism in England*. Oxford UP, p176.

33 Julius, Anthony (2010) *Trials of the Diaspora: a History of Anti-Semitism in England*. Oxford UP, pp178-184.

34 Julius, Anthony (2010) *Trials of the Diaspora: a History of Anti-Semitism in England*. Oxford UP, pp178-184.

35 Adler, Michael (1899) 'History of the 'Domus Conversorum' from 1290 to 1891', *Transactions JHSE* v4, pp41-49.

36 Chambers, E.K. (1923) The Elizabethan Stage. v3; Oxford: Claredon Press, pp424–5.

37 RCA/N1/1.

Chapter 3. The Return, 17th century

1 Como, David R. (2004), *Oxford Dictionary*

273

of National Biography

2   Phillips, Henry E. I. (1939) 'An Early Stuart Judaising Sect', *Transactions JHSE* v15, p67.

3   Roth, Cecil (1955) 'The Middle Period of Anglo-Jewish History (1290-1655) Reconsidered', *Transactions JHSE* v19, p12.

4   Samuel, Edgar (1988) 'The Readmission of the Jews to England in 1656, in the Context of English Economic Policy', *Transactions JHSE* v31, pp153-155.

5   Roth, Cecil (1955) 'The Middle Period of Anglo-Jewish History (1290-1655) Reconsidered', *Transactions JHSE* v19, p12. John Warner, Bishop of Rochester, was described in a satirical piece published in 1641 as someone who 'had many rusty bagges in his Chests. On which dish he did eate so immoderately, that whosoever looked on him, supposed he had a Hogshead' — probably alluding to his attempts at self-promotion and pursuit of worldly gain'. (Clement, Catharina (2008) 'Role of the Cathedral 1640-1660'. Transcript of the lecture given on 21 June. Unpublished.).

6   Samuel, Edgar (1988) 'The Readmission of the Jews to England in 1656, in the Context of English Economic Policy', *Transactions JHSE* v31, pp160-161.

7   Daniel 12:7.

8   Deuteronomy 28:64.

9   Roth, Cecil (1949) *A History of the Jews in England*. 2nd ed. Oxford: Clarendon Press, pp161-162.

10   Levy, S. (1908) 'Anglo-Jewish Historiography', *Transactions JHSE* v6, p6.

11   Samuel, Edgar (1988) 'The Readmission of the Jews to England in 1656, in the Context of English Economic Policy', *Transactions JHSE* v31, p165.

12   Samuel, Edgar (1988) 'The Readmission of the Jews to England in 1656, in the Context of English Economic Policy', *Transactions JHSE* v31, pp165-166. See note 54.

13   Roth, Cecil (1924) 'New Light on the Resettlement', *Transactions JHSE* v11, pp131-133.

14   Roth, Cecil (1949) *A History of the Jews in England*. 2nd ed. Oxford: Clarendon Press, pp165-166.

15   Only after the Toleration Act of 1689 did public synagogues became a feasibility. However, the community were brave enough to build a public synagogue for their worship only in 1701 (Diamond, A.S. (1970) 'The Community of the Resettlement, 1656-1684: a Social Survey', *Transactions JHSE* v24, p134).

16   Diamond, A.S. (1970) 'The Community of the Resettlement, 1656-1684: a Social Survey', *Transactions JHSE* v24, p146.

17   Diamond, A.S. (1970) 'The Community of the Resettlement, 1656-1684: a Social Survey', *Transactions JHSE* v24, pp149-150.

18   Woolf, Lucien (1902) 'The Jewry of the Restoration: 1660-1664', *Transactions JHSE* v5, pp10-13.

19   Woolf, Lucien (1902) 'The Jewry of the Restoration: 1660-1664', *Transactions JHSE* v5, p15.

20   Woolf, Lucien (1902) 'The Jewry of the Restoration: 1660-1664', *Transactions JHSE* v5, p16.

21   Levy, S. (1908) 'Anglo-Jewish Historiography', *Transactions JHSE* v6, pp7-8.

22   Lincoln, F. Ashe (1945) 'The Non-Christian Oath in English Law', *Transactions JHSE* v16, pp74-75. The arguments used to determine the admissibility of Jewish evidence in courts were used later in the 18th century to accept evidence from Hindu and Muslim

witnesses.

The final decision on whether a non-Christian witness was able to give evidence was reached in Chancery on 23 February 1744 in the case Omichund v Barker. The problem was because of the doubt if a charge of perjury could be maintained against a non-Christian or anyone not sworn upon the New Testament. The decision stated that 'an Infidel in general cannot be excluded from being a witness'. (Lincoln, F. Ashe (1945) 'The Non-Christian Oath in English Law', *Transactions JHSE* v16, pp73, 76).

23   Roth, Cecil (1949) *A History of the Jews in England*. 2nd ed. Oxford: Clarendon Press, pp179-181.

24   Ashbee, Andrew (2008) 'Lupo, Thomas (bap. 1571?-1627-28?), Violinist and Composer', *Oxford Dictionary of National Biography* (online). London: Oxford UP; accessed 18/11/2018 Available from *www.oxforddnb.com/view/10.1093/ref:odnb/9780198614128.001 0001/ odnb-9780198614128 -e-17199*.

25   Brenchley-Rye, William (1866) 'Visits to Rochester and Chatham Made by Royal, Noble, and Distinguished Personages, English and Foreign, from the Year 1300 to 1783', *Archaeologia Cantiana* v6, pp70-71.

26   Smith, Frederick F. (1928) *A History of Rochester*. London: The Daniel Company, pp184-186.

27   DRC/FTB/10.

28   DRC/FTB/17.

29   DRC/FTB/18.

30   DRC/FTB/18.

31   Chalklin, Christopher W. (1978) *Seventeenth-Century Kent: a Social and Economic History*. Rochester: Hallewell Publications , p173.

In September 1660 the Rochester population was estimated to be 1,113. However,

these were presumably adults over 16, and children were not taken into account. The more accurate figure would be, according to Arnold, 1,600, but even that one is probably an underestimate. (Arnold, A.A. (1914) 'The Poll Tax in Rochester, September 1660', *Archaeologia Cantiana* v30, p9).

32   Smith, Frederick F. (1928) *A History of Rochester*. London: The Daniel Company, p384.

33   MacDougall, Philip (1999) *Chatham Past*. Chichester: Phillimore, p1.

34   MacDougall, Philip (1999) *Chatham Past*. Chichester: Phillimore, p23.

35   Presnail, James (1952) *Chatham: a Story of a Dockyard Town and the Birthplace of the British Navy*. Chatham: Corporation of Chatham, p133.

36   Presnail, James (1952) *Chatham: a Story of a Dockyard Town and the Birthplace of the British Navy*. Chatham: Corporation of Chatham, pp133-134.

37   Steel, D.J. (1974) *National Index of Parish Registers, 3 Sources for Roman Catholic and Jewish Genealogy and Family History*. London: Society of Genealogists, pp968-969.

Chapter 4. Settling in the area, from the 18th to the early 19th century, part 1

1   To become a British subject otherwise than by birth, two procedures existed side by side till 1844 — denization and naturalisation. In the early times a person with a status of a liege subject of the Crown, either by birth or by grant, was known as a 'denizen', and granting of the status was known as denization or endenization.

Originally granted by the king by letters patent, in the 16th century the grant of the denizen status became also possible to obtain by the act of parliament. From the early 17th century the lawyers came to a conclusion that letters patent made the individual in question a denizen only for the future, *ie* from the moment of endenization. As a result, the person was unable to inherit or enable others to inherit from or through him. An act of parliament, on the other hand, could make the person a subject by birth.

This difference in status marked the distinction between the denization (by the letter patent) and naturalisation (by an act of parliament). The clause in the act of 1609 required the acceptance of the Sacrament by the person, who wanted to be naturalised. As a result, Jews as well as Roman Catholics were disqualified for parliamentary naturalisation. The clause remained in the statutes till 1826, when parliament passed a statute (6 George IV, cap. 67) removing the compulsory requirement of taking the Sacrament according to the rites of Church of England before naturalisation, thus achieving the goal of the 'Jew Bill' of 1753.

However, the requirement for the Oaths of Allegiance and Supremacy continued until 1844, when they were substituted by a new oath. An act of parliament (7 & 8 Vic. C66) also empowered the home secretary to grant certificates of naturalisation. However, they did not grant the full status of the British subject till the Naturalisation Act 1870 (33 & 34 Vic c.14) which repealed all the previous acts and also adopted a simplified new oath: 'I,_____ do swear that I will be faithful and bear true allegiance to her majesty Queen Victoria, her heirs and successors, according to law. So help me God.'

In 1844 the cost of naturalisation was less than £1, which resulted in tenfold increase in the numbers of foreigners denizied or naturalised annually. In 1880 the fee was increased to £5, and with some variations, the fee would increase at various times depending on the falling value of money: in 1970 the fee stood at £30, increasing to £1,330 in 2018 (Ross, J.M. (1970) 'Naturalisation of Jews in England', *Transactions JHSE* v24, pp59-61; Roth, Cecil (1949) *A History of the Jews in England*. 2nd ed. Oxford: Clarendon Press, p245; Hyamson, Albert M (1899) 'The Jew Bill of 1753', *Transactions JHSE* v4, p177).

2   Hyamson, Albert M. (1899) 'The Jew Bill of 1753', *Transactions JHSE* v4, p160-173.

3   Roth, Cecil (1949) *A History of the Jews of England*. 2nd ed. Oxford: Clarendon Press, p217.

4   Newman, Aubrey (1978) 'Anglo-Jewry in the 18th Century: Presidential Address', *Transactions JHSE* v27, p1.

5   Burnim, Kalman A. (1992) 'The Jewish Presence in the London theatre, 1666-1800', *Transactions JHSE* v33, p67.

6   Julius, Anthony (2010) *Trials of the Diaspora: a History of Anti-Semitism in England*. Oxford: Oxford UP, p192.

7   Endelman, Todd M. (1999) *The Jews of Georgian England, 1714-1830: Tradition and Change in a Liberal Society*. Michigan: Michigan UP, p31-32.

8   Endelman, Todd M. (1999) *The Jews of Georgian England, 1714-1830: Tradition and Change in a Liberal Society*. Michigan: Michigan UP, p184.

9   Vaynes, Julia H.L., ed. (1882) *The Kentish Garland*. v2; Hertford: Austin & Sons, p784-785.

10 Vaynes, Julia H.L., ed. (1882) *The Kentish Garland*. v2; Hertford: Austin & Sons,

p784-785.

11 Vaynes, Julia H.L., ed. (1882) *The Kentish Garland*. v2; Hertford: Austin & Sons, p613; *Kentish Gazette* 19/11/1771.

12 James, M.A. (1965) *Chatham in 1765. Training Management Centre*; HM Dockyard, Chatham (unpublished).

13 Smith, Frederick F. (1928) *A History of Rochester*. London: The Daniel Company, pp194-196.

14 RCA/02/8.

15 Burnim, Kalman A. (1992) 'The Jewish Presence in the London Theatre, 1666-1800', *Transactions JHSE* v33, p67.

16 Smith, Frederick F. (1928) *A History of Rochester*. London: The Daniel Company, pp246-247; DE402/1/49.

17 *The Alphabetical List of the Freemen for 1807* lists three Jewish names, who pay for the privilege to trade in the city — Solomon Mordecai, jeweller; Israel Levi, fruiterer, and a shopkeeper Cohan. Bearing in mind the chronological arrangement of the list, it is possible that Solomon Mordecai became a freeman earlier than Israel Levi. However, no record for Mordecai's admission survived.

18 CO 23/3/1934.

19 CH2/9.

20 CH2/14.

21 Levi Israel died in 1802, leaving his estate of £5 to his niece, Rachael Israel.

Michael Abraham (or Abrahams) was probably a son of John and Elizabeth and was baptised as a child in 1746 at St Mary's Church, Chatham. Abraham was a business partner of Israel Levi (died in 1802) and Solomon Mordecai. Abraham died in 1826 at the age of 76. There is a discrepancy about his age, if he was baptised in 1746. However, the date of birth and age did not bear such significance as they do these days. Age records may show fluctuation during the person's time and are to be treated with caution. Michael Abraham was buried in the Chatham synagogue burial ground.

Abraham Moses (Chatham), salesman, is probably a son of Abraham and Jane Moses. He was baptised on 25 August 1751 at St Mary's Church, Chatham. The father lived his life, probably outwardly, as a Christian, which is confirmed by the parish records and the wording in his will. He died in 1776 and was buried at St Mary's Church graveyard. Abraham Moses Jr reverted to Judaism.

Solomon Mordecai — Solomon ben Mordecai (1730-1816) — is presumably father or identical to Solomon Mordecai Rochester, whose name with the date 1782 is in a copy of the Sepher haHaim in the Jews' College Library.

Isaac Abraham — also known as Isaac Chatham, was one of the founders of the Sheerness Jewish community. The earliest record from 1799 shows a property in Blue Town occupied at the time by an Isaac Abraham. He is most probably the person referred to in the records of the Great Synagogue as 'Isaac Chatham of Sheerness'. Described as a tobacconist in the leases for the synagogue, he refers to himself as a pawnbroker in his will. (Roth, Cecil (1950) *The Rise of Provincial Jewry*. London: Jewish Monthly, p50).

22 CH2/14.

23 Kadish, Sharman (2011) 'Jewish Funerary Architecture in Britain and Ireland since 1656', *Jewish Historical Studies* v43, p62.

24 Kadish, Sharman (2011) 'Jewish Funerary Architecture in Britain and Ireland since 1656', *Jewish Historical Studies* v43, p59.

25 Fridman, Irina (2015) *A Fitting Memorial: A Brief History of Chatham Synagogue*. Rochester: Chatham Memorial

Synagogue, p10.

26 *The Circumcision Register 1765-1818* together with *The Wedding Register 1775-99* ascribed to Rabbi Ash of Dover, MSS/160 2332, Jewish Museum.

27 Only in 1793 the courts recognised the competence of Beth Din to decide on validity of Jewish marriages. (Roth, Cecil (1949) *A History of the Jews in England.* 2nd ed. Oxford: Clarendon Press, p246).

28 Endelman, Todd M. (1999) *The Jews of Georgian England, 1714-1830: Tradition and Change in a Liberal Society.* Michigan: Michigan UP, p224.

29 Dulley, A.J F. (1962) 'People and Homes in the Medway Towns: 1687-1783', *Archaeologia Cantiana* v77, p170.

30 Newman, Aubrey (1978) 'Anglo-Jewry in the 18th Century: Presidential Address', *Transactions JHSE* v27, p5.

Lord George Gordon (1751-93), was the eccentric son of a duke and an MP who, in 1780, as self-appointed head of the Protestant Association, incited a mob of 50,000 to march on Parliament to present a petition against Catholic Emancipation. It turned into a riot and the army was brought in, killing or injuring 450. Gordon was acquitted of high treason but later excommunicated by the Archbishop of Canterbury. In 1787 he converted to Judaism and was later imprisoned for defamation. He died in Newgate Jail.

31 Dulley, A.J.F. (1962) 'People and Homes in the Medway Towns: 1687-1783', *Archaeologia Cantiana* v77, p172.

Chapter 5. Settling in the Area, from the 18th to the early 19th Century, part two

1 Formed in 1792, the London Corresponding Society was a radical organisation with a goal of reforming the political system. The society's key aim was to ensure universal suffrage for British men and annual parliaments. Its membership consisted primarily of artisans, tradesmen, and shopkeepers. Suspicious of a possible French influence on the society and its radical aims, the government of William Pitt the Younger outlawed it by a parliamentary act in 1799.

2 Jones, John Gale (1997; 1796) *Sketch of a Political Tour through Rochester, Chatham, Maidstone, Gravesend, &c , Including Reflections on the Tempers and Dispositions of the Inhabitants of Those Places, and on the Progress of the Societies Instituted for the Purpose of Obtaining a Parliamentary Reform. Part the First.* Rochester: Baggins Book Bazaar in Association with Bruce Aubry, p.17; p26. The book was originally published in London in 1796.

3 Jones, John Gale (1997; 1796) *Sketch of a Political Tour through Rochester, Chatham, Maidstone, Gravesend, &c , Including Reflections on the Tempers and Dispositions of the Inhabitants of Those Places, and on the Progress of the Societies Instituted for the Purpose of Obtaining a Parliamentary Reform. Part the First.* Rochester: Baggins Book Bazaar in Association with Bruce Aubry, p37.

4 Endelman, Todd M. (1999) *The Jews of Georgian England, 1714-1830: Tradition and Change in a Liberal Society.* Michigan: Michigan UP, pp69-70.

5 Rubens, Alfred (1955) 'Portrait of Anglo-Jewry 1656-1836', *Transactions JHSE* v19, p35.

6 Green, Geoffrey L. (1989) *The Royal Navy and Anglo-Jewry 1740-1820: Traders and Those Who Served.* London: Green, p234; ADM 73-56; ADM 73-043.

7 '5 October 1787 Jacobs, David, Age 17, height 5'0'. Dark brown hair, sallow

complexion pitted with smallpox. Smart boy, reads well. Discharged as a servant to Lt Hewitt *HMS Sandwich* on 20 October 1787 at Chatham.' (Green, Geoffrey L. (1989) *The Royal Navy and Anglo-Jewry 1740-1820: Traders and Those Who Served.* London: Green, p224; MSY/K/1; ADM 36-10526).

8   Green, Geoffrey L. (1989) *The Royal Navy and Anglo-Jewry 1740-1820: Traders and Those Who Served.* London: Green, p55.

9   Isaac Samuel went to join *HMS Royal William* on 8 February 1800 (Green, Geoffrey L. (1989) *The Royal Navy and Anglo-Jewry 1740-1820: Traders and Those Who Served.* London: Green, p55, 236; ADM 36-13638; ADM 36-15357).

10   Green, Geoffrey L. (1989) *The Royal Navy and Anglo-Jewry 1740-1820: Traders and Those Who Served.* London: Green, pp 131-133, p138.

11   Green, Geoffrey L. (1989) *The Royal Navy and Anglo-Jewry 1740-1820: Traders and Those Who Served.* London: Green, pp145, 146; ADM 1/4440 piece 243; Secretarial Papers.

12   Rabbi means 'my teacher' in Hebrew. The rabbi is a spiritual leader of the community and requires approval from the chief rabbi. In addition to the authority in relation to the principles of *Halakhah* (Jewish law), a rabbi has communal responsibilities — conducting weddings, bar mitzvahs, dealing with the welfare of his congregants, etc. In the provincial communities also often called minister, *ie* minister of religion. If used as prenominal title, it is abbreviated to the Rev, such as the Rev Barlin. Reader is a person assisting the minister in various functions, such as leading the services. In small communities the functions of reader and rabbi were often performed by the same person. A *chazan* (cantor) is the same

as reader.

13   CH2/15.

14   Roth, Cecil (1949) *A History of the Jews in England.* 2nd ed. Oxford: Clarendon Press, p246.

15   Esther Cohen (born 1816, Chatham, Kent, England, died June 1907, Brunson, Hampton, South Carolina, USA), daughter of Phoebe née Magnus and a watchmaker, Abraham David Cohen, is mentioned in Lazarus Magnus's will, where he bequeaths her, as his eldest granddaughter, four shares of the Eagle Insurance Company. Esther grew up in New York and attended Columbia University, studying law, where she met and married Gilbert William Martin Williams of South Carolina, a colonel in the Confederate Army, on 3 June 1837 at the Reformed Protestant Dutch Church.
Elizabeth Cohen (born 22/2/1820, Chatham, Kent, died 28/5/1921, New Orleans, Orleans, Louisiana, USA), Esther's sister, married Aaron Cohen (no relation). In 1854 she followed her husband to New Orleans to study surgery. Elizabeth enrolled at the Female Medical College of Pennsylvania and graduated fifth in a class of 36 students. She became the first woman to practise medicine in Louisiana. (Emory, Martin S. and Lewis Perciballi (2019) *The US Branches of the Lazarus Philip Magnus and Sarah Moses Family of Chatham, Kent.* (Unpublished)).

16   CH2/15.

17   Duschinky, C (1921) *From the Rabbinate of the Great Synagogue, London: From 1756-1842* (online). London: Oxford University Press, p265; accessed 8/04/2019. Available from *https://archive.org/details/rabbinateofgreat00dusc/mode/2up.*

18   Dulley, A.J.S. (1962) 'People and Homes in the Medway Towns: 1687-1783',

Archaeologia Cantiana v77, p169.

19 HMSO (1846) *Specimen of a proposed publication of the numbers and ages of the population in the registration districts of England.* London: HMSO.

20 Pfeffer, Jeremy I. (2009) *From Once End of the Earth to the Other: The London Bet Din, 1805-1855, and the Jewish Convicts Transported to Australia.* Brighton: Sussex Academic Press, pp231-232.
The story of Abraham Abrahams, a slopseller from Sheerness is a fascinating one. Two years before his execution, his name is found as a plaintiff in a case of assault against Lieutenant-Colonel Clifford in His Majesty's Service.
The judge awarded damages to Abrahams, which infuriated Clifford. In 1819 Abrahams maintained that his role in the case was exaggerated by falsified statements, and he identified one person in the crowd, which gathered to watch his execution. Reading the narrative constructed by Prof Pfeffer, who unravelled Abrahams's story, one cannot but agree that the 24-year-old young man fell victim of revenge. For the full story, see the above book.

21 Deuteronomy 21:22-23.

22 *The Times*, 26/8/1819.

23 CH2/15 f343. Jonathan Zacharia was born in Poland c.1792. After the end of the Napoleonic wars, young Jonathan moved to England and settled in Chatham. About 1818 he married Amelia Goldsmith (born 1792). The couple had six children: Martha (born 1819); Fannie (born 1820); Rebecca (born 1822), Issachar (born 1825); Lavinia (born 1828) and Jane (born 1832).
Zacharia quickly established himself as a prominent member of the community. In 1823 he was one of the trustees of the synagogue and appears on its lease renewal. In 1832 Jonathan Zacharia moved to New York with his family to seek a better fortune.
Issachar, the only son of Jonathan and Amelia, became a podiatrist and a personal chiropodist to Abraham Lincoln, his political confidant and special emissary. About 1875, Issachar Zacharia, his wife Mary Ann and their two youngest daughters, Clara and Victoria, moved to Brook Street, Mayfair, London. He died on 18 September 1900, aged 73. Zacharia is buried at Highgate Cemetery, London.
For additional information about Issachar Zacharia read Sarna, Jonathan D. and Benjamin Shapell (2015) *Lincoln and the Jews: A History.* New York: Thomas Dunn Books.

24 Rubens, Alfred (1935) 'Early Anglo-Jewish Artists', *Transactions JHSE* v14, pp117-118.

25 Rubens, Alfred (1970) 'Jews and the English Stage, 1667-1850', *Transactions JHSE* v24, p152.

26 Conway, David (2007) 'John Braham — from Meshorrer to Tenor', *Transactions JHSE* v41, p46-47.

27 Conway, David (2007) 'John Braham — from Meshorrer to Tenor', *Transactions JHSE* v41, p48.

28 Lodge of Israel No 280, United Grand Lodge of England. Freemason Membership Registers 1751-1921 (online), accessed 3/3/2018.

29 Rubens, Alfred (1970) 'Jews and the English Stage, 1667-1850', *Transactions JHSE* v24, p153.

30 *Morning Post* 9/5/1814.

31 *Kentish Weekly Post* 6/3/1810.

32 Rubens, Alfred (1970) 'Jews and the English Stage, 1667-1850', *Transactions JHSE* v24, p152.

33   DRb/Pw65/1832/12/1-2.

34   Rubens, Alfred (1970) 'Jews and the English Stage, 1667-1850', *Transactions JHSE* v24, p161.

35   Shaftesley, John M. (1973) 'Jews in English Regular Freemasonry, 1717-1860', *Transactions JHSE* v25, pp154-155.

36   Shaftesley, John M. (1973) 'Jews in English Regular Freemasonry, 1717-1860', *Transactions JHSE* v25, pp151-152.

37   Shaftesley, John M (1973) 'Jews in English Regular Freemasonry, 1717-1860', *Transactions JHSE* v25, p158.

38   Shaftesley, John M (1973) 'Jews in English Regular Freemasonry, 1717-1860', *Transactions JHSE* v25, p158.

39   John Gideon Millingen (1782-1849), a son of Michael Millingen, a Dutch merchant and Elizabeth Westflaten, née Coole, was an army surgeon and a writer. After his retirement in 1823, Millingen was appointed as a physician to the military lunatic asylum at Chatham. In 1837 he was appointed as a resident physician to the Middlesex Pauper Lunatic Asylum at Hanwell.
John Gideon Millingen was a younger brother of James Millingen, archaeologist and numismatist and an uncle of Julius Michael Millingen, a physician to Lord Byron. John Millingen's grandson, Joseph Joseph (1833-40), is buried at the Chatham synagogue burial ground. (Saunders, T.B., and James Faulkner (2008) 'Millingen, John Gideon (1782-1849), army surgeon and writer.' *Oxford Dictionary of National Biography* (online). London: Oxford UP; accessed 20/3/2020 Available from *www.oxforddnb.com/view/10.1093/*

ref:odnb/9780198614128.001 0001/ odnb-9780198614128-e-18759).

40   'Bro Francis Naphtali Solomon of 21 High St Chatham was on Wednesday installed Worshipful Master of the Royal Kent Lodge of Antiquity, No 20, the oldest masonic lodge in the country outside London. Worshipful Bro Solomon is the first Jew to be Master of this Lodge, as is the only Jewish member of it.' (JC 25/3/1927).

Chapter 6. The Road to Emancipation, 1830-58

1   Rubens, Alfred (1955) 'Portrait of Anglo-Jewry 1656-1836', *Transactions JHSE* v19, p50.

2   Roth, Cecil (1949) *A History of the Jews in England*. 2nd ed. Oxford: Clarendon Press, p249.

3   Roth, Cecil (1949) *A History of the Jews in England*. 2nd ed. Oxford: Clarendon Press, pp247-250.

4   Wolf, Lucien (1898) 'The Queen's Jewry — 1837-97', *The Jewish Yearbook 1897-98* (5658), p317.

5   Smith, Frederick F. (1928) *A History of Rochester*. London: The Daniel Company, pp106-107.

6   *Kentish Independent* 23/12/1850.

7   Presnail, James (1952) *Chatham: a Story of a Dockyard Town and the Birthplace of the British Navy*. Chatham: Corporation of Chatham, pp203-207.

8   Hobbes, R.G. (1895) *Reminiscences and Notes of Seventy Years' Life, Travel, and Adventure; Military and Civil; Scientific and Literary*. v2; London: Elliot Stock, p103.

9   JC 9/3/1855.
10 JC 14/11/1856.
11 *SE Gazette* 10/2/1857.
12 *SE Gazette* 11/5/1858.
13 Joyce, Brian (2003) *Dumb Show and Noise: Theatre, Music Hall and Cinema in the Medway Towns*. Rochester: Pocock Press, pp53-56.
14 *SE Gazette* 2/11/1863.
15 CBA/AM3/3.
16 Smith, Frederick F. (1928) *A History of Rochester*. London: The Daniel Company, pp138-139.
17 RG 10/11/1840.
18 Wheatley, Sydney W. (1992) *Historical Notes, Rochester St Margaret*. Rochester: City of Rochester Society, p102.
19 CO 23/3/1934.
20 JC 15/4/1853.
21 JC 17/2/1871; CO 4/2/1871.
22 Wolf, Lucien (1898) 'The Queen's Jewry — 1837-97', *The Jewish Yearbook 1897-98* (5658), p318.
23 Cantor, Geoffrey (2012) 'Anglo-Jewry in 1851: The Great Exhibition and Political Emancipation', *Transactions JHSE* v44, p113-114.
24 Dickens, Charles (1837) *The Posthumous Papers of the Pickwick Club*. The quote appears in chapter 2 and was written in May 1836.
25 HMSO (1846) *Specimen of a proposed publication of the numbers and ages of the population in the registration districts of England*. London: HMSO.
26 Julius, Anthony (2010) *Trials of the Diaspora: a History of Anti-Semitism in England*. Oxford: Oxford UP, pp199-204.
27 Julius, Anthony (2010) *Trials of the Diaspora: a History of Anti-Semitism in England*. Oxford: Oxford UP, pp199-204.
28 Julius, Anthony (2010) *Trials of the Diaspora: a History of Anti-Semitism in England*. Oxford: Oxford UP, pp199-204.
29 Julius, Anthony (2010) *Trials of the Diaspora: a History of Anti-Semitism in England*. Oxford: Oxford UP, p201.
30 Cantor, Geoffrey (2012) 'Anglo-Jewry in 1851: the Great Exhibition and Political Emancipation', *Transactions JHSE* v44, pp115-116.
31 *The Reformer and Chatham Literary Gazette*, December 1852.
32 JC 15/4/1853.
33 *Morning Herald* 18/3/1853.
34 JC 25/3/1853.
35 DRc/Azz/3/1.
36 U513/O/2.
37 JC 15/4/1853.
38 U1210/Z3.
39 Wolf, Lucien (1898) 'The Queen's Jewry — 1837-97', *The Jewish Yearbook 1897-98* (5658), p323.
40 JC 7/5/1858. Even after the legislation, the worry remained that Jews could be excluded easily from parliament by another act. The danger was removed when a uniform oath that might be taken by members of all religious denominations substituted the Oaths of Allegiance, Supremacy, and Abjuration in 1860. In 1885 Nathan Rothschild was created a peer, thus confirming the admissibility of Jews to the House of Lords. Chancellorship was the prerogative of the members of Church of England only until 1890 (Wolf, Lucien (1898) 'The Queen's Jewry — 1837-97', *The Jewish Yearbook 1897-98* (5658), p324).

Chapter 7. The Reforms, 1830-70

1   JC 5/12/1873.
2   JC 16/12/1853.
3   Wolf, Lucien (1898) 'The Queen's Jewry — 1837-97', *The Jewish Yearbook 1897-98*

(5658), p314.

4   Wolf, Lucien (1898) 'The Queen's Jewry — 1837-97', *The Jewish Yearbook 1897-98* (5658), p315.

5   Lipman V.D. (1961) 'The Age of Emancipation', in V.D. Lipman ed. *Three Centuries of Anglo-Jewish History*. Cambridge: JHSE, p84.

6   JC 18/7/1845.

7   Lipman, V.D. (1954) *Social History of the Jews in England*. London: Watts, pp38-9.

8   Lipman, V.D. (1954) *Social History of the Jews in England*. London: Watts, p37.

9   JC 2/9/1853.

10 JC 16/9/1853.

11 Lipman, V.D. (1951) 'A Survey of Anglo-Jewry in 1851', *Transactions JHSE* v17, pp173-4.

12 JC 4/11/1853.

13 JC 9/12/1853.

14 JC 16/12/1853.

15 JC 23/12/1853.

16 JC 3/2/1854.

17 JC 15/9/1854.

18 Karaite Judaism is a Jewish religious movement that recognises only the supreme authority of the written Torah in relation to Halakhah (Jewish law). Karaite Judaism does not recognise the Talmud and subsequent works as the authoritative interpretations of the Torah, in contrast to mainstream rabbinic Judaism.

19 Leviticus 19:18; *Maidstone Journal* 28/02/1854.

20 *Maidstone Journal* 14/3/1854.

21 JC 26/10/1855; *Maidstone Journal* 20/5/1856.

22 JC 13/5/1959.

23 JC 28/11/1902.

24 JC 23/4/1880.

25 JC 16/1/1874.

26 Hobbes, R.G. (1895) *Reminiscences and Notes of Seventy Years' Life, Travel, and Adventure; Military and Civil; Scientific and Literary*. v2, London: Elliot Stock, pp101-102.

27 Dickens, Charles (1851) 'One Man in a Dockyard', *Household Words* v3.

28 Hobbes, R.G. (1895) *Reminiscences and Notes of Seventy Years' Life, Travel, and Adventure; Military and Civil; Scientific and Literary*. v2, London: Elliot Stock, pp102-103.

29 *Maidstone Journal* 28/2/1854.

30 CN 24/9/1887.

31 On 26 August 1827 Tsar Nicholas I issued his *ustav rekrutskoi povinnosti* (statute on conscription duty). The ustav cancelled the requirement of Jews to provide money ransom instead of conscripts and made Jews of the Russian Empire bound to personal army service. All recruits, including Jews, had to serve 25 years in the army.

    Jews were required to provide conscripts between the ages of 12 and 25 in comparison with other conscripts, who were between 18 and 35. The system pursued the agenda of making Jews 'useful' and productive, which meant that those who were drafted were most susceptible to external influence. The Jewish conscripts though legally entitled to religious freedom, in reality faced bullying and persecution for doing so; anti-Jewish feeling permeated every level of the military.

    By the Crimean War of 1854-56 the quota for conscripts doubled for Russians and quadrupled for Jews, with Jewish communal leaders had long exhausted their pool of 'non-useful' members. To fulfil the ever-growing quota, khappers (catchers) were employed. Khappers would catch Jews of any age and any status and hand them over to the conscription centres. (*www.yivoencyclopedia.org/article.aspx/*

Military_Service_in_Russia, accessed 14/7/2019).

32 JC 29/9/1854.

33 Waters, M. (1981) 'The Dockyard Work-Force: a Picture of Chatham Dockyard *c.*1860', *Archaeologia Cantiana* v97, p79.

34 The Railway Saloon was formerly known as the Granby Head pub. It was renamed by James Atkins to celebrate the arrival of the railway in Strood, linking the Medway Towns with London.

35 Joyce, Brian (2003) *Dumb Show and Noise: Theatre, Music Hall and Cinema in the Medway Towns*. Rochester: Pocock Press, pp53-56.

36 Hobbes, R.G. (1895) *Reminiscences and Notes of Seventy Years' Life, Travel, and Adventure; Military and Civil; Scientific and Literary*. v2, London: Elliot Stock, p103.

37 JC 18/7/1902.

38 JC 18/7/1902.

39 JC 19/3/1858.

40 JC 18/7/1902.

41 *The Times* 17/1/1850.

42 *London Daily News* 10/2/1859; *Kentish Gazette* 15/2/1859; *Huddersfield Chronicle* 12/2/1859.

43 Joseph and Sara Pyke were ancestors of several notable British personalities.

Lionel Edward Pyke, their second son, was born in Chatham on 21 April 1854. He was educated at Rochester Cathedral Grammar School and at London University (today's University College London), gaining Bachelor of Arts and Latin Legum Baccalaureus (law)degrees. On 3 November 1874 he entered as a student of the Inner Temple and was called to the Bar on 13 June 1877. In 1880 he became a member of the Council of the Anglo-Jewish Association and served on the executive committee from 1882 until his death.

In February 1892 he was appointed Queen's Counsel and immediately became the leader of the branch of the Admiralty Court designated as the Probate, Divorce, and Admiralty Division.

In 1895 Pyke unsuccessfully contested the Wilton division, Wiltshire, as a Liberal candidate. He died suddenly on 26 March 1899 in Brighton. (JC 31/3/1899; *Jewish World* 31/3/1899).

Geoffrey Nathaniel Joseph Pyke, Lionel's son and Joseph and Sara's grandson, born on 9 November 1893 was an English journalist, educationalist and an inventor. As a journalist he travelled to Germany at the break of the First World War under a false passport but was soon arrested and interned. He escaped and made his way back to England.

He is particularly remembered for his unconventional proposals for weapons of war, such as pykrete — a frozen ice alloy, consisting of sawdust, wood pulp and ice, which he saw as prime candidate material for a supersized aircraft carrier for the British Royal Navy during the Second World War (project Habakkuk). He died 21 February 1948.

Magnus Alfred Pyke, born on 29 December 1908 was another grandson of Joseph and Sara. Son of their youngest son Robert Bond Pyke, Magnus Pyke became an English nutritional scientist, governmental scientific adviser, writer and presenter. He became particularly famous as a television personality in the 1970s and 1980s, promoting science to lay people. He died on 19 October 1992.

Another member of this extended family, Montagu Alexander Pyke (13 April 1874-September 1935) was an eccentric cinema pioneer in London. The Montagu Pyke pub in Soho is a nod to the 16th (and final) cinema he built in 1911.

44 HMSO (1846) *Specimen of a proposed publication of the numbers and ages of the population in the registration districts of England*. London: HMSO.

45 Yates, Nigel (1984) 'The Major Kentish Towns in the Religious census of 1851', *Archaeologia Cantiana* v100, pp400-401.

46 JC 23/7/1847.

47 Lipman, V.D. (1951) 'A Survey of Anglo-Jewry in 1851', *Transactions JHSE* v17, p178.

48 Lipman, V.D., ed. (1961) *Three Centuries of Anglo-Jewish History*. Cambridge: JHSE, pp35-37.

49 Dickens, Charles (1851) 'One Man in a Dockyard', *Household Words* v3.

50 *http://jewishencyclopedia.com/articles/10227-maas-joseph*, accessed 17/01/2019.

51 JC 16/3/1877.

52 CN 3/4/1869.

53 JC 26/4/1867).

54 Wills, Stella (1951) 'The Anglo-Jewish Contribution to the Education Movement for Women in the 19th century', *Transactions JHSE* v17, p269.

55 Larkin, Tony (1997) 'Jewish Schools, in Northfleet and Gravesend', *Transactions of the Gravesend Historical Society No 43*, p21.

56 Larkin, Tony (1997) 'Jewish Schools, in Northfleet and Gravesend', *Transactions of the Gravesend Historical Society No 43*, p23; Brown, Malcolm (1996) 'The Jews of Gravesend before 1915', *Transactions JHSE* v35, pp119-139.

57 Deuteronomy 15:11.

58 Kaddish is the prayer sequence regularly recited during the synagogue service. It includes thanksgiving and praise, concluding with a prayer for universal peace. The best-known form of Kaddish is a prayer for the dead.

59 Lipman, V.D., ed. (1961) *Three Centuries of Anglo-Jewish History*. Cambridge: JHSE, p42.

60 N/J/305.

61 Schischa, A. (1973) 'Bibliographical Serendipity', *Transactions Misc JHSE* v25, p238.

62 N/J/305.

63 Census 1841 HO107/491/4; JC 10/12/1847.

64 *SE Gazette* 21/10/1856.

65 CO 18/12/1900. Lazarus and Mindela Polack had nine children: David (born 1855); Joseph (born 1856); Cecily (born 1858); James (born 1859); Isaac (born 1861); Emmanuel (born 1863); Bona (born 1864); Flora (born 1867); Philip (born 1869).

66 JC 3/7/1875.

67 *Evening Standard* 9/12/1844.

68 JC 18/11/1853.

69 JC 5/8/1853.

70 CN 21/7/1860.

71 JC 18/7/1856.

72 *Sheerness Guardian* 3/9/1859.

73 *Sheerness Guardian* 12/5/1860.

74 *Sheerness Guardian* 14/7/1860.

75 *The Times* 19/7/1860.

76 ILN 21/7/1860.

77 *The Times* 19/7/1860.

78 *Sheerness Guardian* 2/10/1858.

79 *Sheerness Guardian* 4/10/1862.

80 *London Gazette* 13/1/1860.

81 *Sheerness Guardian* 1/9/1860.

82 *Sheerness Guardian* 1/9/1860; JC 14/9/1860; *The Times* 26/8/1864.

83 JC 18/5/1860. The 4th Kent Artillery Volunteer Corps at Sheerness, raised on 9 January 1860 was amalgamated on 23 January 1867 with 13th Corps as its third battalion.

84 N/J/305/22.

85 CO 23/3/1934.

86 JC 18/11/1853.
87 N/J/305/22.
88 JC 26/7/1867.
89 Jamilly, Edward (1953) 'Anglo-Jewish Architects, and Architecture in the 18th and 19th Centuries', *Transactions JHSE* v18, p133.
90 Jamilly, Edward (1953) 'Anglo-Jewish Architects, and Architecture in the 18th and 19th Centuries', *Transactions JHSE* v18, p129.
91 Jamilly, Edward (1953) 'Anglo-Jewish Architects, and Architecture in the 18th and 19th Centuries', *Transactions JHSE* v18, p129.
92 JC 16/10/1868.
93 JC 24/6/1870.
94 Jamilly, Edward (1953) 'Anglo-Jewish Architects, and Architecture in the 18th and 19th Centuries', *Transactions JHSE* v18, p137.
95 *The Builder* 23/12/1905, p684.
96 Kadish, Sharman (2004) 'The 'Cathedral Synagogues' of England', *Transactions JHSE* v39, p55.
97 Kadish, Sharman (2004) 'The 'Cathedral Synagogues' of England', *Transactions JHSE* v39, p55.
98 Kadish, Sharman (2004) 'The 'Cathedral Synagogues' of England', *Transactions JHSE* v39, pp54-55.
99 Kadish, Sharman (2004) 'The 'Cathedral Synagogues' of England', *Transactions JHSE* v39, p55.
100 JC 24/6/1870.
101 Proverbs 3:16.
102 JC 24/6/1870.
103 Kadish, Sharman (2004) 'The 'Cathedral Synagogues' of England', *Transactions JHSE* v39, pp71-72.
104 CN 18/6/1870.
105 CN 18/6/1870.
106 JC 24/6/1870.
107 JC 24/6/1870.
108 JC 24/6/1870; CN 18/6/1870.
109 JC 24/6/1870.
110 JC 24/6/1870; CN 18/6/1870.
111 JC 24/6/1870.
112 JC 24/6/1870; CN 25/6/1870.
113 JC 24/6/1870.
114 CN 27/9/1873; JC 25/3/1875; JC 4/4/1879; JC 18/1/1889.

Chapter 8. After the Emancipation, 1870-1914

1   CN 16/7/1870. The Elementary Education Act 1870 created a framework for compulsory schooling of children between the ages of five and twelve in England and Wales. Before that, access to education was voluntary: children of better-off parents attended boarding private schools; children of poorer families were able to attend voluntary schools, but many did not receive education of any sort.
2   JC 27/5/1870.
3   The bill became the Universities Tests Act in 1871.
4   JC 5/8/1892; JC 10/1/1896.
5   CN 23/7/1870.
6   CN 23/7/1870.
7   CN 23/7/1870.
8   *Songs in Henry Russell's Vocal and Pictorial Entertainment entitled The Far West; or, the Emigrant's Progress from the Old World to the New; and Negro Life, in Freedom and in Slavery.* London: Chapman, 1850; CN 23/7/1870.
9   CN 23/7/1870.
10 CN 23/7/1870.
11 CN 23/7/1870; JC 29/7/1870.
12 JC 11/12/1885.
13 CN 6/8/1870.
14 JC 9/8/1878.
15 *Whitstable Times and Herne Bay Herald*

10/4/1880.

16 CN 18/1/1896; JC 30/3/1894. Sir Julian Goldsmid, Bart, born 8 October 1838, was a son of Frederick David Goldsmid, MP and Caroline, née Samuel, daughter of Phillip Samuel. He was a descendant of a Polish Jew Uri Halevi from Emden in East Friesland, one of the founders of Amsterdam Jewish community in 1593. The first Goldsmid to settle in England was Aaron Goldsmid from Emden, who arrived there in 1765. Julian Goldsmid was educated at University College (today's University College London), of which his grandfather, Sir Isaac Lyon Goldsmid, was one of the principal founders, and of which Julian Goldsmid himself was a fellow and treasurer. After his university career, Goldsmid was called to the Bar, which he abandoned on the death of his father, whom he succeeded as MP for Honiton in March 1868. A nephew of Francis Goldsmid, MP, Julian Goldsmid succeeded him in baronetcy in 1878. Goldsmid was active in an emancipation campaign to allow Jews to enter parliament. During his tenure as MP for Rochester (1870-80) he was active in support of Romanian Jews. In 1885 he was elected as first member for South-West St Pancras, which he represented as a Liberal Unionist till his death. Goldsmid was chairman of the Submarine Telegraph Company before its dissolution, chairman of the Imperial and Continental Gas Company, and a director of the London, Brighton and South Coast Railway. In the Jewish community, he was president of the Anglo-Jewish Association, chairman of the Russo-Jewish Committee, president of the Jews' Infant School, chairman of the Council of the West London Synagogue of British Jews and also on the committee of the Jews' Free School.
In 1868 Julian Goldsmid married Virginia, née Phillipson. The couple had eight daughters. The family resided in Somehill, near Tunbridge Wells. Virginia died in 1892. Goldsmid suffered from rheumatic gout, complicated later by other malignant symptoms. He died aged 57 on 7 January 1896 and was buried at Kingsbury Road Cemetery in the London borough of Hackney. (JC 5/8/1892; JC 10/01/1896).

17 JC 15/4/1881.

18 JC 15/4/1881.

19 CN 9/2/1884.

20 CN 10/5/1884.

21 CN 10/5/1884.

22 CN 10/5/1884.

23 CN 10/5/1884. The Rev Lazarus Polack died on 21 November 1900 at the residence of his son James L. Polack, principal of Craufurd College, Maidenhead. He was 87. A cultured man and a proficient violinist, he was a Jew of intense piety and a man of simple habits, humble and modest. He had nine children, eight of whom survived him, including the above James L. Polack and the Rev Joseph Polack, BA, housemaster of Clifton College, Bristol. Lazarus's wife, Mindela, had died in 1879 at the age of 49 and was buried in the Chatham Memorial Synagogue cemetery. (JC 23/11/1900; N/J/305).

24 JC 9/2/1884.

25 JC 1/4/1938.

26 *Thanet Advertiser* 25/3/1938.

27 JC 7/8/1885.

28 JC 1/4/1938.

29 *The Jewish Yearbook 1897-98* (5658).

30 *The Jewish Yearbook 1897-98* (5658).

31 JC 24/6/1891; JC 23/9/2892;

JC 27/5/1892.

32 JC 1/4/1938.

33 JC 2/10/1896.

34 JC 4/3/1892.

35 JC 13/5/1892.

36 JC 1/4/1898.

37 CO 7/5/1892.

38 Aubry, Bruce (2005) *Red Flows the Medway: a Labour History of the Medway Towns*. Rochester: Pocock Press, p81.

39 CN 1/2/1896.

40 JC 18/1/1895.

41 JC 9/3/1895.

42 JC 1/4/1938; CO 30/10/1886.

43 JC 30/1/1891.

44 JC 16/3/1890.

45 JC 30/1/1891.

46 JC 4/3/1892.

47 JC 21/12/1894.

48 JC 1/4/1938.

49 JC 15/11/1895.

50 JC 30/1/1891.

51 JC 24/9/1897.

52 JC 10/12/1880.

53 JC 27/7/1900.

54 CO 14/1/1882; CO 30/10/1886.

55 CO 14/1/1882.

56 JC 10/12/1880.

57 Bloom, Cecil (1992) 'The Politics of Immigration, 1881-1905', *Transactions JHSE* v33, p188.

58 CN 18/2/1882.

59 CN 25/2/1882; JC 24/2/1882.

60 JC 21/4/1899.

61 Finestein, Israel (1961) 'The New Community', in V.D. Lipman, ed. *Three Centuries of Anglo-Jewish History*. Cambridge: JHSE, p111.

Saul Isaac's brother, Samuel Isaac was the army contractor whose firm was ruined after supporting the Southern states during the American Civil War. Samuel Isaacs formed the company that built the first Mersey Tunnel, opened by the Prince of Wales in 1885 (Jamilly, Edward (2003) 'Patrons, clients, designers and developers: the Jewish contribution to secular building in England', *Transactions JHSE* v38, p88). Additional reading about Isaac and his family: Jolles, Michael (1998) *Samuel Isaac, Saul Isaac and Nathaniel Isaacs*. London: Jolles Publications.

62 JC 21/4/1911; CO 5/7/1913.

63 CO 5/7/1913. Robert Sebag-Montefiore was keenly interested in national defence. In 1904, while still an undergraduate at Oxford, he was nominated by Lord Harris as Second Lieutenant in the Royal East Kent Mounted Rifles, later East Kent Yeomanry. Owing chiefly to his effort, the Rochester Troop was formed in 1912; he also raised the Ramsgate Troop a few years earlier. Subsequently, he was promoted to the rank of captain.

War broke out and at the end of September 1915 he went with his regiment, the Royal East Kent Yeomanry to Gallipoli, and on 23 October was wounded in the thigh, left shoulder and right knee when a bomb accidentally exploded in a trench. Sebag-Montefiore died at the 17th General Hospital, Alexandria, four weeks later, on 19 November.

He was married to Miss Ida Samuel, daughter of Sir Marcus Samuel, Bart, and Lady Samuel, of Mote Park, Maidstone. (CO 5/7/1913; CO 27/11/15).

64 CO 4/12/1875.

65 Jolles, Michael (1998) *Samuel Isaac, Saul Isaac, and Nathaniel Isaac*. London: Jolles Publications, p31. Jane Magnus (born 1827) was married to Henry Jacob Nathan, of Gerrard Street, Soho, London, costumier, son of Joseph Nathan. The ceremony took place at the Sun Hotel on 13 September 1848. Marriage was

solemnised by the Rev Jehiel Phillips. (*SE Gazette* 19/9/1848).

Sara Magnus (born 1829) was married to Joseph Pyke, fourth son of Lewis Eliazer Pyke, clerk to the Great Synagogue, London. The ceremony took place on 16 January 1850 at her father's house. The marriage was solemnised by the Rev Jehiel Phillips. (*The Times*, 17/1/1850).

Cordelia Magnus (born 1831) was married on 22 June 1854 to Coleman Defries, son of Jonas.

Elizabeth Magnus (born 1835) was married to Manuel Castello, a broker of Stock Exchange on 31 October 1855. The ceremony took place at 25 Middleton Square, London, (JC 2/11/1855).

66 *The Times* 4/4/1850.

67 JC 13/12/1872; CN 21/12/1872
Jane Nathan (née Magnus) died on 10 December 1872 at Randolph Crescent, Maida Vale, London, and was interred at Chatham Memorial Synagogue burial ground. Her coffin was brought to Chatham on Sunday morning, 15 December, by train, with a large number of mourners. A hearse, five mourning coaches, and a carriage were waiting at the Chatham station. The cortege proceeded along Railway Street and High Street, to the cemetery. Simon Magnus joined the procession from his house in the High Street. Family, friends, members of the Chatham Jewish community and numerous inhabitants of the Medway Towns assembled to pay a last tribute to Mrs Nathan.

The funeral service was performed by the rabbi, the Rev L. Polack. The remains were placed in a vault by the ashes of her brother, Captain Lazarus Simon Magnus. After the interment, the synagogue was crowded with the sympathising

congregation. Rabbi Polack officiated, and a solemn and eloquent address was delivered by the Rev Professor Marks. The stone-setting ceremony took place a year later, in early June 1873. That September, Henry Jacob Nathan, of Tichborne Street and 4 Randolph Crescent, Maida Vale, London, presented the synagogue a handsome cover for the reader's desk in memory of his wife. The cloth was of rich white silk, with gold fringe, and bore an inscription in Hebrew, beautifully embroidered in gold: 'The gift of Henry Jacob Nathan, in memory of his wife, Jane, daughter of Simon Magnus, A.M. 5634.' (JC 13/12/1872; CN 21/12/1872; CN 7/6/1873).

68 CO 4/12/1875.

69 N/J/305.

70 JC 7/11/1879; CN 1/11/1879, CO 1/11/1879.

71 CO 1/11/1879.

72 Joyce, Brian (2003) *Dumb Show and Noise: Theatre, Music Hall and Cinema in the Medway Towns*. Rochester: Pocock Press, pp69-86.

73 CO 27/11/1897; JC 21/3/1902; CO 22/3/1902; JC 28/3/1902.

74 *Jewish Yearbook* 1897/98 (5658).

75 JC 7/1/1910.

76 BOD, *www.jewishgen.org*, accessed 18/3/2007.

77 *Jewish Yearbook* 1897-98 (5658).

78 BOD, *www.jewishgen.org*, accessed 18/3/2007.

79 G/ME/WI.

80 G/ME/WI; JC 13/7/1894.

81 G/ST.

82 Elman, Peter (1951) 'The Beginnings of the Jewish Trade Union Movement in England', *Transactions JHSE* v17, p53.

83 Bloom, Cecil (1992) 'The Politics of Immigration, 1881-1905', *Transactions*

JHSE v33, p187.

84 Elman, Peter (1951) 'The Beginnings of the Jewish Trade Union Movement in England', *Transactions JHSE* v17, p53.

85 Bloom, Cecil (1992) 'The Politics of Immigration, 1881-1905', *Transactions JHSE* v33, p187.

86 *Sankt-Peterburgskie Vedomosti* newspaper 8(20)/3/1881 No 65.

87 The Pale of Settlement. Statutes of 1804 and 1835 described the provinces where the Jewish population of the Russian Empire was permitted to reside: the Lithuanian provinces of Vilna, Kovno, and Grodno; the Belorussian provinces of Minsk, Vitebsk, and Mogilev; the Ukrainian provinces of Volhynia, Podolia, Kiev, Chernigov, Poltava, Kherson, and Ekaterinoslav; the Crimean province of Taurida; and the Moldavian province of Bessarabia. Established Jewish communities, though not new settlements, were tolerated in Courland (Kurland) province, and in Riga and Shlok in Lifland province. (*yivoencyclopedia.org/article.aspx/ Pale_of_Settlement*, accessed 23/12/2019).

88 During the reign of Alexander II (1855-81), the authorities relaxed restrictions of the Pale for privileged categories of Jews deemed economically productive, or satisfying the official agenda of Jewish acculturation into Russian society. The groups included merchants of the First Guild (1859), holders of academic degrees (1861), and some military veterans (1862). In 1865 Jewish master craft workers were permitted to leave the Pale, a provision that potentially applied to 20 per cent of the Jewish population. However, the taxing process and bureaucratic regulations meant that very few could leave the Pale. (*yivoencyclopedia.org/article.aspx/ Pale_of_Settlement*, accessed 23/12/2019).

89 Lipman, V.D. (1954) *Social History of the Jews in England 1850-1950*. London: Watts, p85.

90 *www.britannica.com/topic/pale-restricted-area*, accessed 23/12/2019.

91 Lipman, V.D (1954) *Social History of the Jews in England 1850-1950*. London: Watts, p86.

92 Lipman, V.D. (1954) *Social History of the Jews in England 1850-1950*. London: Watts, p91.

93 Elman, Peter (1951) 'The Beginnings of the Jewish Trade Union Movement in England', *Transactions JHSE* v17, p54.

94 JC 1/4/1910.

95 JC 6/12/1906.

96 Cesarani, David (1998) 'Reporting Antisemitism: *The Jewish Chronicle* 1879-1979', in Jones, Sian, Tony Kushner and Sarah Pearce, eds. *Cultures of Ambivalence and Contempt. Studies in Jewish-Non-Jewish Relations*. London: Valentine Mitchell, p255.

97 Wolf, Lucien (1898) 'The Queen's Jewry — 1837-97', *The Jewish Yearbook 1897-98* (5658), p339.

98 Bloom, Cecil (1992) 'The Politics of Immigration, 1881-1905', *Transactions JHSE* v33, pp188-189.

99 Bloom, Cecil (1992) 'The Politics of Immigration, 1881-1905', *Transactions JHSE* v33, p194; Jeyes, S.H. (1/7/1891) 'Foreign pauper Immigration', *Fortnightly Review* L (N.S.) 22; 19.

100 Bloom, Cecil (1992) 'The Politics of Immigration, 1881-1905', *Transactions JHSE* v33, p195.

101 Bloom, Cecil (1992) 'The Politics of Immigration, 1881-1905', *Transactions JHSE* v33, p95; White, Arnold (1894) *The English Democracy: its Promises and Perils*. London: Swan Sonnenschein, p170.

102 Bloom, Cecil (1992) 'The Politics of

Immigration, 1881-1905', *Transactions JHSE* v33, p196.

103 Bloom, Cecil (1992) 'The Politics of Immigration, 1881-1905', *Transactions JHSE* v33, p195; Fox, S.N. (1888) 'The Invasion of pauper Foreigners', *Contemporary Review* v53, p864.

104 Bloom, Cecil (1992) 'The Politics of Immigration, 1881-1905', *Transactions JHSE* v33, p194.

105 CO 26/7/1902.

106 CO 13/5/1899.

107 CO 11/8/1900.

108 CO 16/7/1904.

109 N/J/305.

110 Bloom, Cecil (1992) 'The Politics of Immigration, 1881-1905', *Transactions JHSE* v33, pp208-209.

111 JC 23/10/1891.

112 JC Supplement 31/10/1913.

113 CO 21/10/1911.

Chapter 9. The Great War, 1914-18

1   Baldwin, Ronald A. (1998) *The Gillingham Chronicles: a History of Gillingham, Kent.* Gillingham: Baggins Book Bazaar, pp280-282.

2   Pendlebury, Alyson (2006) *Portraying 'the Jew' in First World War Britain.* London: Valentine Mitchell, p52.

3   Pendlebury, Alyson (2006) *Portraying 'the Jew' in First World War Britain.* London: Valentine Mitchell, p55.

4   CO 21/11/1914.

5   CO 1/11/1916.

6   CO 6/7/1918.

7   Baldwin, Ronald A. (1998) *The Gillingham Chronicles: a History of Gillingham, Kent.* Gillingham: Baggins Book Bazaar, pp280-282.

8   Pendlebury, Alyson (2006) *Portraying 'the Jew' in First World War Britain.* London:

Valentine Mitchell, pp60-61.

9   Adolph Fehrenbach, resident of Gillingham, was naturalised in 1910 (HO 144/1076/192246). Albin Fehrenbach, resident of Rochester was naturalised in 1898 (HO 334/27/10175). Edward Fehrenbach, resident of Chatham was naturalised in 1913 (HO 144/1251/233973). Emil Fehrenbach, resident of Strood, was naturalised in 1894 (HO 334/21/8064).

10 CO 17/10/1914.

11 CO 21/11/1914.

12 CO 20/5/1916.

13 CN 22/8/1914.

14 CN 24/10/1914.

15 Pendlebury, Alyson (2006) *Portraying 'the Jew' in First World War Britain.* London: Valentine Mitchell, pp150-151.

16 CN 5/6/1915.

17 CN/15/5/1915.

18 CO 22/5/1915.

19 The outfitter L. Levy was no relation to the former Mayor of Rochester, John Lewis Levy.

20 CN 5/6/1915; CO 5/6/1915.

21 CO 5/6/1915.

22 CN 5/6/1915; CO 5/6/1915.

23 12th (Service) Battalion of the Middlesex Regiment was formed in Mill Hill, London, in August 1914 as part of the Second Kitchener's Army. In September 1914 it was attached to the 54th Brigade of the 18th Eastern Division, which served on the Western Front from spring 1915, taking part in most of the significant actions in France. In total, the division suffered more than 46,500 casualties during the Great War, of whom 13,727 died. The 12th Battalion was disbanded in France on 13 February 1918.

24 Shub, Irina (2008) 'Not Forgotten after 90 Years', *Shemot* v16(3) pp13-15 Lieutenant

Albert Isaacs was buried at the Chatham Synagogue burial ground. In 2008 a request was made to the Commonwealth War Commission to recognise him as a casualty of war, which was granted. It was impossible to establish with precision where Isaacs's grave was. As a result, a stone was erected on the approximate spot.

25 Cesarani, David (1998) 'Reporting Antisemitism: *The Jewish Chronicle* 1879-1979', in Jones, Sian, Tony Kushner and Sarah Pearce, eds. *Cultures of Ambivalence and Contempt. Studies in Jewish-Non-Jewish Relations.* London: Valentine Mitchell, pp259-260.

26 JC 20/7/1917.

27 CO 23/6/1917.

28 CO 27/11/1915.

29 CN 8/7/1917.

30 Pendlebury, Alyson (2006) *Portraying 'the Jew' in First World War Britain.* London: Valentine Mitchell, pp65-66.

31 Pendlebury, Alyson (2006) *Portraying 'the Jew' in First World War Britain.* London: Valentine Mitchell, pp69-70.

32 CN 9/5/1917; CN 19/05/1917; CO 19/05/1917. The initial report about the death of Lazarus Jacobs was published by the *Chatham News* on 9 May 1917. The same issue contained a report of another suicide, that of 31-year-old Private John Deebank of Hornsey, attached to the Queen's Royal West Surrey Regiment, who shot himself at Gore Court Camp, Sittingbourne.

33 Genesis 9:5.

34 Baba Kama 90b.

35 Mishneh Torah, Hilchot Avel 1:11.

36 Aruch Hashulchan, Yoreh De'ah 345:5.

37 Pendlebury, Alyson (2006) *Portraying 'the Jew' in First World War Britain.* London: Valentine Mitchell, pp69-70.

38 The revolution took place in March 1917, according to the Gregorian calendar, but Russians know it as the February Revolution because the country was then using the Julian calendar, which is 13 days 'behind'. Russia changed to the Gregorian calendar, aligning it with the West, in February 1918.

39 Cesarani, David (1998) 'Reporting Antisemitism: *The Jewish Chronicle* 1879-1979', in Jones, Sian, Tony Kushner and Sarah Pearce eds. *Cultures of Ambivalence and Contempt. Studies in Jewish-Non-Jewish Relations.* London: Valentine Mitchell, pp260-261.

40 Pendlebury, Alyson (2006) *Portraying 'the Jew' in First World War Britain.* London: Valentine Mitchell, pp69-70.

41 CO 27/4/1918.

42 CO 15/7/1916; CO 25/11/1916.

43 CO 19/5/1917.

44 CO 23/6/1917.

45 CO 13/4/1918.

46 Staatsarchiv Hamburg; Hamburg, Deutschland; *Hamburger Passagierlisten*; Volume: 373-7 I, *VIII A 1 Band 223*; Page: 1289; Microfilm No: *K_1814.*

47 HO 334/58/22506.

48 CO 29/7/1916; CO 23/11/1916; CO 3/2/1917.

49 CO 12/5/1917; CO 4/8/1917.

50 CO 25/8/1917.

51 CO 27/10/1917.

52 CO 10/11/1917.

53 CO 25/3/1916.

54 CO 29/9/1917.

55 CO 25/3/1916.

56 CO 4/3/1916.

57 CO 25/3/1916.

58 CO 4/3/1916; C/A/2/15; CO 25/3/1916.

59 CO 15/4/1916.

60 C/A/2/15; WO 372/16/49439.

61 CO 29/7/1916; CO 14/10/1916; CO

28/10/1916.
62 CO 23/12/1916.
63 CN 5/6/1915.
64 JC 13/10/1916.
65 In peace time the Rev Herman
Shandel was a preacher at the private
Montefiore synagogue in Ramsgate. (JC
28/1/1916; JC 4/2/1916; JC 3/5/1916;
JC 16/6/1916; JC 23/6/1916; JC
27/10/1916; JC 3/11/1916).
66 CO 4/7/1903.
67 CN 5/6/1915; *The Times* 3/6/1915; CN
15/6/1915.
68 JC 10/1/1902.
69 JC 31/1/1919; CO 25/1/1919; CO
1/2/1919.
70 *Kent Messenger* 14/1/1939.

Chapter 10. The Turbulent Peaceful Years, 1919-39

1 JC 3/11/1922.
2 CO 11/11/1921.
3 JC 27/10/1922.
4 JC 13/7/1923; JC 27/7/1923; JC
10/8/1923.
5 In 1920 it was decided to commemorate
the naval dead of the three home
ports — Plymouth, Portsmouth and
Chatham — who had no grave. Sir Robert
Lorimer designed all three memorials to
a single pattern. The Chatham memorial,
overlooking the town, was built on the
Great Lines at Brompton. It comprises
a Portland stone obelisk supported by
four buttresses, on which the names
of the dead were inscribed, and was
surmounted by copper sphere supported
by figures representing the four winds. It
was unveiled by Edward, Prince of Wales,
in 1924 (Joyce, Brian and Sophie Miller
(2014) *Gillingham and Around from Old
Photographs*. Stroud: Amberley, p27).

6 JC 2/5/1924.
7 Pendlebury, Alyson (2006) *Portraying 'the
Jew' in First World War Britain*. London:
Valentine Mitchell, p201.
8 JC 1/1/1926.
9 Turner, David (1993) *Fascism and Anti-
Fascism in the Medway Towns 1927-40*.
Rochester: Kent Anti-Fascist Action
Committee, pp6-7.
10 CN 14/11/1924.
11 CN 21/5/1926; CO 15/4/1927.
12 Cesarani, David (1998) 'Reporting
Antisemitism: *The Jewish Chronicle* 1879-
1979', in Jones, Sian, Tony Kushner and
Sarah Pearce eds. *Cultures of Ambivalence
and Contempt. Studies in Jewish-Non-Jewish
Relations*. London: Valentine Mitchell,
pp264-265.
13 Turner, David (1993) *Fascism and Anti-
Fascism in the Medway Towns 1927-40*.
Rochester: Kent Anti-Fascist Action
Committee, p11.
14 Pendlebury, Alyson (2006) *Portraying 'the
Jew' in First World War Britain*. London:
Valentine Mitchell, pp201-202.
15 Turner, David (1993) *Fascism and Anti-
Fascism in the Medway Towns 1927-40*.
Rochester: Kent Anti-Fascist Action
Committee, pp11-12.
16 Turner, David (1993) *Fascism and Anti-
Fascism in the Medway Towns 1927-40*.
Rochester: Kent Anti-Fascist Action
Committee, pp13-16.
17 Turner, David (1993) *Fascism and Anti-
Fascism in the Medway Towns 1927-40*.
Rochester: Kent Anti-Fascist Action
Committee, p17.
18 Cesarani, David (1998) 'Reporting
Antisemitism: *The Jewish Chronicle* 1879-
1979', in Jones, Sian, Tony Kushner and
Sarah Pearce eds. *Cultures of Ambivalence
and Contempt. Studies in Jewish-Non-Jewish
Relations*. London: Valentine Mitchell,

p265.

19 Turner, David (1993) *Fascism and Anti-Fascism in the Medway Towns 1927-40.* Rochester: Kent Anti-Fascist Action Committee, p19.

20 Pendlebury, Alyson (2006) *Portraying 'the Jew' in First World War Britain.* London: Valentine Mitchell, pp198-99.

21 Pendlebury, Alyson (2006) *Portraying 'the Jew' in First World War Britain.* London: Valentine Mitchell, p199.

22 Turner, David (1993) *Fascism and Anti-Fascism in the Medway Towns 1927-40.* Rochester: Kent Anti-Fascist Action Committee, pp20-22.

23 CO 3/11/1934.

24 Turner, David (1993) *Fascism and Anti-Fascism in the Medway Towns 1927-40.* Rochester: Kent Anti-Fascist Action Committee, p22.

25 Turner, David (1993) *Fascism and Anti-Fascism in the Medway Towns 1927-40.* Rochester: Kent Anti-Fascist Action Committee, p23.

26 CO 26/6/1936; CN 26/6/1936.

27 Pendlebury, Alyson (2006) *Portraying 'the Jew' in First World War Britain.* London: Valentine Mitchell, p91.

28 CO 26/6/1936; CN 26/6/1936.

29 CN 12/7/1936.

30 *Whitstable Times* 5/12/1936.

31 CO 26/6/1936; CN 26/6/1936; CN 4/12/1936.

32 Turner, David (1993) *Fascism and Anti-Fascism in the Medway Towns 1927-40.* Rochester: Kent Anti-Fascist Action Committee, p20; p 37; CO 3/11/1934; CO 27/4/1938; CN 9/4/1938.

33 CN 16/10/1936; CO 14/5/1938; CO 15/11/1938; CO 17/2/1940.

34 Turner, David (1993) *Fascism and Anti-Fascism in the Medway Towns 1927-40.* Rochester: Kent Anti-Fascist Action Committee, p32-33; CO 3/9/1937.

35 CO 12/2/1938; CO 14/5/1938.

36 CO 11/3/1939.

37 *Yorkshire Post* 27/1/1937.

38 Turner, David (1993) *Fascism and Anti-Fascism in the Medway Towns 1927-40.* Rochester: Kent Anti-Fascist Action Committee, p29.

39 *Yorkshire Post* 11/2/1937.

40 Turner, David (1993) *Fascism and Anti-Fascism in the Medway Towns 1927-40.* Rochester: Kent Anti-Fascist Action Committee, p30.

41 Yorkshire Post 27/1/1937.

42 CN 24/4/1938.

43 CN 13/11/1936.

44 JC 15/1/1937; CO 27/4/1938; CN 29/4/1938.

45 CO 27/4/1938; CN 29/4/1938.

46 JC 4/5/1928.

47 JC 22/11/1929; JC 3/7/1931. Samuel Wolfe (Shmuel Zeev ben Eliezer), son of Eliezer Zvi Kushelevich, was born on 7 June 1883 in the Kovno (Kaunas) region of Lithuania. At the age of 17 or 18 Samuel left home for Germany to train as shochet (ritual butcher) but was refused a work permit. As the parents did not want him to return to Tsarist Russia, young Shmuel went to England. He arrived in Liverpool between April 1901 and December 1905 On 26 December 1905 Samuel married Fanny Simons (Fruma bat Abraham Yitzhak) in the synagogue in High St, Leicester. The couple had four children. The next decade Samuel Wolfe and his family lived in Northampton, Derby, Bradford and Westcliffe before arriving to Chatham just after 1924 Samuel Wolfe died in 1970 at the age of 87 (JC 28/8/1970).

48 JC 24/3/1933.

49 CO 2/11/1934; JC 23/11/1934.

50 JC 15/3/1935.
51 JC 27/4/1935.
52 JC 11/12/1936; JC 13/1/1939.
53 CN 12/7/1936.
54 JC 19/5/1939.
55 JC 24/3/1933; CN 2/11/1938.
56 JC 11/12/1936; JC 13/1/1939.
57 JC 2/4/1937.
58 CN 2/11/1938.
59 JC 11/12/1936.
60 CN 12/7/1936.
61 JC 15/3/1935; JC 19/5/1939.
62 *Kent Messenger* 14/1/1939.
63 'Kristallnacht.' *Britannica Library*,
    Encyclopædia Britannica 2018
    library.eb.co.uk/levels/adult/article/
    Kristallnacht/46254, accessed 2/02/2020.
64 CO 26/11/1938.
65 CO 3/12/1938.
66 *Kent Messenger* 14/1/1939.
67 Turner, David (1993) *Fascism and Anti-*
    Fascism in the Medway Towns 1927-40.
    Rochester: Kent Anti-Fascist Action
    Committee, p37.

List of Illustrations

© *Chatham Observer*
Group of Jewish servicemen in Chatham, 1917
The Rev Marks Fenton (*c.*1864-1919)
The Rev Abraham Samet, *c.*1925

The Rev Sam Wolfe, 1930s
The Last Night of Hanukkah by Charles
Spencelayh © Guildhall Museum,
Rochester

Index

The Last Night of Hanukkah, one of the rare images of the Jewish
subject painted by the Rochester artist Charles Spencelayh